THE PHILOSOPHY OF LAW

THE

PHILOSOPHY OF LAW

An Exposition

OF THE

FUNDAMENTAL PRINCIPLES OF JURISPRUDENCE

AS THE

SCIENCE OF RIGHT

BY

IMMANUEL KANT

[1887]

AUGUSTUS M. KELLEY • PUBLISHERS

CLIFTON 1974

English Translation First Published 1887

(*Edinburgh*: T. & T. Clark, *38 George Street*, 1887)

Reprinted 1974 by

Augustus M. Kelley Publishers

Clifton New Jersey 07012

Library of Congress Cataloging in Publication Data

Kant, Immanuel, 1724-1804.
  The philosophy of law.

  Reprint of the 1887 ed. published by T. & T. Clark,
Edinburgh.
  Translation of Metaphysische Anfangsgründe der
Rechtslehre, pt. 1 of the author's Die Metaphysik der
Sitten.
  1. Law--Philosophy. 2. Natural law. 3. Ethics.
I. Title.
Law   340.1   77-146882
ISBN 0-678-01152-4

PRINTED IN THE UNITED STATES OF AMERICA
by SENTRY PRESS, NEW YORK, N. Y. 10013
Bound by A. HOROWITZ & SON, CLIFTON, N. J.

THE PHILOSOPHY OF LAW

An Exposition

OF THE

FUNDAMENTAL PRINCIPLES OF JURISPRUDENCE

AS

THE SCIENCE OF RIGHT.

BY

IMMANUEL KANT

Translated from the German

BY

W. HASTIE, B.D.

EDINBURGH:

T. & T. CLARK, 38 GEORGE STREET.

1887.

'But next to a new History of Law, what we most require is a new Philosophy of Law.'—Sir HENRY SUMNER MAINE.

TRANSLATOR'S PREFACE.

——o——

KANT'S *Science of Right*[1] is a complete exposition of the Philosophy of Law, viewed as a rational investigation of the fundamental Principles of Jurisprudence. It was published in 1796,[2] as the First Part of his *Metaphysic of Morals*,[3] the promised sequel and completion of the *Foundation for a Metaphysic of Morals*,[4] published in 1785. The importance and value of the great thinker's exposition of the Science of Right, both as regards the fundamental Principles of his own Practical Philosophy and the general interest of the Philosophy of Law, were at once recognised. A second Edition, enlarged by an

[1] Rechtslehre.

[2] It appeared soon after Michaelmas 1796, but with the year 1797 on the title-page. This has given rise to some confusion regarding the date of the first Edition, which is now usually quoted as 1796-7. (Schubert, *Kant's Werke*, Bd. ix. viii., and *Biographie*, p. 145.)

[3] Die Metaphysik der Sitten. Erster Theil. Metaphysische Anfangs-gründe der Rechtslehre. Königsberg, 1797.

[4] Grundlegung zur Metaphysik der Sitten. Translated by Willich (1798), Semple (1836), and Abbott (1873).

Appendix, containing Supplementary Explanations of the
Principles of Right, appeared in 1798.[1] The work has
since then been several times reproduced by itself, as
well as incorporated in all the complete editions of
Kant's Works. It was immediately rendered into Latin
by Born[2] in 1798, and again by König[3] in 1800. It
was translated into French by Professor Tissot in 1837,[4]
of which translation a second revised Edition has
appeared. It was again translated into French by M.
Barni, preceded by an elaborate analytical introduction,
in 1853.[5] With the exception of the Preface and
Introductions,[6] the work now appears translated into
English for the first time.

Kant's *Science of Right* was his last great work of an
independent kind in the department of pure Philosophy,

[1] These Supplementary Explanations were appended by Kant to the
First Part of the work, to which most of their detail more directly
apply ; but they are more conveniently appended in this translation to the
whole work, an arrangement which has also been adopted by the other
Translators.

[2] Initia Metaphysica Doctrinæ Juris. Immanvelis Kantii Opera ad
philosophiam criticam. Latine vertit Fredericus Gottlob Born. Volumen
quartum. Lipsiæ, MDCCLXXXXVIII.

[3] Elementa Metaphysica Juris Doctrinæ. Latine vertit G. L. König.
Amstel. 1800, 8. (Warnkönig and others erroneously refer it to Gotha.)

[4] Principes Métaphysiques du Droit, par Emm. Kant, etc. Paris, 1837.

[5] Eléments Métaphysiques de la Doctrine du Droit, etc. Paris, 1853.

[6] The Preface and the Introductions (*infra*, pp. 1-58, 259-265) have
been translated by Mr. Semple. See *The Metaphysic of Ethics by*

and with it he virtually brought his activity as a master of thought to a close.[1] It fittingly crowned the rich practical period of his later philosophical teaching, and he shed into it the last effort of his energy of thought. Full of years and honours he was then deliberately engaged, in the calm of undisturbed and unwearied reflection, in gathering the finally matured fruit of all the meditation and learning of his life. His three immortal Critiques of *the Pure Reason* [2] (1781), *the Practical Reason* [3] (1788), and *the Judgment* [4] (1790), had unfolded all the theoretical Principles of his Critical Philosophy, and established his claim to be recognised as at once the most profound and the most original thinker of the modern world. And as the experience of life deepened around and within him, towards the sunset, his

Immanuel Kant, translated by J. W. Semple, Advocate. Fourth Ed. Edited with Introduction by Rev. Henry Calderwood, LL.D., Professor of Moral Philosophy, University of Edinburgh. Edin. : T. & T. Clark, 1886.—These are indispensable parts of the present work, but they have been translated entirely anew.

[1] He ceased lecturing in 1797 ; and the only works of any importance published by himself subsequent to the *Rechtslehre*, were the *Meta-physische Anfangsgründe der Tugendlehre* in 1797, and *Der Streit der Facultäten* and the *Anthropologie* in 1798. The *Logik* was edited by Jäsche in 1800 ; the *Physische Geographie* by Rink in 1802, and the *Pädagogik*, also by Rink, in 1803, the year before Kant's death.

[2] Kritik der reinen Vernunft. Translated anew by Max Müller (1881).

[3] Kritik der praktischen Vernunft. Translated by Abbott.

[4] Kritik der Urtheilskraft. Translated into French by M. Barni.

interest had been more and more absorbed and concentrated in the Practical. For to him, as to all great and comprehensive thinkers, Philosophy has only its beginning in the theoretical explanation of things; its chief end is the rational organization and animation and guidance of the higher life in which all things culminate. Kant had carried with him through all his struggle and toil of thought, the cardinal faith in God, Freedom, and Immortality, as an inalienable possession of Reason, and he had beheld the human Personality transfigured and glorified in the Divine radiance of the primal Ideas. But he had further to contemplate the common life of Humanity in its varied ongoings and activities, rising with the innate right of mastery from the bosom of Nature and asserting its lordship in the arena of the mighty world that it incessantly struggles to appropriate and subdue to itself. In the natural chaos and conflict of the social life of man, as presented in the multitudinous and ever-changing mass of the historic organism, he had also to search out the Principles of order and form, to vindicate the rationality of the ineradicable belief in human Causation, and to quicken anew the lively hope of a higher issue of History. The age of the Revolution called and inspired him to his task. With keen vision he saw a new world suddenly born before him, as the blood-stained product of a motion long toiling in

the gloom, and all old things thus passing away ; and he
knew that it was only the pure and the practical Reason,
in that inmost union which constitutes the birthright of
Freedom, that could regulate and harmonize the future
order of this strongest offspring of time. And if it was
not given to him to work out the whole cycle of the
new rational ideas, he at least touched upon them all,
and he has embodied the cardinal Principle of the
System in his *Science of Right* as the philosophical
Magna Charta of the age of political Reason and the
permanent foundation of all true Philosophy of Law.

Thus produced, Kant's *Science of Right* constituted an
epoch in jural speculation, and it has commanded the
homage of the greatest thinkers since. Fichte, with
characteristic ardour and with eagle vision, threw his
whole energy of soul into the rational problem of Right,
and if not without a glance of scorn at the sober limitations of the ' old Lectures ' of the aged professor, he yet
acknowledges in his own more aerial flight the initial
safety of this more practical guidance.[1] In those early
days of eager search and high aspiration, Hegel, stirred
to the depths by Kant, and Fichte, and Schelling, wrote
his profound and powerful essay on the Philosophy of

[1] Fichte's Nachgelassene Werke, 2 Bd. System der Rechtslehre (1804),
498, etc. (Bonn, 1834.) Fichte's Grundlage des Naturrechts (1796), as he
himself points out, was published before Kant's *Rechtslehre*, but its principles
are all essentially Kantian. (Translated by Kroeger, Philadelphia, 1870.)

Right, laden with an Atlantean burden of thought and strained to intolerable rigidity and severity of form, but his own highest achievement only aimed at a completer integration of the Principles differentiated by Kant.[1] It was impossible that the rational evangel of universal freedom and the seer-like vision of a world, hitherto groaning and travailing in pain but now struggling into the perfection of Eternal Peace and Good-will, should find a sympathetic response in Schopenhauer, notwithstanding all his admiration of Kant; but the racy cynicism of the great Pessimist rather subsides before him into mild lamentation than seeks the usual refuge from its own vacancy and despair in the wilful caustic of scorching invective and reproach.[2] Schleiermacher, the greatest theologian and moralist of the Century, early discerned the limitations of the à priori formalism, and supplemented it by the comprehensive conceptions of the primal dominion and the new order of creation, but he owed his critical and dialectical ethicality mainly to Kant.[3] Krause, the leader of the latest and largest

[1] Hegel's Werke, Bd. i. Philosophische Abhandlungen, iv. *Ueber die Wissenschaftlichen Behandlungsarten des Naturrechts* (1802-3); and the Grundlinien der Philosophie des Rechts, oder Naturrecht und Staatswissenschaft im Grundrisse (1821). Werke, Bd. viii. (*passim*). Dr. J. Hutchison Stirling's *Lectures on the Philosophy of Law* present a most incisive and suggestive introduction to Hegel's Philosophy of Right.

[2] Die beiden Grundprobleme der Ethik (1841), pp. 118-9.

[3] Grundlinien einer Kritik der bisherigen Sittenlehre (1803). Entwurf

thought in this sphere—at once intuitive, radical, and
productive in his faculty, analytic, synthetic, and organic
in his method, and real, ideal, and historic in his product
—caught again the archetypal perfectibility of the human
reflection of the Divine, and the living conditions of the
true progress of humanity. The dawn of the thought of
the new age in Kant rises above the horizon to the
clear day, full-orbed and vital, in Krause.[1] All the
continental thinkers and schools of the century in this
sphere of Jurisprudence, whatever be their distinctive
characteristics or tendencies, have owned or manifested
their obligations to the great master of the Critical
Philosophy.

eines Systems der Sittenlehre, herausg. von A. Schweizer (1835). Grundriss der philosophischen Ethik, von A. Twesten (1841). Die Lehre vom
Staat, herausg. von Ch. A. Brandes (1845).

[1] Grundlage des Naturrechts (1803). Abriss des Systems der Philosophie des Rechts oder des Naturrechts (1828). Krause is now universally recognised as the definite founder of the organic and positive school
of Natural Right. His principles have been ably expounded by his two
most faithful followers, Ahrens (*Cours de Droit Naturel*, 7th ed. 1875) and
Röder (*Grundzüge des Naturrechts o. der Rechtsfilosofie*, 2 Auf. 1860).
Professor J. S. del Rio of Madrid has vividly expounded and enthusiastically
advocated Krause's system in Spanish. Professor Lorimer of the Edinburgh University, while maintaining an independent and critical attitude
towards the various Schools of Jurisprudence, is in close sympathy with
the Principles of Krause (*The Institutes of Law: a Treatise of the Principles of Jurisprudence as determined by Nature*, 2nd ed. 1880, and *The
Institutes of the Law of Nations*). He has clearly indicated his agreement
with the Kantian School, *so far as its principles go* (*Instit.* p. 336, n.).

The influence of the Kantian Doctrine of Right has thus been vitally operative in all the subsequent progress of jural and political science.[1] Kant, here as in every other department of Philosophy, summed up the fragmentary and critical movement of the Eighteenth Century, and not only spoke its last word, but inaugurated a method which was to guide and stimulate the highest thought of the future. With an unwonted blending of speculative insight and practical knowledge, an ideal universality of conception and a sure grasp of the reality of experience, his effort, in its inner depth, vitality, and concentration, contrasts almost strangely with the trivial formalities of the Leibnitzio-Wolffian Rationalists on the one hand,[2] and with the pedantic

[1] This applies to the latest German discussions and doctrines. The following works may be referred to as the most important recent contributions, in addition to those mentioned above (such as Ahrens and Röder, xi. n.) :—Trendelenburg, Naturrecht auf dem Grunde der Ethik, 2 Auf. 1868. Post, Das Naturgesetz des Rechts, 1867. W. Arnold, Cultur und Rechtsleben, 1865. Ulrici, Naturrecht, 1873. Zoepfl, Grundriss zu Vorlesungen über Rechtsphilosophie, 1878. Rudolph von Ihering, Der Zweck im Recht, i. 1877, ii. 1883. Professor Frohschammer of Munich has discussed the problem of Right in a thoughtful and suggestive way from the standpoint of his original and interesting System of Philosophy, in his new volume, *Ueber die Organisation und Cultur der menschlichen Gesellschaft*, Philosophische Untersuchungen über Recht und Staat, sociales Leben und Erziehung, 1885.

[2] Leibnitz, Nova Methodus discendæ docendæque Jurisprudentiæ, 1767. Observationes de principio Juris. Codex Juris Gentium, 1693–1700.

Wolff, Jus Naturæ Methodo Scientifica pertractatum, Lips. 8 Tomi.

tediousness of the Empiricists of the School of Grotius
on the other.[1] Thomasius and his School, the expounders
of the Doctrine of Right as an independent Science,
were the direct precursors of the formal method of
Kant's System.[2] Its firm and clear outline implies the
substance of many an operose and now almost unread-
able tome; and it is alive throughout with the quick,
keen spirit of the modern world. Kant's unrivalled
genius for distinct division and systematic form, found
full and appropriate scope in this sphere of thought. He

1740-48.   Institutiones Juris Naturæ et Gentium, Halæ, 1754.   (In
French by *Luzac*, Amsterdam, 1742, 4 vols.)   Vernünftige Gedanken.

Vatel, Le Droit des Gens, Leyden, 1758.   Edited by Royer-Collard,
Paris, 1835.   English translation by Chitty, 1834.   [For the other works
of this school, see Ahrens, i. 323-4, or Miller's *Lectures*, p. 411.]

[1] Grotius, De Jure Belli ac Pacis, lib. iii. 1625.   Translated by
Barbeyrae into French, 1724 ; and by Whewell into English, 1858.

Pufendorf, Elementa Juris Universalis, 1660.   De Jure Naturæ et
Gentium, 1672.   [English translation by Kennett, 1729.]

Cumberland, De Legibus Naturæ Disquisitio Philosophica, London,
1672.   Translated into English by Towers, Dublin, 1750.

Cocceji, Grotius illustratus, etc., 3 vols. 1744-7.   [See Miller, 409.]   '

[2] Christian Thomasius (1655-1728) first clearly distinguished between
the Doctrine of Right and Ethics, and laid the basis of the celebrated
distinction of Perfect and Imperfect Obligations as differentiated by the
element of Constraint.   See Professor Lorimer's excellent account of
Thomasius and of Kant's relation to his System, *Inst. of Law*, p. 288 ;
and Röder, i. 240.   The principal works of this School are : Thomasius,
Fundamenta juris naturæ et gentium ex sensu communi deducta, 1705.
Gerhard, Delineatio juris naturalis, 1712.   Gundling, Jus Naturæ et
gentium.   Koehler, Exercitationes, 1728.   Achenwall, Prolegomena Juris
naturalis, and Jus Naturæ, 1781.

had now all his technical art as an expounder of Philosophy in perfect control, and after the hot rush through
the first great Critique he had learned to take his time.
His exposition thus became simplified, systematized, and
clarified throughout to utmost intelligibility. Here, too,
the cardinal aim of his Method was to wed speculative
thought and empirical fact, to harmonize the abstract
universality of Reason with the concrete particularities of
Right, and to reconcile the free individuality of the
citizen with the regulated organism of the State. And
the least that can be said of his execution is, that he has
rescued the essential principle of Right from the debase-
ment of the antinomian naturalism and arbitrary politi-
cality of Hobbes[1] as well as from the extravagance of the
lawless and destructive individualism of Rousseau,[2] while
conceding and even adopting what is substantially true
in the antagonistic theories of these epochal thinkers;
and he has thereby given the birthright of Freedom
again, full-reasoned and certiorated, as 'a possession for
ever' to modern scientific thought. With widest and

[1] Hobbes, De Cive, 1642. Leviathan seu de civitate ecclesiastica et
civili, 1651. On Hobbes generally, see Professor Croom Robertson's
Monograph in 'Blackwood's Philosophical Classics.'

[2] L'origine et les fondements de l'inégalité parmi les hommes, Dijon,
1751. Contrat social, 1762. Rousseau's writings were eagerly read by
Kant, and greatly influenced him. On Rousseau generally, see John
Morley's Rousseau, Lond. 1878.

furthest vision, and with a wisdom incomparably superior
to the reactionary excitement of the great English
Orator,[1] he looked calmly beyond 'the red fool-fury of
the Seine' and all the storm and stress of the time, to
the sure realization of the one increasing purpose that
runs through the ages. The burden of years chilled
none of his sympathies nor dimmed any of his hopes for
humanity ; nor did any pessimistic shadow or murmur
becloud his strong poetic thought, or disturb 'the
mystical lore' of his eventide. And thus at the close of
all his thinking, he made the Science of Right the very
corner-stone of the social building of the race, and the
practical culmination of all Religion and all Philosophy.

It is not meant that everything presented here by
Kant is perfect or final. On the contrary, there is
probably nothing at all in his whole System of Philosophy—whose predominant characteristics are criticism,
initiation, movement — that could be intelligently so
regarded ; and the admitted progress of subsequent
theories of Right, as briefly indicated above, may be
considered as conceding so much. It must be further
admitted of Kant's *Science of Right* that it presents

---

[1] Burke is assigned to the Historical School of Jurisprudence by
Ahrens, who not inaptly designates him 'the Mirabeau of the anti-
revolution' (i. 53). See the *Reflections on the French Revolution* (1790).
Stahl gives a high estimate of Burke as 'the purest representative of
Conservatism.'

KANT'S PHILOSOPHY OF LAW.

everywhere abundant opening and even provocation for
' Metacriticism ' and historical anticriticism, which have
certainly not been overlooked or neglected. But it *is*
meant withal that the Philosophy of Jurisprudence has
really flourished in the Nineteenth Century only where
Kant's influence has been effective, and that the higher
altitudes of jural science have only come into sight
where he has been taken as a guide. The great critical
thinker *set* the problem of Right anew to the pure
Speculative Reason, and thus accomplished an intellectual transformation of juridical thought corresponding to
the revolutionary enthusiasm of liberty in the practical
sphere. It is only from this point of view that we can
rightly appreciate or estimate his influence and significance. The all-embracing problem of the modern metamorphosis of the institutions of Society in the free State,
lies implicitly in his apprehension. And in spite of his
negative aspect, which has sometimes entirely misled
superficial students, his solution, although betimes tenta-
tive and hesitating, is in the main faithful to the highest
ideal of humanity, being foundationed on the eternity of
Right and crowned by the universal security and peace
of the gradually realized Freedom of mankind. As Kant
saved the distracted and confused thought of his time
from utter scepticism and despair, and set it again with
renewed youth and enthusiasm on its way, so his spirit

seems to be rising again upon us in this our hour of
need, with fresh healing in his wings.   Our Jurists must
therefore also join the ever increasing throng of contemporary thinkers in the now general *return to Kant*.[1] Their
principles are even more conspicuously at hazard than
any others, and the whole method of their science, long
dying of intellectual inanition and asphyxia, must seek
the conditions of a complete renovation.   It is only thus,
too, that the practical Politician will find the guidance of
real principle in this agitated and troubled age in which
the foundations of Government as well as of Right are
so daringly scrutinised and so manifestly imperilled,[2]
and in which he is driven by the inherent necessary

[1] 'The very cry of the hour is, Fichte and Schelling are dead, and Hegel,
if not clotted nonsense, is unintelligible ; let us go back to Kant.   See,
too, in other countries, what a difference the want of Kant has made.'
Dr. J. H. Stirling, *Mind*, No. xxxvi.   'Within the last ten years many
voices have been heard, both in this country and in Germany, bidding us
return to Kant, as to that which is alone sound and hopeful in Philosophy ; that which unites the prudence of science with the highest
speculative enterprise that is possible without idealistic extravagances.'
Professor E. Caird, *Journal of Speculative Philosophy*, vol. xiv. 1, 126.
'From Hegel, we must, I think, still return upon Kant, seeking fresh
hope for Philosophy in a continued use of the critical method.'   Professor
Calderwood, *Introduction to Kant's Metaphysic of Ethics*, p. xix.

[2] The Socialistic and Communistic Doctrines of Owen (1771–1858),
Fourier (1777–1837), Saint-Simon (1760–1825), Louis Blanc, Proudhon,
and Cabet, 'considered as aberrations in the development of Right,' are
sketched by Ahrens (i. § 12) with his characteristic discrimination and
fairness.   The principles of the contemporary English Socialism will be

implication of local politics to face the inevitable issue
of world-wide complications and the universal problem
of human solidarity. And thus only, as it now appears,
will it be possible to find a Principle that will at once
be true to the most liberal tendency of the time, and
yet do justice to its most conservative necessities.
Of criticism and comment, blind adulation and
unjust depreciation of Kant's system of Right, there
has been, as already hinted, abundance and even more
than enough. Every philosophical Jurist has had to
define more or less explicitly his attitude towards the
Kantian standpoint. The original thinkers of the
dogmatic Schools—Fichte, Schelling,[1] Hegel, and Krause,

---

found summed up in *A Summary of the Principles of Socialism written
for the Democratic Federation*, by H. M. Hyndman and William Morris
(1884). Compare also Hyndman's *The Historical Basis of Socialism in
England*, and *To-day* and *Justice*, the organs of the Social Democracy.

[1] Schelling's contributions to the Science of Right have hardly
received the attention they deserve. The absorption of his thought in
the Philosophy of Nature left him less free to devote himself to the
Philosophy of History, but it is mainly to him that the idea of the
systematic objectivity and the organic vitality of the State, in
its latest forms, is due. Hegel and Krause have severally adopted
and developed the two sides of this conception. Compare Schelling's
Abhandlung über das Naturrecht in *Fichte and Niethammer's Journal*,
iv. and v. ; and his *Vorlesungen über die Methode des akademischen
Studiums*, p. 146, etc. See Stahl's excellent account of Schelling's
Doctrine, *Philosophie des Rechts*, i. 403-14, and *The Journal of
Speculative Philosophy*, vol. xiii. No. 3, vi., 'Schelling on History and
Jurisprudence.'

—have made it the starting-point of their special efforts, and have elaborated their own conceptions by positive or negative reference to it. The recent Theological School of Stahl and Baader, De Maistre and Bonald,[1] representing the Protestant and Papal reaction from the modern autonomy of Reason, has yet left the Kantian principle unshaken, and has at the best only formulated its doctrine of a universal Divine order in more specific Christian terms. The Historical School of Hugo and Savigny[2] and Puchta,[3]—which is also that of Bentham, Austin

[1] Stahl and Baader represent the Neo-Schellingian standpoint in their philosophical doctrines.—F. J. Stahl, *Die Philosophie des Rechts*, 3 Bde., 3 Auf. 1865 (an important and meritorious work).—Franz von Baader's *Sämmtliche Werke*, 16 Bde. 1851–60. (Cf. Franz Hoffmann's *Beleuchtung des Angriffs auf Baader in Thilo's Schrift :* ' Die theologisikende Rechts- und Staatslehre,' 1861.)—Joseph de Maistre, *Soirées de St. Petersburg*, Paris, 1821. *Mémoires*, etc., par A. Blanc, 1858.—L'Abbé de Bonald, *Législation primitive*, 1821.

[2] Hugo (1768–1844) is usually regarded as the founder, and Savigny (1778–1861) as the chief representative of the Historical School. Hugo, *Lehrbuch des Naturrechts als einer Philosophie des positiven Rechts*, 1799, 3 Auf. 1820. Frederich Carl von Savigny, *Vom Beruf unserer Zeit für Gesetzgebung und Rechtswissenschaft*, 1814 ; *System des heutigen Römischen Rechts*, 1840. (See Guthrie's translation of Savigny, *Treatise on the Conflict of Laws*, with an excellent Preface. T. & T. Clark.)

[3] The Historical School, as Ahrens shows, must be carried back so as to include such thinkers as Cujas, the great French Jurist of the 16th century, who called the History of Right his ' hameçon d'or ; ' Montesquieu (1689–1755), whose well-known book, *L'Esprit des Lois* (1748), ran through twenty-two editions in a few years ; and the Neapolitan Vico (1688–1744), the founder of the ' New Science ' of History. Vico is only now becoming properly appreciated. See Professor's Flint's able and

and Buckle, Sir George C. Lewis and Sir Henry
Sumner Maine, and Herbert Spencer,—with all its
apparent antagonism, has only so far supplemented
the rational universality of Kant by the necessary
counterpart of an historical Phenomenology of the rise
and development of the positive legal institutions, as
the natural evolution and verification in experience of
the juridical conceptions.[1] The conspicuous want of a
criterion of Right in the application of the mere his-

instructive ' Vico ' in Blackwood's *Philosophical Classics.* ' In his work,
De universi juris uno principio et fine (1820), Vico divides the whole
Science of Right into three parts : (1) the Philosophy of Right, (2) the
History of Right, and (3) the Art of applying the Philosophy to facts.
He distinguishes profoundly in Laws the spirit or will of the legislator
(*mens legis*) and the reason of the law (*ratio legis*), which consists in the
accordance of a law with historical facts and with the eternal principles
of the True and Good ' (Ahrens). The contemporary Historical School
does not yet occupy so philosophical a position.

[1] Sir Henry Sumner Maine, the most eminent English representative
of the Historical School, continues to regard ' the philosophy founded on
the hypothesis of a state of nature ' as ' still the greatest antagonist of the
Historical Method ' (*Ancient Law*, pp. 90, 91) ; but this is evidently said in
disregard of the transformation of Rousseau's theory by Kant, and the
contributions to the application of the Historical Method by Hegel and
his school, in whose principle the historic evolution is an essential
element. Sir H. S. Maine's own contributions cannot be too highly
recommended for their thoroughness and suggestiveness. He has gathered
much of his original and pregnant matter from direct-acquaintance with
India, where, as is the case with the forms of nature, the whole genesis
and stratification of the forms of Society are presented livingly to view.
(*Ancient Law*, 1861, 7th ed. 1880. *Village Communities in the East
and West*, 4th ed. 1881. *Early History of Institutions*, 1874.)

torical Method to the manifold, contingent, and vari-
able institutions of human society, has been often
signalized ; and the representatives of the School have
been driven again, especially in their advocacy of
political liberalism, upon the rational principles of
Freedom.[1]

The Civil Jurists who have carried the unreasoning
admiration of the Roman Law almost to the idolatry of
its letter, and who are too apt to ignore the movement
of two thousand years and all the aspirations of the
modern Reason, could not be expected to be found in
sympathy with the Rational Method of Kant. Their
multiplied objections to the details of his exposition,
from Schmitthenner [2] to the present day, are, however,
founded upon an entire misapprehension of the purpose
of his form. For while Kant rightly recognised the

[1] Extremes meet in the moral indifference of the universal naturalism
of the ultra-historical School and the abstract absolute rationalism of
Spinoza. It was Grotius who first clearly distinguished between positive
fact and rational idea in the sphere of Right, and thus originated the
movement of modern 'jural' speculation. For evidence of the statement
in the text, see Bentham's *Works*, Buckle's *History of Civilisation*, Mill
on *Liberty*, and especially Puchta's *Encyclopädie*, introductory to his
Cursus der Institutionen, 6 Auf. 1865. The standpoint of the Historical
School has been thoroughly reviewed by Stahl, i. 570-90 ; Ahrens, i.
51-61 ; and Röder, i. 266-279.

[2] 'Ueber den Charakter und die Aufgaben unserer Zeit in Beziehung auf
Staat und Staatswissenschaft,' Giess. 1832. Zwölf Bücher vom Staate,
1839. See Rosenkranz's *Geschichte der Kant'schen Philosophie*, p. 268.

Roman Law as the highest embodiment of the juridical
Reason of the ancient world, and therefore expounded
his own conceptions by constant reference to it, he
clearly discerned its relativity and its limitations ; and
he accordingly aims at unfolding everywhere through its
categories the juridical idea in its ultimate purity. In
Kant the juridical Idea first attains its essential self-
realization and productivity, and his system of Private
Right is at once freer and more concrete than the
Systems of Hobbes and Rousseau, because it involves
the ancient civil system, corrected and modernized by
regard to its rational and universal principles. This
consideration alone will meet a host of petty objections,
and guard the student against expecting to find in this
most philosophical exposition of the Principles of Right
a mere elementary text-book of the Roman Law.[1]

In England, Kant's *Science of Right* seems as yet to

[1] This remark especially applies to the running fire of criticism in Von
Kirchmann's recent *Erläuterungen zu Kant's Metaphysik der Sitten*,
1882. It is a matter of regret that such criticisms cannot be here dealt
with in detail. Kant has himself clearly indicated the position stated
above, as at p. 54, *infra.*—The depth and subtlety of Kant's method, so
far transcending the common modes of juridical thinking in England, are
inseparable from the system, but he has himself given the sufficient reason
for their appearance in it (*infra*, p. 116). Without entering in detail
upon the point, the translator may remark with regard to one conspicuous, yet irremoveable blot, that he homologates the unanimous
disapprobation of subsequent jurists, and would only refer to Dr.
Hutchison Stirling's drastic castigation of it in his *Lectures*, p. 51. But

have been little studied, and it has certainly exerted but
little influence on English Juridical Science. This has
no doubt been mainly due to the traditional habit of the
national mind, and the complete ascendancy during the
present century of the Utilitarian School of Bentham.[1]
The criterion of Utility found a ready application to the
more pressing interests of Political and Legal Reform,
and thus responding to the practical legislative spirit of
the time, its popular plausibilities completely obscured or
superseded all higher rational speculation. By Austin
the system was methodically applied to the positive
determination of the juridical conceptions, under aid of
the resources of the German Historical School, with the
result that Right was made the mere 'creature' of positive
law, and the whole Rational Method pretentiously condemned as irrational 'jargon.'   In Austin[2] we have only

of this and other difficulties in so original and originative a work can
only be said in the meantime :
          'Sunt delicta tamen, quibus ignovisse velimus.'
And every reader and student should be ready to apply the Horatian
rule here too :
          ' Verum ubi plura nitent . . . non ego paucis
          Offendar maculis, quas aut incuria fudit
          Aut humana parum cavit natura.'
[1] Fragment on Government, 1776. Essay on Political Tactics, 1791.
Principles of Morals and Legislation, 1780. Traités de Legislation, 1802.
[2] Province of Jurisprudence determined, or Philosophy of Positive Law,
1832. Lectures on Jurisprudence, edited by his Widow.
Austin (1790–1859) has been greatly overestimated as a Jurist by his

KANT'S PHILOSOPHY OF LAW.

the positive outcome of Hobbes and Hume and Bentham. The later forms of this legal positivism have not been fruitful in scientific result, and the superficiality and infutility of the standpoint are becoming more and more apparent. Nor does the Utilitarian Principle,[1] with all

friends and followers. The affectionate tributes of his widow may be borne with, but it is more extraordinary to find Professor Sheldon Amos characterizing him as 'the true founder of the Science of Law' (S. Amos, *The Science of Law*, p. 4). Here is Austin's estimate of Kant's *Science of Right:* 'A treatise darkened by a philosophy which, I own, is my aversion, but abounding, I must needs admit, with traces of rare sagacity. He has seized a number of notions, complex and difficult in the extreme, with distinction and precision which are marvellous, considering the scantiness of his means. For of positive systems of law he had scarcely the slightest tincture; and the knowledge of the principles of jurisprudence, which he borrowed from other writers, was drawn, for the most part, from the muddiest sources; from books about the fustian which is styled the Law of Nature.' (*Lectures*, iii. 157.) And here is his account of the German Jurists generally : 'It is really lamentable that the instructive and admirable books which many of the German Jurists have certainly produced, should be rendered inaccessible, or extremely difficult of access, by the thick coat of obscuring jargon with which they have wantonly incrusted their necessarily difficult science' (ii. 405). Comment on this is superfluous. In the same breath a more condemnatory judgment is dealt out even to Sir W. Blackstone. So long as such statements passed as philosophical criticism there was no possibility for a genuine Philosophy of Law in England. Austin, notwithstanding his English reputation, is entirely ignored by the German Jurists. He seems to have known only enough of German to consult the more popular productions of the Historical School. Dr. Hutchison Stirling has dealt with Austin's commonplace Hedonism in a severe way, and yet not too severely, in his *Lectures on the Philosophy of Law (sub fin.)*.

[1] Utilitarianism has been the subject of incessant discussion in England down to its latest systematic exposition in Sidgwick's *Methods of Ethics*.

its seeming justice and humanity, appear capable of
longer satisfying the popular mind with its deepening
Consciousness of Right, or of resolving the more fundamental political problems that are again coming into
view. In this connection we may quote and apply the
authority of Sir Henry Sumner Maine when he says:[1]
'There is such widespread dissatisfaction with existing
theories of jurisprudence, and so general a conviction that
they do not really solve the questions they pretend to
dispose of, as to justify the suspicion that some line
of inquiry necessary to a perfect result has been in-
completely followed, or altogether omitted by their
authors.' The present unsatisfactory condition of the
Science of Right in England—if not in Scotland[2]—could
not be better indicated.

On the Continent the system has also been carefully and ably reviewed by
Th. Jouffroy (*Cours de droit naturel*, 1835), Ahrens (i. 48, but less fully
in the later editions), I. H. Fichte (*Die philosophischen Lehren von Recht,
Staat und Sitte*, 1850), De Wal (Prysverhandeling van het Natuurregt,
1833), and particularly by the Italian Jurists (Röder, i. 108).

[1] Ancient Law, p. 118.

[2] Much more may be justly claimed for Scotland than for England
since the middle of the last century in regard to the cultivation of the
Philosophy of Right. The Scottish School of Philosophy started on this
side from Grotius and Thomasius. Gershom Carmichael edited Pufendorf
with praiseworthy notes. Hutchison discussed the doctrine of Right with
fulness and care in his *System of Moral Philosophy* (1755). Hume, in
consistency with the method of his Intellectual Philosophy, derationalized
the conceptions of Justice and Right, and resolved them into empirical
products of public Utility (*Treatise on Human Nature*, 1739. *Essays,*

In these circumstances, no other alternative is left for us but a renewed and deepened appeal to the universal principle of Reason, as the essential condition of all true progress and certainty. And in the present dearth of philosophical origination and the presence of the un-assimilated products of well-nigh a century of thought, it seems as if the prosecution of this Method of all methods

1742). Reid, leading the realistic reaction, examined this side of Hume's speculation with his characteristic earnestness, and advanced by his practical principle of Common Sense to positions akin to those of Kant's Practical Reason (*Active Powers*, 1788, Essay V. c. iii. *Of Systems of Natural Jurisprudence*, and the following chapters on Hume's Utili-tarianism). Henry Home, Lord Kames, prosecuted the same method with more juridical knowledge (*Principles of Equity ; Historical Law Tracts*, 1758 ; *Sketches of the History of Man*). The movement was carried on by Adam Ferguson (*Principles of Moral and Political Science*, 1792 ; *Essay on the History of Civil Society*, 1767), Dugald Stewart (see especially the account of the Grotian School in the *Dissertation*, 1815), and Dr. Thomas Brown (*Lectures*). Sir James Mackintosh wrote a *Discourse on the Study of the Law of Nature and Nations*, 1835. The cultivation of the Philosophy of Law has never been extinct in the Scottish Universities. Since the revival of the Chair of Public Law in the University of Edinburgh in 1862, Professor Lorimer has done much by his devotion and erudition to further the cultivation of the subject. (See the reference to his own works, *supra*, xi. n.) One of his pupils, Mr. W. G. Miller, Lecturer on Public Law in the University of Glasgow, has published a series of excellent Lectures on the subject, displaying exten-sive knowledge and critical acumen, with general regard to the Hegelian standpoint (*Lectures on the Philosophy of Law*, designed mainly as an introduction to the study of International Law, 1884). Professor Flint's important work on the *Philosophy of History in France and Germany*, and Professor Edward Caird's recent book on Comte's *Social Philosophy*, may also be referred to in this connection.

can only now be fruitfully carried on by *a return to Kant* and advance through his System. Enough has perhaps already been said to indicate the recognised importance of the Kantian standpoint, and even to point to the rich fields of thought and inquiry that open everywhere around it to the student. Into these fields it was the original intention of the translator to attempt to furnish some more definite guidance by illustrative comment and historical reference in detail, but this intention must be abandoned meanwhile, and all the more readily as it must be reckoned at the most but a duty of subordinate obligation and of secondary importance. The Translation is therefore sent forth by itself in reliance upon its intelligibility as a faithful rendering of the original, and in the hope that it will prove at once a help to the Students and an auxiliary to the Masters of our present juridical science.   W. H.

EDINBURGH, *January* 1887.

_____

BIBLIOGRAPHICAL NOTE.

RÖDER remarks (i. 254) that by far the most of the later philosophical writers on Natural Right—'*nomen illis legio !*'—follow the system of Kant and Fichte, which is in the main identical in principle with that of Thomasius. It was impossible to refer to them in detail in these prefatory remarks, but it may be useful to quote the following as the more

important works on the subject from this standpoint since the appearance
of Kant's *Rechtslehre* :—

A. Mellin, Grundlegung zur Metaphysik der Rechte, 1796.

P. J. A. Feuerbach, Kritik des natürlichen Rechts, 1796.

H. Stephani, Grundlinien der Rechtswissenschaft, 1797.

Ph. Schmutz, Erklärung der Rechte des Menschen u. des Bürgers,
1798. Handbuch der Rechtsphilosophie, 1807.

R. Gerstäcker, Metaphysik des Rechts, 1802.

L. Bendavid, Versuch einer Rechtslehre, 1802.

K. H. v. Gros, Lehrbuch des Naturrechts, 1802. 6 Ausg. 1841.

Friès, Philosophische Rechtslehre u. Kritik aller positiven Gesetz
Gebung, 1803.

L. N. Jacob, Philosophische Rechtslehre, 2 A. 1802.

K. S. Zachariä, Anfangsgründe der Philosoph. Privatrechts, 1804.

Philosophische Rechtslehre o. Naturrecht u. Staatslehre, 1819.

Vierzig Bucher vom Staate, 1839–43.

Chr. Weiss, Lehrbuch der Philosophie des Rechts, 1804.

A. Bauer, Lehrbuch des Naturrechts, 1808. 3 Ausg. 1825.

J. C. F. Meister, Lehrbuch des Naturrechts, 1809.

Dreśch, Systematische Entwickelung der Grundbegriffe u. Grundprin-
zipien des gesammten Privatrechts, Staatsrechts, und Volkerrechts,
1810, 1822.

V. Zeiller, Naturrecht, 1813.

W. F. Krug, Dikäologie oder philosophische Rechtslehre, 1817, 1830.

Eschenmeyer, Normalrecht, 2 Thle. 1819.

S. Beck, Lehrbuch des Naturrechts, 1820.

V. Droste-Hülshoff, Lehrbuch des Naturrechts o. der Rechtsphilosophie, 1823, 1831.

Pölitz, Natur- und Volkerrecht, Staats- und Staatenrecht, 1823, 1825.

J. Haus, Elementa doctrinæ philosophiæ sive juris naturalis. Gondavi,
1824.

K. von Rotteck, Lehrbuch des Vernunftrechts und der Staatswissenschaft, 4 Bde. 1829–34, 1841.

Ant. Virozsil, Epitome juris naturalis. Pesthini, 1839.

F. Fischer, Naturrecht und natürliche Staatslehre, 1848.

G. Schilling, Lehrbuch des Naturrechts, 1859.

Besides these a considerable number of similar German works might be referred to by Schaumann, Heydenreich, Klein, A. Thomas, Weiss, J. K. Schmid, T. M. Zachariä, Stöckhardt, E. Reinhold, Schnabel, Pfitzer, and others.

Of the French works, from the Kantian standpoint, may be quoted (Ahrens, i. 326):—

M. Bussart, Elements de droit naturel privé, Fribourg en Suisse, 1836.

V. Belime, Philosophie du droit. Paris, 1844, 4 ed. 1881.

In Italy, where the Philosophy of Law has been cultivated 'with great zeal and intelligence' (Ahrens, i. 327; Röder, *Krit. Zeitschrift für Rechtswiss.* xv. 1, 2, 3), the Kantian system has been ably discussed by Mancini, Mamiani, Rosmini, Poli, and others. Its chief representatives have been—

Baroli, Diritto naturale privato e publico, 6 vol. Cremona, 1837.

Tolomei, Corso elementare di diritto naturale, 2 ed. Padova, 1855.

Soria di Crispan, Filosofia di diritto publico. (Philosophie du droit public. Brux. 1853–4.) Transl. into French.

Rosmini-Serbati, Filosofia del diritto, 1841. (In part Kantian.)

[Since writing the foregoing Preface there has come to hand the important work, 'La Vita del Diritto, nei suoi rapporti colla Vita Sociale: Studio comparativo di Filosofia Giuridica. Per Giusseppe Carle, Professore ordinario di Filosofia de Diritto nella R. Universita di Torino.' Its comprehensive method and profound insight add to the already ample evidence of the 'great zeal and intelligence' with which the Philosophy of Law is now being cultivated by the countrymen of Vico, the natural successors of Antistius Labeo, and Papinian. Professor Carle points out the relation of Kant not only to Rosmini, but also to Mamiani and others. His view of the importance and influence of the Kantian System is in accord with the brief indications ventured in these Prefatory hints. It is impossible to quote his exposition here, but attention may be directed to P. ii. L. i. Cap. ii. § 3, 'Emmanuele Kant come iniziatore del metodo rationale nello studio del diritto naturale;' and L. ii. Cap. v. 'Ulteriore svolgimento,' etc.—TR.]

CONTENTS.

—o—

KANT'S METAPHYSICAL PRINCIPLES OF THE SCIENCE OF RIGHT.

PAGE

PREFATORY EXPLANATIONS, ... 3

PROLEGOMENA.

GENERAL INTRODUCTION TO THE METAPHYSIC OF MORALS.

I. Relations of the Faculties of the Human Mind to the Moral
Laws, ... 9
II. The Idea and Necessity of a Metaphysic of Morals, . . 15
III. The Division of a Metaphysic of Morals, . . . 20

GENERAL DIVISIONS OF THE METAPHYSIC OF MORALS.

I. Division of the Metaphysic of Morals as a System of Duties
generally, ... 24
II. Division of the Metaphysic of Morals according to Relations
of Obligation, ... 26
III. Division of the Metaphysic of Morals according to its Principles and Method, ... 27
IV. General Preliminary Conceptions defined and explained, . 28

INTRODUCTION TO THE SCIENCE OF RIGHT.

GENERAL DEFINITIONS AND DIVISIONS.

A. What the Science of Right is, ... 43
B. What is Right? 44
C. Universal Principle of Right, ... 45
D. Right is conjoined with the Title to compel, . . . 47
E. Strict Right; Compulsion, Freedom, Universal Laws, . 47
F. Supplementary Remarks on Equivocal Right, . . . 50

  I. Equity, ... 50
  II. The Right of Necessity, ... 52

DIVISION OF THE SCIENCE OF RIGHT.

	PAGE
A. General Division of the Duties of Right, . .	54
B. Universal Division of Rights, ...	55
I. Natural Right and Positive Right, . . .	55
II. Innate Right and Acquired Right, . . .	55
There is only one Innate Right, the Birthright of Freedom, ...	56
C. Methodical Division of the Science of Right, . . .	58

THE SCIENCE OF RIGHT.

PART FIRST: PRIVATE RIGHT.

THE SYSTEM OF THOSE LAWS WHICH REQUIRE NO EXTERNAL PROMULGATION.

The Principles of the Exteral Mine and Thine.

PRIVATE RIGHT.

CHAPTER FIRST.

Of the Mode of having anything External as one's own.

1. The Meaning of 'Mine' in Right, ...	61
2. Juridical Postulate of the Practical Reason, . . .	62
3. Possession and Ownership, ...	64
4. Exposition of the Conception of the External Mine and Thine, ...	64
5. Definition of the Conception of the External Mine and Thine, ...	66
6. Deduction of the Conception of Juridical Possession of an External Object, ...	67
7. Application of the Principle of the possibility of an External Mine and Thine to Objects of Experience, . . .	72
8. To have anything External as one's own is only possible in a Juridical or Civil State of Society, . . .	76
9. An External Mine and Thine in the State of Nature only provisory, ...	78

CHAPTER SECOND.

The Mode of Acquiring anything External.

10. The General Principle of External Acquisition, . .	81

First Section : Principles of Real Right.

PAGE

11. What is a Real Right? 85
12. The First Acquisition of a Thing can only be that of the
    Soil, ... 87
13. Every part of the Soil may be originarily acquired, . . 88
14. The Juridical Act of this original Acquisition is Occupancy, . 89
15. Peremptory and Provisory Acquisition, . . . 90
16. Conception of a Primary Acquisition of the Soil, . . 94
17. Deduction of the Conception of original primary Acquisition, 95
    Property, ... 98

Second Section : Principles of Personal Right.

18. Nature and Acquisition of Personal Right, . . . 100
19. Acquisition by Contract, ... 101
20. What is acquired by Contract? 104
21. Acceptance and Delivery, ... 105

Third Section : Principles of Personal Right that is Real in Kind.

22. Nature of Personal Right of a Real Kind, . . . 108
23. What is acquired in the Household, ... 109

RIGHTS OF THE FAMILY AS A DOMESTIC SOCIETY.

Title First : Conjugal Right (Husband and Wife).

24. The Natural Basis of Marriage, ... 109
25. The Rational Right of Marriage, ... 110
26. Monogamy and Equality in Marriage, . . . 111
27. Fulfilment of the Contract of Marriage, . . . 113

Title Second : Parental Right (Parent and Child).

28. The Relation of Parent and Child, ... 114
29. The Rights of the Parent, ... 116

Title Third : Household Right (Master and Servant).

30. Relation and Right of the Master of a Household, . . 118

SYSTEMATIC DIVISION OF ALL THE RIGHTS CAPABLE OF
BEING ACQUIRED BY CONTRACT.

PAGE

31. Division of Contracts, ... 121

Illustrations : I. What is Money ? 125

II. What is a Book ? . . . 129

The Unauthorized Publishing of Books, . 130

Confusion of Personal Right and Real Right, . . 131

EPISODICAL SECTION : THE IDEAL ACQUISITION OF
EXTERNAL OBJECTS OF THE WILL.

32. The Nature and Modes of Ideal Acquisition, . . . 132

33. I. Acquisition by Usucapion, ... 133

34. II. Acquisition by Inheritance, ... 136

35. III. The Right of a good Name after Death, . . . 138

CHAPTER THIRD.

ACQUISITION CONDITIONED BY THE SENTENCE OF A
PUBLIC JUDICATORY.

36. How and what Acquisition is subjectively conditioned by
the Principle of a Public Court, ... 141

37. I. The Contract of Donation, ... 143

38. II. The Contract of Loan, ... 144

39. III. The Revindication of what has been Lost, . . 147

40. IV. Acquisition of Security by taking of an Oath, . . 151

TRANSITION

FROM THE MINE AND THINE IN THE STATE OF NATURE
TO THE MINE AND THINE IN THE JURIDICAL STATE
GENERALLY.

41. Public Justice as related to the Natural and the Civil State, . 155

42. The Postulate of Public Right, ... 157

PART SECOND: PUBLIC RIGHT.

THE SYSTEM OF THOSE LAWS WHICH REQUIRE PUBLIC PROMULGATION.

The Principles of Right in Civil Society.

PAGE

43. Definition and Division of Public Right, . . . 161

PUBLIC RIGHT.

I. RIGHT OF THE STATE AND CONSTITUTIONAL LAW.

44. Origin of the Civil Union and Public Right, . . . 163
45. The Form of the State and its Three Powers, . . 165
46. The Legislative Power and the Members of the State, . 166
47. Dignities in the State and the Original Contract, . . 169
48. Mutual Relations and Characteristics of the Three Powers, . 170
49. Distinct Functions of the Three Powers. Autonomy of the State, ... 171

Constitutional and Juridical Consequences arising from the Nature of the Civil Union.

A. Right of the Supreme Power. Treason ; Dethronement ; Revolution ; Reform, ... 174
B. Land Rights. Secular and Church Lands. Rights of Taxation ; Finance ; Police ; Inspection, . . 182
C. Relief of the Poor. Foundling Hospitals. The Church, 186
D. The Right of assigning Offices and Dignities in the State, ... 190
E. The Right of Punishing and of Pardoning, . . 194
50. Constitutional Relations of the Citizen to his Country and to other Countries. Emigration ; Immigration ; Banishment ; Exile, ... 205
51. The Three Forms of the State. Autocracy ; Aristocracy ; Democracy, ... 206
52. Historical Origin and Changes. A Pure Republic. Representative Government, ... 208

II. THE RIGHT OF NATIONS AND INTERNATIONAL LAW.

53. Nature and Division of the Right of Nations, . . 213
54. The Elements of the Right of Nations, . . . 214
55. Right of going to War as related to the Subjects of the State, 215
56. Right of going to War in relation to Hostile States, . . 218

PAGE

57. Right during War, ...   219
58. Right after War, ...   221
59. The Rights of Peace, ...   222
60. Right as against an unjust Enemy, ...   223
61. Perpetual Peace and a Permanent Congress of Nations,   .   224

III. THE UNIVERSAL RIGHT OF MANKIND.

62. Nature and Conditions of Cosmopolitical Right,   .   .   226

    CONCLUSION, ...   229

SUPPLEMENTARY EXPLANATIONS OF PRINCIPLES OF RIGHT.

OCCASION AND OBJECT OF THESE SUPPLEMENTARY EXPLANATIONS.

Objection as to the Faculty of Desire, ...   234

   I. Logical Preparation for the preceding Conception of Right,   235
  II. Justification of the Conception of a Personal Right of a
      Real Kind, ...   237
 III. Examples of Real-Personal Right,   .   .   .   238
  IV. Confusion of Real and Personal Right,   .   .   241
   V. Addition to the Explanation of the Conception of Penal
      Right, ...   243
  VI. On the Right of Usucapion,   .   .   .   245
 VII. On Inheritance and Succession,   .   .   .   247
VIII. The Right of the State in relation to Perpetual Founda-
      tions for the benefit of the Subjects,   .   .   249
      A. Hospitals, ...   250
      B. Churches, ...   251
      C. The Orders in the State,   .   .   .   253
      D. Primogeniture and Entail,   .   .   .   254
  IX. Concluding Remarks on Public Right and Absolute Submis-
      sion to the Sovereign Authority, .   .   .   255

APOLOGIA.

Kant's Vindication of his Philosophical Style,   .   .   259

THE METAPHYSICAL PRINCIPLES

OF

THE SCIENCE OF RIGHT

AS CONTAINED IN

THE METAPHYSIC OF MORALS.

BY

IMMANUEL KANT.

Translated from the German.

treated as a System of Principles that originate in Reason ; and, as such, it might be properly designated 'The Meta-physic of Right.' But the conception of Right, purely rational in its origin though it be, is also applicable to cases presented in experience ; and, consequently, a Metaphysical System of Rights must take into considera-tion the empirical variety and manifoldness of these cases in order that its Divisions may be complete. For com-pleteness and comprehensiveness are essential and indis-pensable to the formation of a rational system. But, on the other hand, it is impossible to obtain a complete survey of all the details of experience, and where it may be attempted to approach this, the empirical conceptions embracing those details cannot form integral elements of the system itself, but can only be introduced in subordinate observations, and mainly as furnishing examples illustrative of the General Principles. The only appropriate designa-tion for the First Part of a Metaphysic of Morals, will, therefore, be THE METAPHYSICAL PRINCIPLES OF THE SCIENCE OF RIGHT. And, in regard to the practical appli-cation to cases, it is manifest that only an approximation to systematic treatment is to be expected, and not the attainment of a System complete in itself. Hence the same method of exposition will be adopted here as was followed in the former work on 'The Metaphysical Prin-ciples of the Science of Nature.' The Principles of Right which belong to the rational system will form the leading

portions of the text, and details connected with Rights
which refer to particular cases of experience, will be
appended occasionally in subordinate remarks. In this
way a distinction will be clearly made between what is a
Metaphysical or rational Principle, and what refers to the
empirical Practice of Right.

.　　.　　.　　.　　.　　.　　.　　.

Towards the end of the work, I have treated several
sections with less fulness of detail than might have been
expected when they are compared with what precedes
them. But this has been intentionally done, partly
because it appears to me that the more general principles
of the later subjects may be easily deduced from what has
gone before; and, also, partly because the details of the
Principles of Public Right are at present subjected to so
much discussion, and are besides so important in themselves, that they may well justify delay, for a time, of a
final and decisive judgment regarding them.

PROLEGOMENA.

GENERAL INTRODUCTION
TO
THE METAPHYSIC OF MORALS.

GENERAL INTRODUCTION TO THE
METAPHYSIC OF MORALS.

I.

THE RELATION OF THE FACULTIES OF THE HUMAN MIND TO THE MORAL LAWS.

The Practical Faculty of Action.—THE ACTIVE FACULTY OF THE HUMAN MIND, as the Faculty of Desire in its widest sense, is the Power which man has, through his mental representations, of becoming the cause of objects corresponding to these representations. The capacity of a Being to act in conformity with his own representations, is what constitutes the Life of such a Being.

The Feeling of Pleasure or Pain.—It is to be observed, *first*, that with Desire or Aversion there is always connected PLEASURE or PAIN, the susceptibility for which is called FEELING. But the converse does not always hold. For there may be a Pleasure connected, not with the desire of an object, but with a mere mental representation, it being indifferent whether an object corresponding to the representation exist or not. And, *second*, the Pleasure or Pain connected with the object of desire does not always precede the activity of Desire; nor can it be regarded in every case as the cause, but it may as well be the Effect of that activity. The capacity of experiencing Pleasure or Pain on the occasion of a

mental representation, is called 'Feeling,' because Pleasure and Pain contain only what is *subjective* in the
relations of our mental activity.   They do not involve
any relation to an object that could possibly furnish a
knowledge of it as such; they cannot even give us a
knowledge of our own mental state.   For even Sensa-
tions,[1] considered apart from the qualities which attach to
them on account of the modifications of the Subject,—as,
for instance, in reference to Red, Sweet, and such like,—
are referred as constituent elements of knowledge to
Objects, whereas Pleasure or Pain felt in connection with
what is red or sweet, express absolutely nothing that is
in the Object, but merely a relation to the Subject.
And for the reason just stated, Pleasure and Pain considered in themselves cannot be more precisely defined.
All that can be further done with regard to them is
merely to point out what consequences they may have
in certain relations, in order to make the knowledge of
them available practically.

[1] The Sensibility as the Faculty of Sense, may be defined by reference to
the subjective Nature of our Representations generally.   It is the Understanding that first refers the subjective Representations to an object; it
alone *thinks* anything by means of these Representations.   Now, the subjective nature of our Representations might be of such a kind that they could
be related to Objects so as to furnish knowledge of them, either in regard
to their Form or Matter—in the former relation by pure Perception, in
the latter by Sensation proper.   In this case the Sense-faculty, as the
capacity for receiving objective Representations, would be properly called
Sense-perception.   But mere mental Representation from its subjective
nature cannot, in fact, become a constituent of objective knowledge,
because it contains merely the relation of the Representations to the
Subject, and includes nothing that can be used for attaining a knowledge
of the object.   In this case, then, this receptivity of the Mind for subjective representations is called FEELING.   It includes the effect of the
Representations, whether sensible or intellectual, upon the Subject; and
it belongs to the Sensibility, although the Representation itself ˙may
belong to the Understanding or the Reason.

Practical Pleasure, Interest, Inclination.—The Pleasure, which is necessarily connected with the activity of Desire, when the representation of the object desired affects the capacity of Feeling, may be called *Practical Pleasure*. And this designation is applicable whether the Pleasure is the cause or the effect of the Desire. On the other hand, that Pleasure which is not necessarily connected with the Desire of an object, and which, therefore, is not a pleasure in the existence of the object, but is merely attached to a mental representation alone, may be called Inactive Complacency, or mere *Contemplative Pleasure*. The Feeling of this latter kind of Pleasure, is what is called *Taste*. Hence, in a System of Practical Philosophy, the Contemplative Pleasure of Taste will not be discussed as an essential constituent conception, but need only be referred to incidentally or episodically. But as regards *Practical* Pleasure, it is otherwise. For the determination of the activity of the Faculty of Desire or Appetency, which is necessarily preceded by this Pleasure as its cause, is what properly constitutes DESIRE in the strict sense of the term. Habitual Desire, again, constitutes *Inclination;* and the connection of Pleasure with the activity of Desire, in so far as this connection is judged by the Understanding to be valid according to a general Rule holding good at least for the individual, is what is called *Interest*. Hence, in such a case, the Practical Pleasure is an Interest of the Inclination of the individual. On the other hand, if the Pleasure can only follow a preceding determination of the Faculty of Desire, it is an Intellectual Pleasure, and the interest in the object must be called a rational Interest; for were the Interest sensuous, and not based only upon pure Principles of

Reason, Sensation would necessarily be conjoined with the Pleasure, and would thus determine the activity of the Desire. Where an entirely pure Interest of Reason must be assumed, it is not legitimate to introduce into it an Interest of Inclination surreptitiously. However, in order to conform so far with the common phraseology, we may allow the application of the term 'Inclination' even to that which can only be the object of an 'Intellectual' Pleasure in the sense of a habitual Desire arising from a pure Interest of Reason. But such Inclination would have to be viewed, not as the Cause, but as the Effect of the rational Interest; and we might call it the *non-sensuous* or RATIONAL INCLINATION (*propensio intellectualis*).—Further, *Concupiscence* is to be distinguished from the activity of Desire itself, as a stimulus or incitement to its determination. It is always a sensuous state of the mind, which does not itself attain to the definiteness of an act of the Power of Desire.

The Will generally as Practical Reason.—The activity of the Faculty of Desire may proceed in accordance with Conceptions; and in so far as the Principle thus determining it to action is found in the mind, and not in its object, it constitutes *a Power of acting or not acting according to liking.* In so far as the activity is accompanied with the Consciousness of the Power of the action to produce the Object, it forms an act of *Choice;* if this consciousness is not conjoined with it, the Activity is called a *Wish.* The Faculty of Desire, in so far as its inner Principle of determination as the ground of its liking or Predilection lies in the Reason of the Subject, constitutes THE WILL. The Will is therefore the Faculty of active Desire or Appetency, viewed not so much in relation to the action—which is the relation of the act of Choice—as rather in relation to the Principle that determines the power of Choice to the action. It has, in itself, properly no special Principle of determination, but in so far as it may determine the voluntary act of Choice, it is THE PRACTICAL REASON ITSELF.

The Will as the Faculty of Practical Principles.— Under the Will, taken generally, may be included the volitional act of *Choice*, and also the mere act of *Wish*, in so far as Reason may determine the Faculty of Desire in its activity. The act of Choice that can be determined by *pure Reason*, constitutes the act of Free-will. That act which is determinable only by Inclination as a sensuous impulse or stimulus would be irrational brute Choice (*arbitrium brutum*). The human act of Choice, however, as human, is in fact *affected* by such impulses or stimuli, but is not *determined* by them ; and it is, therefore, not pure in itself when taken apart from the acquired habit of determination by Reason. But it may be determined to action by the pure Will. The *Freedom* of the act of volitional Choice, is its independence of being *determined* by sensuous impulses or stimuli. This forms the *negative* conception of the Free-will. The *positive* Conception of Freedom is given by the fact that the Will is the capability of Pure Reason to be practical of itself. But this is not possible otherwise than by the Maxim of every action being subjected to the condition of being practicable as a universal Law. Applied as Pure Reason to the act of Choice, and considered apart from its objects, it may be regarded as the Faculty of Principles ; and, in this connection, it is the source of Practical Principles. Hence it is to be viewed as a law-giving Faculty. But as the *material* upon which to construct a Law is not furnished to it, it can only make

the *form* of the Maxim of the act of Will, in so far as
it is available as a universal Law, the supreme Law and
determining Principle of the Will. And as the Maxims,
or Rules of human action derived from subjective causes,
do not of themselves necessarily agree with those that
are objective and universal, Reason can only prescribe
this supreme Law as an absolute Imperative of prohibition or command.

The Laws of Freedom as Moral, Juridical, and Ethical.—
The Laws of Freedom, as distinguished from the Laws
of Nature, are *moral* Laws. So far as they refer only
to external actions and their lawfulness, they are called
Juridical; but if they also require that, as Laws, they
shall themselves be the determining Principles of our
actions, they are *Ethical*. The agreement of an action
with Juridical Laws, is its *Legality*; the agreement of
an action with Ethical Laws, is its *Morality*. The Freedom to which the former laws refer, can only be Freedom
in external practice; but the Freedom to which the
latter laws refer, is Freedom in the internal as well as
the external exercise of the activity of the Will in so
far as it is determined by Laws of Reason. So, in
Theoretical Philosophy, it is said that only the objects
of the external senses are in Space, but all the objects
both of internal and external sense are in Time; because
the representations of both, as being representations, so
far belong all to the internal sense. In like manner,
whether Freedom is viewed in reference to the external
or the internal action of the Will, its Laws, as pure
practical Laws of Reason for the free activity of the
Will generally, must at the same time be inner Principles for its determination, although they may not
always be considered in this relation.

II.

THE IDEA AND NECESSITY OF A METAPHYSIC OF MORALS.

The Laws of Nature Rational and also Empirical.—It has been shown in *The Metaphysical Principles of the Science of Nature*, that there must be Principles *à priori* for the Natural Science that has to deal with the objects of the external senses. And it was further shown that it is possible, and even necessary, to formulate a System of these Principles under the name of a 'Metaphysical Science of Nature,' as a preliminary to Experimental Physics regarded as Natural Science applied to particular objects of experience. But this latter Science, if care be taken to keep its generalizations free from error, may accept many propositions as universal on the evidence of experience, although if the term 'Universal' be taken in its strict sense, these would necessarily have to be deduced by the Metaphysical Science from Principles *à priori*. Thus Newton accepted the principle of the Equality of Action and Reaction as established by experience, and yet he extended it as a universal Law over the whole of material Nature. The Chemists go even farther, grounding their most general Laws regarding the combination and decomposition of the materials of bodies wholly upon experience ; and yet they trust so completely to the Universality and Necessity of those laws, that they have no anxiety as to any error being found in propositions founded upon experiments conducted in accordance with them.

Moral Laws à priori and Necessary.—But it is otherwise with Moral Laws. These, in contradistinction to Natural Laws, are only valid *as* Laws, in so far as they can be rationally established *à priori* and comprehended as *necessary*. In fact, conceptions and judgments regarding ourselves and our conduct have no *moral* significance, if they contain only what may be learned from experience ; and when any one is, so to speak, misled into making a Moral Principle out of anything derived from this latter source, he is already in danger of falling into the coarsest and most fatal errors.

If the Philosophy of Morals were nothing more than a Theory of Happiness (*Eudæmonism*), it would be absurd to search after Principles *à priori* as a foundation for it. For however plausible it may sound to say that Reason, even prior to experience, can comprehend by what means we may attain to a lasting enjoyment of the real pleasures of life, yet all that is taught on this subject *à priori* is either tautological, or is assumed wholly without foundation. It is only Experience that can show what will bring us enjoyment. The natural impulses directed towards nourishment, the sexual instinct, or the tendency to rest and motion, as well as the higher desires of honour, the acquisition of knowledge, and such like, as developed with our natural capacities, are alone capable of showing in what those enjoyments are to be *found*. And, further, the knowledge thus acquired, is available for each individual merely in his own way ; and it is only thus he can learn the means by which he has to *seek* those enjoyments. All specious rationalizing *à priori*, in this connection, is nothing at bottom but carrying facts of Experience up to generalizations by induction (*secundum principia generalia non universalia*) ; and the generality thus attained . is still so limited that numberless exceptions must be allowed to every individual in order that he may adapt the choice of his mode of life to his own particular inclinations and his capacity for pleasure. And, after all, the individual has really to acquire his Prudence at the cost of his own suffering or that of his neighbours.

But it is quite otherwise with the Principles of Morality. They lay down Commands for every one without regard to his particular inclinations, and merely because and so far as he is free, and has a practical Reason. Instruction in the Laws of Morality is not drawn from observation of oneself or of our animal nature, nor from perception of the course of the world in regard to what happens, or how men act.[1] But Reason commands how we *ought* to act, even although no example of such action were to be found; nor does Reason give any regard to the Advantage which may accrue to us by so acting, and which Experience could alone actually show. For, although Reason allows us to seek what is for our advantage in every possible way, and although, founding upon the evidence of Experience, it may further promise that greater advantages will probably follow on the average from the observance of her commands than from their transgression, especially if Prudence guides the conduct, yet the authority of her precepts as *Commands* does not rest on such considerations. They are used by Reason only as Counsels, and by way of a counterpoise against seductions to an opposite course, when adjusting beforehand the equilibrium of a partial balance in the sphere of Practical Judgment, in order thereby to secure the decision of this Judgment, according to the due weight of the à *priori* Principles of a pure Practical Reason.

[1] This holds notwithstanding the fact that the term 'Morals,' in Latin *Mores*, and in German *Sitten*, signifies originally only *Manners* or *Mode of Life*.

The Necessity of a Metaphysic of Morals.—'META-
PHYSICS' designates any System of Knowledge à priori
that consists of pure Conceptions. Accordingly a
Practical Philosophy not having Nature, but the Freedom of the Will for its object, will presuppose and
require a Metaphysic of Morals. It is even a *Duty*
to have such a Metaphysic; and every man does, indeed,
possess it in himself, although commonly but in an
obscure way. For how could any one believe that he
has a source of universal Law in himself, without Principles à priori ? And just as in a Metaphysic of Nature
there must be principles regulating the application of
the universal supreme Principles of Nature to objects
of Experience, so there cannot but be such principles in
the Metaphysic of Morals; and we will often have to deal
objectively with the particular *nature* of man as known
only by Experience, in order to show in it the consequences of these universal Moral Principles. But this
mode of dealing with these Principles in their particular
applications will in no way detract from their rational
purity, or throw doubt on their à priori origin. In other
words, this amounts to saying that a Metaphysic of
Morals cannot be founded on Anthropology as the
Empirical Science of Man, but may be applied to it.

Moral Anthropology.—The counterpart of a Metaphysic
of Morals, and the other member of the Division of
Practical Philosophy, would be a Moral Anthropology, as
the Empirical Science of the Moral Nature of Man. This
Science would contain only the subjective conditions
that hinder or favour the *realization* in practice of the
universal moral Laws in human Nature, with the means
of propagating, spreading, and strengthening the Moral
Principles,—as by the Education of the young and the

instruction of the people,—and all other such doctrines and precepts founded upon experience and indispensable in themselves, although they must neither precede the metaphysical investigation of the Principles of Reason, nor be mixed up with it. For, by doing so, there would be a great danger of laying down false, or at least very flexible Moral Laws, which would hold forth as unattainable what is not attained only because the Law has not been comprehended and presented in its purity, in which also its strength consists. Or, otherwise, spurious and mixed motives might be adopted instead of what is dutiful and good in itself; and these would furnish no certain Moral Principles either for the guidance of the Judgment or for the discipline of the heart in the practice of Duty. It is only by Pure Reason, therefore, that Duty can and must be prescribed.

Practical Philosophy in relation to Art.—The higher Division of Philosophy, under which the Division just mentioned stands, is into Theoretical Philosophy and Practical Philosophy. Practical Philosophy is just Moral Philosophy in its widest sense, as has been explained elsewhere.[1] All that is practicable and possible, according to Natural Laws, is the special subject of the activity of Art, and its precepts and rules entirely depend on the Theory of Nature. It is only what is practicable according to Laws of Freedom that can have Principles independent of Theory, for there is no Theory in relation to what passes beyond the determinations of Nature. Philosophy therefore cannot embrace under its practical Division a *technical* Theory, but only a *morally practical* Doctrine. But if the dexterity of the Will in acting according to Laws of Freedom, in contradistinction to

[1] In the *Critique of the Judgment* (1790).

Nature, were to be also called an *Art*, it would necessarily indicate an Art which would make a System of
Freedom possible like the System of Nature. This
would truly be a Divine Art, if we were in a position by
means of it to realize completely what Reason prescribes
to us, and to put the Idea into practice.

III.

The Division of a Metaphysic of Morals.

Two Elements involved in all Legislation.—All Legislation, whether relating to internal or external action,
and whether prescribed *à priori* by mere Reason or laid
down by the Will of another, involves two Elements :—
1st, a LAW which represents the action that ought to
happen as necessary *objectively*, thus making the action
a Duty ; 2nd, a MOTIVE which connects the principle
determining the Will to this action with the Mental representation of the Law *subjectively*, so that the Law makes
Duty the motive of the Action. By the first element,
the action is represented as a Duty, in accordance with
the mere theoretical knowledge of the possibility of
determining the activity of the Will by practical Rules.
By the second element, the Obligation so to act, is
connected in the Subject with a determining Principle of
the Will as such.

Division of Duties into Juridical and Ethical.—All
Legislation, therefore, may be differentiated by reference
to its Motive-principle.[1] The Legislation which makes

---

[1] This ground of Division will apply, although the action which it
makes a duty may coincide with another action, that may be otherwise
looked at from another point of view. For instance, Actions may in all
cases be classified as external.

an Action a Duty, and this Duty at the same time a Motive, is *ethical*. That Legislation which does not include the Motive - principle in the Law, and consequently admits another Motive than the idea of Duty itself, is *juridical*. In respect of the latter, it is evident that the motives distinct from the idea of Duty, to which it may refer, must be drawn from the subjective (pathological) influences of Inclination and of Aversion, determining the voluntary activity, and especially from the latter; because it is a Legislation which has to be compulsory, and not merely a mode of attracting or persuading. The agreement or non-agreement of an action with the Law, without reference to its Motive, is its *Legality*; and that character of the action in which the idea of Duty arising from the Law, at the same time forms the Motive of the Action, is its *Morality*.

Duties specially in accord with a Juridical Legislation, can only be external Duties. For this mode of Legislation does not require that the idea of the Duty, which is internal, shall be of itself the determining Principle of the act of Will; and as it requires a motive suitable to the nature of its laws, it can only connect what is external with the Law. Ethical Legislation, on the other hand, makes internal actions also Duties, but not to the exclusion of the external, for it embraces everything which is of the nature of Duty. And just because ethical Legislation includes within its Law the internal motive of the action as contained in the idea of Duty, it involves a characteristic which cannot at all enter into the Legislation that is external. Hence, Ethical Legislation cannot as such be external, not even when proceeding from a Divine Will, although

it may receive Duties which rest on an external Legislation *as Duties*, into the position of motives, within its
own Legislation.

Jurisprudence and Ethics distinguished.—From what
has been said, it is evident that all Duties, merely
because they are duties, belong to Ethics; and yet the
Legislation upon which they are founded is not on that
account in all cases contained in Ethics.   On the contrary, the Law of many of them lies outside of Ethics.
Thus Ethics commands that I must fulfil a promise
entered into by Contract, although the other party might
not be able to compel me to do so.   It adopts the Law
'*pacta sunt servanda*,' and the Duty corresponding to it,
from Jurisprudence or the Science of Right, by which
they are established.   It is not in Ethics, therefore, but
in Jurisprudence, that the principle of the Legislation
lies, that 'promises made and accepted must be kept.'
Accordingly, Ethics specially teaches that if the Motive-
principle of external compulsion which Juridical Legislation connects with a Duty is even let go, the idea of
Duty alone is sufficient of itself as a Motive.   For were
it not so, and were the Legislation itself not juridical,
and consequently the Duty arising from it not specially
a Duty of Right as distinguished from a Duty of Virtue,
then Fidelity in the performance of acts, to which the
individual may be bound by the terms of a Contract,
would have to be classified with acts of Benevolence and
the Obligation that underlies them, which cannot be
correct.   To keep one's promise is not properly a Duty
of Virtue, but a Duty of Right; and the performance of
it can be enforced by external Compulsion.   But to
keep one's promise, even when no Compulsion can be
applied to enforce it, is, at the same time, a virtuous

action, and a proof of Virtue. Jurisprudence as the Science of Right, and Ethics as the Science of Virtue, are therefore distinguished not so much by their different Duties, as rather by the difference of the Legislation which connects the one or the other kind of motive with their Laws.

, Ethical Legislation is that which *cannot* be external, although the Duties it prescribes *may* be external as well as internal. Juridical Legislation is that which may also be external. Thus it is an external duty to keep a promise entered into by Contract ; but the injunction to do this merely because it is a duty, without regard to any other motive, belongs exclusively to the *internal* Legislation. It does not belong thus to the ethical sphere as being a particular kind of duty or a particular mode of action to which we are bound,— for it is an external duty in Ethics as well as in Jurisprudence, — but it is because the Legislation in the case referred to is internal, and cannot have an external Lawgiver, that the Obligation is reckoned as belonging to Ethics. For the same reason, the Duties of Benevolence, although they are external Duties as Obligations to external actions, are, in like manner, reckoned as belonging to Ethics, because they can only be enjoined by Legislation that is internal.—Ethics has no doubt its own peculiar Duties,—such as those towards oneself,— but it has also Duties in common with Jurisprudence, only not under the same mode of *Obligation*. In short, the peculiarity of Ethical Legislation is to enjoin the performance of certain actions merely because they are Duties, and to make the Principle of Duty itself—whatever be its source or occasion—the sole sufficing motive of the activity of the Will. Thus, then, there are many

ethical Duties that are *directly* such ; and the inner
Legislation also makes the others—all and each of them
—*indirectly* Ethical.

The *Deduction* of the Division of a System is the
proof of its completeness as well as of its continuity,
so that there may be a logical transition from the
general conception divided to the members of the
Division, and through the whole series of the subdivisions without any break or leap in the arrangement (*divisio per saltum*). Such a Division is one of
the most difficult conditions for the architect of a
System to fulfil. There is even some doubt as to
what is the *highest Conception* that is primarily
divided into *Right* and *Wrong* (*aut fas aut nefas*).
It is assuredly the conception of the activity of the
Free-will in general. In like manner, the expounders
of Ontology start from ' *Something* ' and ' *Nothing*,'
without perceiving that these are already members of
a Division for which the highest divided conception
is awanting, and which can be no other than that of
' *Thing* ' in general.

GENERAL DIVISIONS OF THE METAPHYSIC
OF MORALS.

I.

DIVISION OF THE METAPHYSIC OF MORALS AS A SYSTEM
OF DUTIES GENERALLY.

1. All Duties are either Duties of Right, that is,
JURIDICAL DUTIES (*Officia Juris*), or Duties of Virtue,
that is, ETHICAL DUTIES (*Officia Virtutis s. ethica*).
Juridical Duties are such as may be promulgated by
external Legislation ; Ethical Duties are those for which

such legislation is not possible. The reason why the latter cannot be properly made the subject of external Legislation is because they relate to an End or final purpose, which is itself, at the same time, embraced in these Duties, and which it is a Duty for the individual to have as such. But no external Legislation can cause any one to adopt a particular intention, or to propose to himself a certain purpose; for this depends upon an internal condition or act of the mind itself. However, external actions conducive to such a mental condition may be commanded, without its being implied that the individual will of necessity make them an End to himself.

But why, then, it may be asked, is the Science of Morals or Moral Philosophy, commonly entitled— especially by Cicero—the Science of *Duty* and not also the Science of *Right*, since Duties and Rights refer to each other ? The reason is this. We know our own Freedom—from which all Moral Laws and consequently all Rights as well as all Duties arise—only through the Moral Imperative, which is an immediate injunction of Duty; whereas the conception of Right as a ground of putting others under Obligation has afterwards to be developed out of it.

2. In the Doctrine of Duty, Man may and ought to be represented in accordance with the nature of his faculty of Freedom, which is entirely supra-sensible. He is, therefore, to be represented purely according to his Humanity as a Personality independent of physical determinations (*homo noumenon*), in distinction from the same person as a Man modified with these determinations (*homo phenomenon*). Hence the conceptions of Right and End when referred to Duty, in view of this twofold quality, give the following Division :—

DIVISION OF THE METAPHYSIC OF MORALS

ACCORDING TO THE OBJECTIVE RELATION OF THE LAW TO DUTY.

I. JURIDICAL DUTIES to ONESELF or OTHERS.

I. THE RIGHT OF HUMANITY in our own Person (Juridical Duties towards Oneself).

II. THE RIGHT OF MANKIND in Others (Juridical Duties towards Others).

PERFECT DUTY.

II. ETHICAL DUTIES to ONESELF or OTHERS.

III. THE END OF HUMANITY in our Person (Ethical Duties towards Oneself).

IV. THE END OF MANKIND in Others (Ethical Duties towards Others).

IMPERFECT DUTY.

II.

DIVISION OF THE METAPHYSIC OF MORALS ACCORDING TO RELATIONS OF OBLIGATION.

As the Subjects between whom a relation of Right to Duty is apprehended—whether it actually exist or not — admit of being conceived in various juridical relations to each other, another Division may be proposed from this point of view, as follows :—

DIVISION POSSIBLE ACCORDING TO THE SUBJECTIVE RELATION OF THOSE WHO BIND UNDER OBLIGATIONS, AND THOSE WHO ARE BOUND UNDER OBLIGATIONS.

1.	2.
The juridical Relation of Man to Beings *who have neither Right nor Duty.*	The juridical Relation of Man to Beings who have both Rights and Duties.
VACAT.—There is no such Relation. For such Beings are irrational, and they neither put us under Obligation, nor can we be put under Obligation by them.	ADEST.—There is such a Relation. For it is the Relation of Men to Men.

3.	4.
The juridical Relation of Man to Beings who have only Duties and no Rights.	The juridical Relation of Man to a Being who has only Rights and no Duties—(GOD).
VACAT.—There is no such Relation. For such Beings would be Men without juridical Personality, as Slaves or Bondsmen.	VACAT.—There is no such Relation in mere Philosophy, because such a Being is not an object of possible experience.

A *real* relation between Right and Duty is therefore found, in this scheme, only in No. 2. The reason why such is not likewise found in No. 4 is, because it would constitute a *transcendent* Duty, that is, one to which no corresponding subject can be given that is external and capable of imposing Obligation. Consequently the Relation from the theoretical point of view is here merely *ideal*; that is, it is a Relation to an object of thought which we form for ourselves. But the conception of this object is not entirely *empty*. On the contrary, it is a fruitful conception in relation to ourselves and the maxims of our inner morality, and therefore in relation to practice generally. And it is in this bearing, that all the Duty involved and practicable for us in such a merely ideal relation lies.

III.

DIVISION OF THE METAPHYSIC OF MORALS.

AS A SYSTEM OF DUTIES GENERALLY.

According to the constituent Principles and the Method of the System.

I. PRINCIPLES, { I. DUTIES OF RIGHT, { I. Private Right. II. Public Right.

II. DUTIES OF VIRTUE, ETC.—And so on, including all that refers not only to the Materials, but also to the Architectonic Form of a scientific system of Morals, when the Metaphysical investigation of the elements has completely traced out the Universal Principles constituting the whole.

II. METHOD, . { I. DIDACTICS. II. ASCETICS.

IV.

GENERAL PRELIMINARY CONCEPTIONS DEFINED AND EXPLAINED.

(Philosophia practica universalis.)

Freedom.—The conception of FREEDOM is a conception of pure Reason. It is therefore *transcendent* in so far as regards *Theoretical* Philosophy; for it is a conception for which no corresponding instance or example can be found or supplied in any possible experience. Accordingly Freedom is not presented as an object of any theoretical knowledge that is possible for us. It is in no respect a constitutive, but only a regulative conception; and it can be accepted by the Speculative Reason as at most a merely negative Principle. In the practical sphere of Reason, however, the reality of Freedom may be demonstrated by certain Practical Principles which, as Laws, prove a causality of the Pure Reason in the process of determining the activity of the Will, that is independent of all empirical and sensible conditions. And thus there is established the fact of a pure Will existing in us as the source of all moral conceptions and laws.

Moral Laws and Categorical Imperatives.— On this positive conception of Freedom in the practical relation certain unconditional practical Laws are founded, and they specially constitute MORAL LAWS. In relation to us as human beings, with an activity of Will modified by sensible influences so as not to be conformable to the pure Will, but as often contrary to it, these Laws appear as IMPERATIVES commanding or prohibiting certain

actions; and as such they are CATEGORICAL or UNCON-
DITIONAL IMPERATIVES. Their categorical and unconditional character distinguishes them from the *Technical
Imperatives* which express the prescriptions of Art, and
which always command only conditionally. According
to these Categorical Imperatives, certain actions are
allowed or *disallowed* as being morally possible or impossible; and certain of them or their opposites are
morally necessary and obligatory. Hence, in reference
to such actions, there arises the conception of a Duty
whose observance or transgression is accompanied with a
Pleasure or Pain of a peculiar kind, known as Moral
Feeling. We do not, however, take the Moral Feelings or
Sentiments into account, in considering the practical
Laws of Reason. For they do not form the foundation
or principle of practical Laws of Reason, but only the subjective *Effects* that arise in the mind on the occasion of
our voluntary activity being determined by these Laws.
And while they neither add to nor take from the objective validity or influence of the moral Laws in the judgment of Reason, such Sentiments may vary according to
the differences of the individuals who experience them.

**The following Conceptions are common to Jurisprudence
and Ethics as the two main Divisions of the Metaphysic of Morals.**

Obligation.—OBLIGATION is the Necessity of a free
Action when viewed in relation to a Categorical Imperative of Reason.

An IMPERATIVE is a practical Rule by which an
Action, otherwise contingent in itself, is *made* necessary. It is distinguished from a practical Law, in

that such a Law, while likewise representing the
Action as necessary, does not consider whether it is
internally necessary as involved in the nature of the
Agent—say as a holy Being—or is contingent to him,
as in the case of Man as we find him; for, where the
first condition holds good, there is in fact no Imperative. Hence an Imperative is a Rule which not only
represents but *makes* a subjectively contingent action
necessary; and it, accordingly, represents the Subject
as being (morally) *necessitated* to act in accordance
with this Rule. — A Categorical or Unconditional
Imperative is one which does not represent the action
in any way *mediately* through the conception of an
End that is to be attained by it; but it presents the
action to the mind as objectively necessary by the
mere representation of its form as an action, and thus
makes it necessary. Such Imperatives cannot be put
forward by any other practical Science than that which
prescribes Obligations, and it is only the Science of
Morals that does this. All other Imperatives are
technical, and they are altogether conditional. The
ground of the possibility of Categorical Imperatives,
lies in the fact that they refer to no determination of
the activity of the Will by which a purpose might be
assigned to it, but solely to its FREEDOM.

The Allowable.—Every Action is ALLOWED (*licitum*)
which is not contrary to Obligation ; and this Freedom
not being limited by an opposing Imperative, constitutes
a Moral Right as a warrant or title of action (*facultas
moralis*). From this it is at once evident what actions
are DISALLOWED or illicit (*illicita*).

Duty.— Duty is the designation of any Action to
which any one is bound by an obligation. It is therefore the subject - matter of all Obligation. Duty as
regards the Action concerned, may be one and the same,
and yet we may be bound to it in various ways.

The Categorical Imperative, as expressing an Obligation in respect to certain actions, is a morally practical Law. But because Obligation involves not merely practical Necessity expressed in a Law as such, but also actual *Necessitation*, the Categorical Imperative is a Law either of Command or Prohibition, according as the doing or not doing of an action is represented as a Duty. An Action which is neither commanded nor forbidden, is merely *allowed*, because there is no Law restricting Freedom, nor any Duty in respect of it. Such an Action is said to be *morally indifferent* (*indifferens, adiaphoron, res meræ facultatis*). It may be asked whether there *are* such morally indifferent actions ; and if there are, whether in addition to the preceptive and prohibitive Law (*lex præceptiva et prohibitiva, lex mandati et vetiti*), there is also required a Permissive Law (*lex permissiva*), in order that one may be free in such relations to act, or to forbear from acting, at his pleasure ? If it were so, the moral Right in question would not, in all cases, refer to actions that are indifferent in themselves (*adiaphora*) ; for no special Law would be required to establish such a Right, considered according to Moral Laws.

Act ; Agent.—An Action is called an ACT—or moral Deed—in so far as it is subject to Laws of Obligation, and consequently in so far as the Subject of it is regarded with reference to the Freedom of his choice in the exercise of his Will. The AGENT—as the actor or doer of the deed—is regarded as, through the act, the *Author* of its effect ; and this effect, along with the action itself, may be *imputed* to him, if he previously knew the Law, in virtue of which an Obligation rested upon him.

Person ; Imputation.—A PERSON is a Subject who is capable of having his actions *imputed* to him. Moral Personality is, therefore, nothing but the Freedom of a

rational Being under Moral Laws; and it is to be distinguished from psychological Freedom as the mere
faculty by which we become conscious of ourselves in
different states of the Identity of our existence. Hence
it follows that a Person is properly subject to no other
Laws than those he lays down for himself, either alone
or in conjunction with others.

Thing.—A THING is what is incapable of being the
subject of Imputation. Every object of the free activity
of the Will, which is itself void of freedom, is therefore called a Thing (*res corporealis*).

Right and Wrong.—RIGHT or WRONG applies, as a
general quality, to an Act (*rectum aut minus rectum*), in
so far as it is in accordance with Duty or contrary to
Duty (*factum licitum aut illicitum*), no matter what may
be the subject or origin of the Duty itself. An act that
is contrary to Duty is called a *Transgression* (*reatus*).

Fault ; Crime.—An *unintentional* Transgression of a
Duty, which is, nevertheless, imputable to a Person, is
called a mere FAULT (*culpa*). An *intentional* Transgression—that is, an act accompanied with the consciousness
that it *is* a Transgression—constitutes a CRIME (*dolus*).

Just and Unjust.—Whatever is juridically in accordance with External Laws, is said to be JUST (*Jus,
iustum*); and whatever is not juridically in accordance
with external Laws, is UNJUST (*unjustum*).

Collision of Duties.—A COLLISION OF DUTIES OR OBLI-
GATIONS (*collisio officiorum s. obligationum*) would be the
result of such a relation between them that the one
would annul the other, in whole or in part. Duty and
Obligation, however, are conceptions which express the
objective practical *Necessity* of certain actions, and two
opposite Rules cannot be objective and necessary at

the same time; for if it is a Duty to act according to one of them, it is not only no Duty to act according to an opposite Rule, but to do so would even be contrary to Duty. Hence a *Collision* of Duties and Obligations is entirely inconceivable (*obligationes non colliduntur*). There may, however, be two grounds of Obligation (*rationes obligandi*), connected with an individual under a Rule prescribed for himself, and yet neither the one nor the other may be sufficient to constitute an actual Obligation (*rationes obligandi non obligantes*); and in that case the one of them is not a Duty. If two such grounds of Obligation are actually in collision with each other, Practical Philosophy does not say that the stronger *Obligation* is to keep the upper hand (*fortior obligatio vincit*), but that the stronger *ground* of Obligation is to maintain its place (*fortior obligandi ratio vincit*).

Natural and Positive Laws.—Obligatory Laws for which an external Legislation is possible, are called generally *External Laws*. Those External Laws, the obligatoriness of which can be recognised by Reason *à priori* even without an external Legislation, are called NATURAL LAWS. Those Laws, again, which are not obligatory without actual External Legislation, are called POSITIVE LAWS. An External Legislation, containing pure Natural Laws, is therefore conceivable; but in that case a previous Natural Law must be presupposed to establish the authority of the Lawgiver by the Right to subject others to Obligation through his own act of Will.

Maxims.—The Principle which makes a certain action a Duty, is a Practical Law. The Rule of the Agent or Actor, which he forms as a Principle for himself on subjective grounds, is called his MAXIM. Hence, even when the Law is one and invariable, the Maxims of the Agent may yet be very different.

The Categorical Imperative.—The Categorical Imperative only expresses generally what constitutes Obligation. It may be rendered by the following Formula: 'Act according to a Maxim which can be adopted at the same time as a Universal Law.' Actions must therefore be considered, in the first place, according to their subjective Principle; but whether this principle is also valid objectively, can only be known by the criterion of the Categorical Imperative. For Reason brings the principle or maxim of any action to the test, by calling upon the Agent to think of himself in connection with it as at the same time laying down a Universal Law, and to consider whether his action is so qualified as to be fit for entering into such a Universal Legislation.

The simplicity of this Law, in comparison with the great and manifold Consequences which may be drawn from it, as well as its commanding authority and supremacy without the accompaniment of any visible motive or sanction, must certainly at first appear very surprising. And we may well wonder at the power of our Reason to determine the activity of the Will by the mere idea of the qualification of a Maxim for the *universality* of a practical Law, especially when we are taught thereby that this practical Moral Law first reveals a property of the Will which the Speculative Reason would never have come upon either by Principles *à priori*, or from any experience whatever; and even if it had ascertained the fact, it could never have theoretically established its possibility. This practical Law, however, not only discovers the fact of that property of the Will, which is FREEDOM, but irrefutably establishes it. Hence it will be less surprising to find that the Moral Laws are *undemonstrable*, and yet *apodictic*, like the mathematical Postulates; and that they, at the same time, open up before us a whole field of practical knowledge, from which Reason, on its theoretical side, must find itself entirely excluded with its speculative idea of Freedom and all such ideas of the Supersensible generally.

The conformity of an Action to the Law of Duty constitutes its *Legality ;* the conformity of the Maxim of the Action with the Law constitutes its *Morality.* A *Maxim* is thus a *subjective* Principle of Action, which the individual makes a Rule for himself as to how in fact he *will* act.

On the other hand, the Principle of Duty is what Reason absolutely, and therefore objectively and universally, lays down in the form of a Command to the individual, as to how he *ought* to act.

The SUPREME PRINCIPLE of the Science of Morals accordingly is this : ' Act according to a Maxim which can likewise be valid as a Universal Law.' — Every Maxim which is not qualified according to this condition, is contrary to Morality.

> Laws arise from the Will, viewed generally as Practical Reason ; Maxims spring from the activity of the Will in the process of Choice. The latter in Man, is what constitutes free-will. The Will which refers to nothing else than mere Law, can neither be called free nor not free ; because it does not relate to actions immediately, but to the giving of a Law for the Maxim of actions; it is therefore the Practical Reason itself. Hence as a Faculty, it is absolutely necessary in itself, and is not subject to any external necessitation. It is, therefore, only the act of *Choice* in the voluntary process, that can be called *free.*

The Freedom of the act of Will, however, is not to be defined as a Liberty of Indifference (*libertas indifferentiæ*), that is, as a capacity of choosing to act for or against the Law. The voluntary process, indeed, viewed as a *phenomenal* appearance, gives many examples of this choosing in experience ; and some have accordingly so defined the free-will. For Freedom, as it is first made knowable by the Moral Law, is known only as a *negative* Property in us, as constituted by the fact of not being *necessitated* to act by sensible principles of determination. Regarded as a *noumenal* reality, however, in reference to Man as a pure rational Intelligence, the act of the Will cannot be at all *theoretically* exhibited ; nor can it therefore be explained how this power can act *necessitatingly* in relation to the sensible activity in the process of Choice, or consequently in what the positive quality of Freedom consists. Only thus much we can see into and comprehend, that although Man, as a Being *belonging to the world of Sense*, exhibits—as experience shows—a capacity of choosing not only *conformably* to the Law but also *contrary* to it, his Freedom as a rational Being *belonging to the world of Intelligence* cannot be defined by reference merely to sensible appearances. For sensible phenomena cannot make a supersensible object—such as free-will is—intelligible ; nor can Freedom ever be placed in the mere fact that the rational Subject can make a choice in conflict with his own Lawgiving Reason, although experience may prove that it happens often enough, notwithstanding our inability to conceive how it is possible. For it is one thing to admit a proposition as based on experience, and another thing to make it the *defining Principle* and the universal differentiating mark of the act of free-will, in its distinction from the *arbitrium brutum s. servum ;* because the empirical proposition does not assert that any particular characteristic *necessarily* belongs to the conception in question, but this is

requisite in the process of Definition.—Freedom in
relation to the internal Legislation of Reason, can
alone be properly called a Power; the possibility of
diverging from the Law thus given, is an incapacity
or want of Power. How then can the former be
defined by the latter? It could only be by a Definition which would add to the practical conception of
the free-will, its *exercise* as shown by experience;
but this would be a *hybrid Definition* which would
exhibit the conception in a false light.

Law; Legislator.—A morally practical LAW is a proposition which contains a Categorical Imperative or
Command. He who commands by a Law (*imperans*)
is the Lawgiver or LEGISLATOR. He is the Author of
the Obligation that accompanies the Law, but he is not
always the Author of the Law itself. In the latter case,
the Law would be positive, contingent, and arbitrary.
The Law which is imposed upon us *à priori* and unconditionally by our own Reason, may also be expressed as
proceeding from the Will of a Supreme Lawgiver or the
Divine Will. Such a Will as Supreme can consequently have only Rights and not Duties; and it only
indicates the idea of a moral Being whose Will is Law
for all, without conceiving of Him as the Author of that
Will.

Imputation; Judgment; Judge.—IMPUTATION, in the
moral sense, is the *Judgment* by which any one is
declared to be the Author or free Cause of an action
which is then regarded as his moral fact or deed, and is
subjected to Law. When the Judgment likewise lays
down the juridical consequences of the Deed, it is judicial
or valid (*imputatio judiciaria s. valida*); otherwise it
would be only adjudicative or declaratory (*imputatio
dijudicatoria*).—That Person—individual or collective—

who is invested with the Right to impute actions judicially, is called a JUDGE or a Court (*judex s. forum*).

Merit and Demerit.—When any one does, in conformity with Duty, *more* than he can be compelled to do by the Law, it is said to be *meritorious* (*meritum*). What is done only in exact conformity with the Law, is *what is due* (*debitum*). And when *less* is done than can be demanded to be done by the Law, the result is moral *Demerit* (*demeritum*) or Culpability.

Punishment; Reward.—The *juridical* Effect or Consequence of a culpable act of Demerit is PUNISHMENT (*poena*); that of a meritorious act is REWARD (*præmium*), assuming that this Reward was promised in the Law and that it formed the motive of the action. The coincidence or exact conformity of conduct to what is due, has no juridical effect.—Benevolent REMUNERATION (*remuneratio s. repensio benefica*) has no place in *juridical* Relations.

The good or bad Consequences arising from the performance of an obligated action—as also the Consequences arising from failing to perform a meritorious action—cannot be imputed to the Agent (*modus imputationis tollens*).

The good Consequences of a meritorious action—as also the bad Consequences of a wrongful action—may be imputed to the Agent (*modus imputationis poneus*).

The degree of the *Imputability* of Actions is to be reckoned according to the magnitude of the hindrances or obstacles which it has been necessary for them to overcome. The greater the natural hindrances in the sphere of sense, and the less the moral hindrance of Duty, so much the more is a good *Deed* imputed as meritorious. This may be seen by considering such examples as rescuing a man who is an entire stranger from great distress, and at very consider-

able sacrifice.—Conversely, the less the natural hindrance, and the greater the hindrance on the ground of Duty, so much the more is a Transgression imputable as culpable.—Hence the state of mind of the Agent or Doer of a deed makes a difference in imputing its consequences, according as he did it in passion or performed it with coolness and deliberation.

INTRODUCTION

TO

THE SCIENCE OF RIGHT.

INTRODUCTION TO THE SCIENCE OF RIGHT.

——o——

GENERAL DEFINITIONS AND DIVISIONS.

A.

What the Science of Right is.

THE SCIENCE OF RIGHT has for its object the Principles of all the Laws which it is possible to promulgate by external legislation. Where there is such a legislation, it becomes in actual application to it, a system of *positive* Right and Law; and he who is versed in the knowledge of this System is called a Jurist or Jurisconsult (*jurisconsultus*). A practical Jurisconsult (*jurisperitus*), or a professional Lawyer, is one who is skilled in the knowledge of positive external Laws, and who can apply them to cases that may occur in experience. Such practical knowledge of positive Right, and Law, may be regarded as belonging to *Jurisprudence* (*Jurisprudentia*) in the original sense of the term. But the theoretical knowledge of Right and Law in Principle, as distinguished from positive Laws and empirical cases, belongs to the pure SCIENCE OF RIGHT (*Jurisscientia*). The Science of Right thus designates the philosophical and systematic knowledge of the Principles of Natural Right. And it is from this Science that the immutable Principles of all positive Legislation must be derived by practical Jurists and Lawgivers.

B.

What is Right?

This question may be said to be about as embarrassing to the Jurist as the well-known question, 'What is Truth?' is to the Logician. It is all the more so, if, on reflection, he strives to avoid tautology in his reply, and recognise the fact that a reference to what holds true merely of the laws of some one country at a particular time, is not a solution of the general problem thus proposed. It is quite easy to state what may be right in particular cases (*quid sit juris*), as being what the laws of a certain place and of a certain time say or may have said; but it is much more difficult to determine whether what they have enacted is right in itself, and to lay down a universal Criterion by which Right and Wrong in general, and what is just and unjust, may be recognised. All this may remain entirely hidden even from the practical Jurist until he abandon his empirical principles for a time, and search in the pure Reason for the sources of such judgments, in order to lay a real foundation for actual positive Legislation. In this search his empirical Laws may, indeed, furnish him with excellent guidance; but a merely empirical system that is void of rational principles is, like the wooden head in the fable of Phædrus, fine enough in appearance, but unfortunately it wants brain.

1. The conception of RIGHT,—as referring to a corresponding Obligation which is the moral aspect of it,—in the *first* place, has regard only to the external and practical

relation of one Person to another, in so far as they can have influence upon each other, immediately or mediately, by their *Actions* as facts. 2. In the *second* place, the conception of Right does not indicate the relation of the action of an individual to the *wish* or the mere desire of another, as in acts of benevolence or of unkindness, but only the relation of his free action to the freedom of *action* of the other. 3. And, in the *third* place, in this reciprocal relation of voluntary actions, the conception of Right does not take into consideration the *matter* of the act of Will in so far as the end which any one may have in view in willing it, is concerned. In other words, it is not asked in a question of Right whether any one on buying goods for his own business realizes a profit by the transaction or not; but only the *form* of the transaction is taken into account, in considering the relation of the mutual acts of Will. Acts of Will or voluntary Choice are thus regarded only in so far as they are *free*, and as to whether the action of one can harmonize with the Freedom of another, according to a universal Law.

RIGHT, therefore, comprehends the whole of the conditions under which the voluntary actions of any one Person can be harmonized in reality with the voluntary actions of every other Person, according to a universal Law of Freedom.

C.

Universal Principle of Right.

' Every Action is *right* which in itself, or in the maxim on which it proceeds, is such that it can co-exist along with the Freedom of the Will of each and all in action, according to a universal Law.'

If, then, my action or my condition generally can co-exist with the freedom of every other, according to a universal Law, any one does me a wrong who hinders me in the performance of this action, or in the maintenance of this condition. For such a hindrance or obstruction cannot co-exist with Freedom according to universal Laws.

It follows also that it cannot be demanded as a matter of Right, that this universal Principle of all maxims shall itself be adopted as my maxim, that is, that I shall make it the *maxim* of my actions. For any one may be free, although his Freedom is entirely indifferent to me, or even if I wished in my heart to infringe it, so long as I do not actually violate that freedom by *my external action*. Ethics, however, as distinguished from Jurisprudence, imposes upon me the obligation to make the fulfilment of Right a *maxim* of my conduct.

The universal Law of Right may then be expressed, thus : ' Act externally in such a manner that the free exercise of thy Will may be able to co-exist with the Freedom of all others, according to a universal Law.' This is undoubtedly a Law which imposes obligation upon me ; but it does not at all imply and still less command that I *ought*, merely on account of this obligation, to limit my freedom to these very conditions. Reason in this connection says only that it *is* restricted thus far by its Idea, and may be likewise thus limited in fact by others ; and it lays this down as a Postulate which is not capable of further proof. As the object in view is not to teach Virtue, but to explain what Right *is*, thus far the Law of Right, as thus laid down, may not and should not be represented as a motive-principle of action.

D.

Right is conjoined with the Title or Authority to compel.

The resistance which is opposed to any hindrance of an effect, is in reality a furtherance of this effect, and is in accordance with its accomplishment. Now, everything that is wrong is a hindrance of freedom, according to universal Laws; and Compulsion or Constraint of any kind is a hindrance or resistance made to Freedom. Consequently, if a certain exercise of Freedom is itself a hindrance of the Freedom that is according to universal Laws, it is wrong; and the compulsion or constraint which is opposed to it is right, as being a *hindering of a hindrance of Freedom,* and as being in accord with the Freedom which exists in accordance with universal Laws. Hence, according to the logical principle of Contradiction, all Right is accompanied with an implied Title or warrant to bring compulsion to bear on any one who may violate it in fact.

E.

Strict Right may be also represented as the possibility of a universal reciprocal Compulsion in harmony with the Freedom of all according to universal Laws.

This proposition means that Right is not to be regarded as composed of two different elements—Obligation according to a Law, and a Title on the part of one who has bound another by his own free choice, to compel him to perform. But it imports that the conception of Right may be viewed as consisting immediately in the possibility of a universal reciprocal Compulsion, in harmony with the Freedom of all. As Right in general has for its

object only what is external in actions, Strict Right, as
that with which nothing ethical is intermingled, requires
no other motives of action than those that are merely
external; for it is then pure Right, and is unmixed with
any prescriptions of Virtue.   A *strict* Right, then, in the
exact sense of the term, is that which alone can be called
wholly external.   Now such Right is founded, no doubt,
upon the consciousness of the Obligation of every individual according to the Law; but if it is to be pure as
such, it neither may nor should refer to this consciousness as a motive by which to determine the free act of
the Will.   For this purpose, however, it founds upon the
principle of the possibility of an external Compulsion,
such as may co-exist with the freedom of every one
according to universal Laws.   Accordingly, then, where it
is said that a Creditor has a right to demand from a
Debtor the payment of his debt, this does not mean
merely that he can bring him to feel in his mind that
Reason obliges him to do this; but it means that he can
apply an external compulsion to force any such one so to
pay, and that this compulsion is quite consistent with
the Freedom of all, including the parties in question,
according to a universal Law.   Right and the Title to
compel, thus indicate the same thing.

The Law of Right, as thus enunciated, is represented as a reciprocal Compulsion necessarily in
accordance with the Freedom of every one, under the
principle of a universal Freedom.   It is thus, as it
were, a representative *Construction* of the conception
of Right, by exhibiting it in a pure intuitive perception *à priori*, after the analogy of the possibility
of the free motions of bodies under the physical Law
of *the Equality of Action and Reaction*.   Now, as in
pure Mathematics, we cannot deduce the properties of

its objects immediately from a mere abstract conception, but can only discover them by figurative construction or representation of its conceptions; so it
is in like manner with the Principle of Right.   It is
not so much the mere formal *Conception* of Right,
but rather that of a universal and equal reciprocal
Compulsion as harmonizing with it, and reduced
under general laws, that makes representation of that
conception possible.   But just as those conceptions
presented in Dynamics are founded upon a merely
formal representation of pure Mathematics as presented
in Geometry, Reason has taken care also to provide
the Understanding as far as possible with intuitive
presentations *à priori* in behoof of a Construction of
the conception of Right.   The Right in geometrical
lines (*rectum*) is opposed as the Straight to that which
is Curved, and to that which is Oblique.   In the first
opposition there is involved an *inner quality* of the
lines of such a nature that there is only one *straight*
or *right* Line possible between two given points.   In
the second case, again, the *positions* of two intersect-
ing or meeting *Lines* are of such a nature that there
can likewise be only *one* line called the Perpendicular,
which is not more inclined to the one side than the
other, and it divides space on either side into two
equal parts.   After the manner of this analogy, the
Science of Right aims at determining what every one
shall have as his *own* with mathematical exactness ;
but this is not to be expected in the ethical Science of
Virtue, as it cannot but allow a certain latitude for
exceptions.   But without passing into the sphere of
Ethics, there are two cases—known as the equivocal
Right of Equity and Necessity—which claim a juridical decision, yet for which no one can be found to
give such a decision, and which, as regards their
relation to Rights, belong, as it were, to the ' *Inter-
mundia* ' of Epicurus.   These we must at the outset
take apart from the special exposition of the Science

of Right, to which we are now about to advance ; and we may consider them now by way of supplement to these introductory Explanations, in order that their uncertain conditions may not exert a disturbing influence on the fixed Principles of the proper doctrine of Right.

F.

Supplementary Remarks on Equivocal Right.

(Jus æquivocum.)

With every Right, in the strict acceptation (*jus strictum*), there is conjoined a Right to compel. But it is possible to think of other Rights of a *wider* kind (*jus latum*) in which the Title to compel cannot be determined by any law. Now there are two real or supposed Rights of this kind — EQUITY and THE RIGHT OF NECESSITY. The first alleges a Right that is without compulsion ; the second adopts a compulsion that is without Right. This equivocalness, however, can be easily shown to rest on the peculiar fact that there are cases of doubtful Right, for the decision of which no Judge can be appointed.

I. EQUITY.

EQUITY (Æquitas), regarded objectively, does not properly constitute a claim upon the moral Duty of benevolence or beneficence on the part of others ; but whoever insists upon anything on the ground of Equity, founds upon his *Right* to the same. In this case, however, the conditions are awanting that are requisite for the function of a Judge in order that he might determine what or what kind of satisfaction can be done to this claim. When one of the partners of a Mercantile Company,

formed under the condition of Equal profits, has, however, *done more* than the other members, and in consequence has also *lost more*, it is *in accordance with Equity*
that he should demand from the Company more than
merely an equal share of advantage with the rest.   But,
in relation to *strict Right*,—if we think of a Judge considering his case,—he can furnish no definite data to
establish how much more belongs to him by the Contract ; and in case of an action at law, such a demand
would be rejected.   A domestic servant, again, who
might be paid his wages due to the end of his year of
service in a coinage that became depreciated within that
period, so that it would not be of the same value to him
as it was when he entered on his engagement, cannot
claim by Right to be kept from loss on account of the
unequal value of the money if he receives the due
amount of it.   He can only make an appeal on the
ground of Equity,—a dumb goddess who cannot claim a
hearing of Right,—because there was nothing bearing on
this point in the Contract of Service, and a Judge cannot
give a decree on the basis of vague or indefinite conditions.

Hence it follows, that a COURT OF EQUITY for the
decision of disputed questions of Right, would involve a
contradiction.   It is only where his own proper Rights
are concerned, and in matters in which he can decide,
that a Judge may or ought to give a hearing to Equity.
Thus, if the Crown is supplicated to give an indemnity
to certain persons for loss or injury sustained in its
service, it may undertake the burden of doing so,
although, according to strict Right, the claim might
be rejected on the ground of the pretext that the parties
in question undertook the performance of the service
occasioning the loss, at their own risk.

The *Dictum* of Equity may be put thus : 'The strictest Right is the greatest Wrong' (*summum jus summa injuria*). But this evil cannot be obviated by the forms of Right although it relates to a matter of Right ; for the grievance that it gives rise to can only be put before a 'Court of Conscience' (*forum poli*), whereas every question of Right must be taken before a CIVIL COURT (*forum soli*).

II. THE RIGHT OF NECESSITY.

The so-called Right of Necessity (*Jus necessitatis*) is the supposed Right or Title, in case of the danger of losing my own life, to take away the life of another who has, in fact, done me no harm. It is evident that, viewed as a doctrine of Right, this must involve a contradiction. For this is not the case of a *wrongful* aggressor making an unjust assault upon my life, and whom I anticipate by depriving him of his own (*jus inculpatæ tutelæ*) ; nor consequently is it a question merely of the recommendation of moderation which belongs to Ethics as the Doctrine of Virtue, and not to Jurisprudence as the Doctrine of Right. It is a question of the allowableness of using violence against one who has used none against me.

It is clear that the assertion of such a Right is not to be understood objectively as being in accordance with what a Law would prescribe, but merely subjectively, as proceeding on the assumption of how a sentence would be pronounced by a Court in the case. There can, in fact, be no *Criminal Law* assigning the penalty of death to a man who, when shipwrecked and struggling in extreme danger for his life, and in order to save it, may thrust

another from a plank on which he had saved himself.
For the punishment threatened by the Law could not
possibly have greater power than the fear of the loss
of life in the case in question. Such a Penal Law would
thus fail altogether to exercise its intended effect ; for the
threat of an Evil which is still *uncertain*—such as Death
by a judicial sentence—could not overcome the fear of
an Evil which is *certain*, as Drowning is in such circumstances. An act of violent self-preservation, then, ought
not to be considered as altogether beyond condemnation
(*inculpabile*); it is only to be adjudged as exempt from
punishment (*impunibile*). Yet this *subjective* condition of
impunity, by a strange confusion of ideas, has been
regarded by Jurists as equivalent to *objective* lawfulness.

The *Dictum* of the Right of Necessity is put in these
terms, ' Necessity has no Law ' (*Necessitas non habet
legem*). And yet there cannot be a necessity that could
make what is wrong lawful.

It is apparent, then, that in judgments relating both to
' Equity ' and ' the Right of Necessity,' the *Equivocations*
involved arise from an interchange of the objective and
subjective grounds that enter into the application of the
Principles of Right, when viewed respectively by Reason
or by a Judicial Tribunal. What one may have good
grounds for recognising as Right in itself, may not find
confirmation in a Court of Justice ; and what he must
consider to be wrong in itself, may obtain recognition in
such a Court. And the reason of this is, that the conception of Right is not taken in the two cases in one and
the same sense.

DIVISION OF THE SCIENCE OF RIGHT.

A.

GENERAL DIVISION OF THE DUTIES OF RIGHT.

(Juridical Duties.)

In this Division we may very conveniently follow ULPIAN, if his three Formulæ are taken in a general sense, which may not have been quite clearly in his mind, but which they are capable of being developed into or of receiving. They are the following :—

1. HONESTE VIVE. 'Live rightly.' Juridical Rectitude, or Honour (*Honestas juridica*), consists in maintaining one's own worth as a man in relation to others. This Duty may be rendered by the proposition, 'Do not make thyself a mere Means for the use of others, but be to them likewise an End.' This Duty will be explained in the next Formula as an Obligation arising out of the *Right* of Humanity in our own Person (*Lex justi*).

2. NEMINEM LÆDE. 'Do Wrong to no one.' This Formula may be rendered so as to mean, 'Do no Wrong to any one, even if thou shouldst be under the necessity, in observing this Duty, to cease from all connection with others and to avoid all Society' (*Lex juridica*).

3. SUUM CUIQUE TRIBUE. 'Assign to every one what is his own.' This may be rendered, 'Enter, if Wrong cannot be avoided, into a Society with others in which every one may have *secured* to him what is his own.'—If this Formula were to be simply translated, 'Give every one *his own*,' it would express an absurdity, for we cannot *give* any one what he already has. If it is to have a definite meaning, it must

therefore run thus, ' Enter into a state in which every one can have what is his own secured against the action of every other ' (*Lex justitiæ*).

These three classical Formulæ, at the same time, represent principles which suggest a Division of the System of Juridical Duties into *Internal Duties, External Duties*, and those *Connecting Duties* which contain the latter as deduced from the Principle of the former by subsumption.

B.

UNIVERSAL DIVISION OF RIGHTS.

I. Natural Right and Positive Right.

The System of Rights, viewed as a scientific System of Doctrines, is divided into NATURAL RIGHT and POSITIVE RIGHT. Natural Right rests upon pure rational Principles *à priori ;* Positive or Statutory Right is what proceeds from the Will of a Legislator.

II. Innate Right and Acquired Right.

The System of Rights may again be regarded in reference to the implied Powers of dealing morally with others as bound by Obligations, that is, as furnishing a legal Title of action in relation to them. Thus viewed, the System is divided into INNATE RIGHT and ACQUIRED RIGHT. Innate Right is that Right which belongs to every one by Nature, independent of all juridical acts of experience. ACQUIRED RIGHT is that Right which is founded upon such juridical acts.

Innate Right may also be called the ' Internal Mine and Thine ' (*Meum vel Tuum internum*) ; for External Right must always be acquired.

There is only one Innate Right, the Birthright of Freedom.

FREEDOM is Independence of the compulsory Will of another; and in so far as it can co-exist with the Freedom of all according to a universal Law, it is the one sole original, inborn Right belonging to every man in virtue of his Humanity.   There is, indeed, an innate EQUALITY belonging to every man which consists in his Right to be independent of being bound by others to anything more than that to which he may also reciprocally bind them.   It is, consequently, the inborn quality of every man in virtue of which he ought to be *his own master by Right* (*sui juris*).   There is, also, the natural quality of JUSTNESS attributable to a man as naturally of *unimpeachable Right* (*justi*), because he has done no Wrong to any one prior to his own juridical actions.   And, further, there is also the innate Right of COMMON ACTION on the part of every man so that he may do towards others what does not infringe their Rights or take away anything that is theirs unless they are willing to appropriate it; such as merely to communicate thought, to narrate anything, or to promise something whether truly and honestly, or untruly and dishonestly (*veriloquium aut falsiloquium*), for it rests entirely upon these others whether they will believe or trust in it or not.[1]   But all these Rights or Titles are already included in the Prin-

---

[1] It is customary to designate every untruth that is spoken *intentionally* as such, although it may be in a frivolous manner, a ' Lie,' or Falsehood (*mendacium*), because it may do harm, at least in so far as any one who repeats it in good faith may be made a laughing-stock of to others on account of his easy credulity.   But in the juridical sense, only that Untruth is called a Lie which immediately infringes the Right of another, such as a false allegation of a Contract having been concluded, when the allegation is put forward in order to deprive some one of what

ciple of Innate FREEDOM, and are not really distinguished from it, even as dividing members under a higher species of Right.

The reason why such a Division into separate Rights has been introduced into the System of Natural Right viewed as including all that is innate, was not without a purpose. Its object was to enable proof to be more readily put forward in case of any controversy arising about an Acquired Right, and questions emerging either with reference to a fact that might be in doubt, or, if that were established, in reference to a Right under dispute. For the party repudiating an obligation, and on whom the burden of proof (*onus probandi*) might be incumbent, could thus methodically refer to his Innate Right of Freedom as specified under various relations in detail, and could therefore found upon them equally as different Titles of Right.

In the relation of Innate Right, and consequently of the Internal ' Mine ' and ' Thine,' there is therefore not *Rights*, but only ONE RIGHT. And, accordingly, this highest Division of Rights into Innate and Acquired, which evidently consists of two members extremely unequal in their contents, is properly placed in the Introduction ; and the subdivisions of the Science of Right may be referred in detail to the External Mine and Thine.

---

is his (*falsiloquium dolosum*). This distinction of conceptions so closely allied is not without foundation ; because on the occasion of a simple statement of one's thoughts, it is always free for another to take them as he may ; and yet the resulting repute that such a one is a man whose word cannot be trusted, comes so close to the opprobrium of directly calling him a Liar, that the boundary-line separating what in such a case belongs to Jurisprudence and what is special to Ethics, can hardly be otherwise drawn.

C.

METHODICAL DIVISION OF THE SCIENCE OF RIGHT.

The highest Division of the System of Natural Right should not be—as it is frequently put—into *'Natural* Right' and '*Social* Right,' but into NATURAL RIGHT and CIVIL RIGHT. The first constitutes PRIVATE RIGHT ; the second, PUBLIC RIGHT. For it is not the ' *Social* state ' but the ' *Civil* state ' that is opposed to the ' State of Nature ; ' for in the ' State of Nature ' there may well be Society of some kind, but there is no ' civil ' Society, as an Institution securing the Mine and Thine by public laws. It is thus that Right, viewed under reference to the state of Nature, is specially called Private Right. The whole of the Principles of Right will therefore fall to be expounded under the two subdivisions of PRIVATE RIGHT and PUBLIC RIGHT.

THE SCIENCE OF RIGHT.

—o—

PART FIRST.

PRIVATE RIGHT.

THE SYSTEM OF THOSE LAWS WHICH REQUIRE
NO EXTERNAL PROMULGATION.

PRIVATE RIGHT.

THE PRINCIPLES OF THE EXTERNAL MINE AND THINE GENERALLY.

CHAPTER FIRST.

OF THE MODE OF HAVING ANYTHING EXTERNAL AS ONE'S OWN.

1.

The meaning of 'Mine' in Right.
(Meum Juris.)

ANYTHING is '*Mine*' *by Right*, or is rightfully Mine, when I am so connected with it, that if any other Person should make use of it without my consent, he would do me a lesion or injury. The subjective condition of the use of anything, is *Possession* of it.

An *external* thing, however, as such could only be mine, if I may assume it to be possible that I can be wronged by the use which another might make of it *when it is not actually in my possession*. Hence it would be a contradiction to have anything External as one's own, were not the conception of Possession capable of two different meanings, as *sensible* Possession that is perceivable by the senses, and *rational* Possession that is perceivable only by the Intellect. By the former is to be understood a *physical* Possession, and by the latter, a purely *juridical* Possession of the same object.

The description of an Object as '*external* to me' may signify either that it is merely 'different and distinct from me as a Subject,' or that it is also 'a thing placed *outside* of me, and to be found elsewhere in space or time.' Taken in the first sense, the term Possession signifies 'rational Possession;' and, in the second sense, it must mean 'Empirical Possession.' A rational or *intelligible* Possession, if such be possible, is Possession *viewed apart from physical holding or detention (detentio).*

2.

Juridical Postulate of the Practical Reason.

It is possible to have any external object óf my Will as Mine. In other words, a Maxim to this effect—were it to become law—that any object on which the Will can be exerted must remain objectively in itself *without an owner*, as 'res nullius,' is contrary to the Principle of Right.

For an object of any act of my Will, is something that it would be *physically* within my power to use. Now, suppose there were things that *by right* should absolutely not be in our power, or, in other words, that it would be wrong or inconsistent with the freedom of all, according to universal Law, to make use of them. On this supposition, Freedom would so far be depriving itself of the use of its voluntary activity, in thus putting *useable* objects out of all possibility of *use*. In practical relations, this would be to annihilate them, by making them *res nullius*, notwithstanding the fact that acts of Will in relation to such things would formally harmonize, in the actual use of them, with the external freedom of all according to universal Laws. Now the pure practical Reason lays down only formal Laws as Principles to regulate the exercise of the Will; and therefore abstracts from the matter of the act of Will, as regards the other qualities of the object, *which is considered only in so far as it is an object of the activity of the Will.* Hence the practical Reason cannot contain, in reference to such an object, an absolute prohibition of its use, because this would involve a contradiction of external freedom with itself.—An object of my free Will, however, is one which I have the physical capability of making some use of at will, since its *use* stands in my power (*in potentia*). This is to be distinguished from having the *object* brought under my disposal (*in potestatem meam reductum*), which supposes not a *capability* merely, but also a particular *act* of the free-will. But in order to consider something merely as an object of my Will as such, it is sufficient to be conscious that I have it in my power. It is therefore an assumption *à priori* of the practical Reason, to regard and treat every object within the range of my free exercise of Will as objectively a possible Mine or Thine.

This Postulate may be called 'a Permissive Law' of the practical Reason, as giving us a special title which we could not evolve out of the mere conceptions of Right generally. And this Title constitutes the Right to impose upon all others an obligation, not otherwise laid upon them, to abstain from the use of certain objects of our free Choice, because we have already taken them into our possession. Reason wills that this shall be recognised as a valid Principle, and it does so as *practical*

Reason; and it is enabled by means of this Postulate
à priori to enlarge its range of activity in practice.

3.

Possession and Ownership.

Any one who would assert the Right to a thing as his,
must be in possession of it as an object. Were he not
its actual possessor or owner, he could not be wronged
or injured by the use which another might make of it
without his consent. For, should anything external to
him, and in no way connected with him by Right, affect
this object, it could not affect himself as a Subject, nor
do him any wrong, unless he stood in a relation of
Ownership to it.

4.

Exposition of the Conception of the External Mine and Thine.

There can only be *three* external Objects of my Will
in the activity of Choice:

(1) A Corporeal *Thing* external to me;

(2) The *Free-will* of another in the performance of a
particular act (*præstatio*);

(3) The *State* of another in relation to myself.

These correspond to the categories of *Substance, Causality*, and *Reciprocity;* and they form the practical
relations between me and external objects, according to
the Laws of Freedom.

> **A.** I can only call a corporeal thing or an object
> in *space* 'mine,' when, *even although not in physical
> possession of it*, I am able to assert that I am in
> possession of it in another real non-physical sense.

Thus, I am not entitled to call an apple *mine* merely because I hold it in my hand or possess it physically; but only when I am entitled to say, 'I possess it, although I have laid it out of my hand, and wherever it may lie.' In like manner, I am not entitled to say of the ground, on which I may have laid myself down, that therefore it is *mine;* but only when I can rightly assert that it still remains in my possession, although I may have left the spot. For any one who, in the former appearances of empirical possession, might wrench the apple out of my hand, or drag me away from my resting-place, would, indeed, injure me in respect of the *inner* 'Mine' of Freedom, but not in respect of the external 'Mine,' unless I could assert that I was in the possession of the Object, even when not actually holding it physically. And if I could not do this, neither could I call the apple or the spot mine.

B. I cannot call the *performance* of something by the action of the Will of another 'Mine,' if I can *only* say 'it has come into my possession *at the same time* with a promise' (*pactum re initum*); but only if I am able to assert 'I am in possession of the Will of the other, so as to determine him to the performance of a particular act, although the time for the performance of it has not yet come.' In the latter case, the promise belongs to the nature of things actually held as possessed, and as an 'active obligation' I can reckon it mine; and this holds good not only if I have *the thing promised*—as in the first case—already in my possession, but even although I do not yet possess it in fact. Hence, I must be able to regard myself in thought as independent of that empirical form of possession that is limited by the condition of time, and as being nevertheless in possession of the object.

C. I cannot call a Wife, a Child, a Domestic, or, generally, any other Person 'mine' merely because I

command them at present as belonging to my household, or because I have them under control, and in
my power and possession. But I can call them
mine, if, although they may have withdrawn themselves from my control and I do not therefore possess
them empirically, I can still say 'I possess them by
my mere Will, provided they exist anywhere in space
or time; and, consequently, my possession of them is
purely juridical.' They belong, in fact, to my possessions, only when and so far as I can assert this as a
matter of Right.

5.

Definition of the conception of the external Mine and Thine.

Definitions are *nominal* or *real.* A nominal Definition
is sufficient merely to *distinguish* the object defined from
all other objects, and it springs out of a complete and
definite *exposition* of its conception. A real Definition
further suffices for a *Deduction* of the conception defined,
so as to furnish a knowledge of the reality of the object.
—The *nominal Definition* of the external 'Mine' would
thus be: 'The external Mine is anything outside of
myself, such that any hindrance of my use of it at will,
would be doing me an injury or wrong as an infringement
of that Freedom of mine which may coexist with the
freedom of all others according to a universal Law.' The
real Definition of this conception may be put thus: 'The
external Mine is anything outside of myself, such that
any prevention of my use of it would be a wrong, *although
I may not be in possession of it* so as to be actually holding it as an object.'—I must be in some kind of possession of an external object, if the object is to be regarded
as *mine;* for, otherwise, any one interfering with this
object would not, in doing so, affect me; nor, consequently, would he thereby do me any wrong. Hence,

according to § 4, a *rational Possession* (*possessio nou-menon*) must be assumed as possible, if there is to be rightly an external ' Mine and Thine.' Empirical Posses-sion is thus only phenomenal possession or holding (detention) of the object in the sphere of sensible *appearance* (*possessio phenomenon*), although the *object* which I possess is not regarded in this practical relation as itself a Phenomenon,—according to the exposition of the Transcendental Analytic in the *Critique of Pure Reason*—but as a Thing in itself. For in the *Critique of Pure Reason* the interest of Reason turns upon the *theoretical* knowledge of the Nature of Things, and how far Reason can go in such knowledge. But here Reason has to deal with the practical determination of the action of the Will according to Laws of *Freedom*, whether the object is perceivable through the senses or merely think-able by the pure Understanding. And Right, as under con-sideration, is a pure practical conception of the Reason in relation to the exercise of the Will under Laws of Freedom.

And, hence, it is not quite correct to speak of ' possessing' a Right *to* this or that object, but it should rather be said that an object is possessed in a *purely juridical* way ; for a Right is itself the rational possession of an Object, and to ' possess a possession,' would be an expression without meaning.

6.

Deduction of the conception of a purely juridical Possession of an External Object.

(Possessio noumenon.)

The question, ' How is an *external Mine and Thine* possible ? ' resolves itself into this other question, ' How is a *merely juridical* or *rational* Possession possible?' And this second question resolves itself again into a third, 'How is a *synthetic* proposition in Right possible *à priori?*'

All Propositions of Right—as juridical propositions—are Propositions *à priori,* for they are practical Laws of Reason (*Dictamina rationis*). But the juridical Proposition *à priori* respecting *empirical Possession* is *analytical;* for it says nothing more than what follows by the principle of Contradiction, from the conception of such possession; namely, that if I am the holder of a thing in the way of being physically connected with it, any one interfering with it without my consent—as, for instance, in wrenching an apple out of my hand—affects and detracts from my freedom as that which is internally Mine; and consequently the maxim of his action is in direct contradiction to the Axiom of Right. The proposition expressing the principle of an empirical rightful Possession, does not therefore go beyond the Right of a Person in reference to himself.

On the other hand, the Proposition expressing the possibility of the Possession of a thing external to me, after abstraction of all the conditions of empirical possession in space and time—consequently presenting the assumption of the possibility of a *Possessio Noumenon*—goes beyond these limiting conditions; and because this Proposition asserts a possession even without physical holding, as necessary to the conception of the external Mine and Thine, it is *synthetical.* And thus it becomes a problem for Reason to show how such a Proposition, extending its range beyond the conception of empirical possession, is possible *à priori.*

In this manner, for instance, the act of taking possession of a particular portion of the soil, is a mode exercising the private free-will without being an act of *usurpation*. The possessor founds upon the innate Right of *common possession* of the surface of the earth, and upon the universal Will corresponding *à priori* to it, which allows a *private Possession* of the soil ; because what are mere things would be otherwise made in themselves and by a Law, into unappropriable objects. Thus a first appropriator acquires originally by primary possession a particular portion of the ground ; and by Right (*jure*) he resists every other person who would hinder him in the private use of it, although while the 'state of Nature' continues, this cannot be done by juridical means (*de jure*), because a public Law does not yet exist.

And although a piece of ground should be regarded as free, or declared to be such, so as to be for the public use of all without distinction, yet it cannot be said that it is thus free by nature and *originally* so, prior to any juridical act. For there would be a real relation already incorporated in such a piece of ground by the very fact that the possession of it was denied to any particular individual; and as this public freedom of the ground would be a prohibition of it to every particular individual, this presupposes a common possession of it which cannot take effect without a Contract. A piece of ground, how-ever, which can only become publicly free by contract, must actually be in the possession of all those associated together, who mutually interdict or suspend each other, from any particular or private use of it.

> This *original* Community of the soil and of the things upon it (*communio fundi originaria*), is an idea which has objective and practical Juridical reality, and is entirely different from the idea of a *primitive* community of things which is a fiction.

For the latter would have had to be *founded* as a form of Society, and must have taken its rise from a Contract by which all renounced the Right of Private Possession, so that by uniting the property owned by each into a whole, it was thus transformed into a common possession. But had such an event taken place, History must have presented some evidence of it. To regard such a procedure as the original mode of taking possession, and to hold that the particular possessions of every individual may and ought to be grounded upon it, is evidently a contradiction.

Possession (*possessio*) is to be distinguished from habitation as mere *residence (sedes)*; and the act of taking possession of the soil in the intention of acquiring it once for all, is also to be distinguished from *settlement* or *domicile* (*incolatus*), which is a continuous private Possession of a place that is dependent on the presence of the individual upon it. We have not here to deal with the question of domiciliary settlement, as that is a secondary juridical act which may follow upon possession, or may not occur at all; for as such it could not involve an original possession, but only a secondary possession derived from the consent of others.

Simple physical Possession, or holding of the soil, involves already certain relations of Right to the thing, although it is certainly not sufficient to enable me to regard it as Mine. Relative to others, so far as they know, it appears as a first possession in harmony with the law of external freedom; and, at the same time, it is embraced in the universal original possession which contains à *priori* the fundamental principle of the possibility of a private possession. Hence to disturb the first occupier or holder of a portion of the soil in his use of it, is a lesion or wrong done to him. The first taking of Possession has therefore a Title of Right (*titulus possessionis*) in its favour, which is simply the principle of the

THE PRINCIPLES OF PRIVATE RIGHT.

original common possession; and the saying that
' It is well for those who are in possession' (*beati
possidentes*), when one is not bound to authenticate
his possession, is a principle of Natural Right that
establishes the juridical act of taking possession, as a
ground of acquisition upon which every first possessor
may found.

It has been shown in the *Critique of Pure Reason*
that in theoretical Principles *à priori*, an intuitional
Perception *à priori* must be supplied in connection
with any given conception; and, consequently, were
it a question of a purely theoretical Principle, something would have to be *added* to the conception of
the possession of an object to make it real. But in
respect of the *practical* Principle under consideration, the procedure is just the converse of the
theoretical process; so that all the conditions of perception which form the foundation of empirical
possession must be abstracted or taken away in
order to *extend* the range of the juridical Conception
beyond the empirical sphere, and in order to be able
to apply the Postulate, that every external object of
the free activity of my Will, so far as I have it in
my power, although not in the possession of it, may
be reckoned as juridically Mine.

The possibility of such a possession, with consequent Deduction of the conception of a non-empirical
possession, is founded upon the juridical Postulate of
the Practical Reason, that ' It is a juridical Duty so
to act towards others that what is external and useable
may come into the possession or become the property
of some one.' And this Postulate is conjoined with
the exposition of the Conception that what is externally one's own, is founded upon a possession, that is
not physical. The possibility of such a possession,
thus conceived, cannot, however, be proved or comprehended in itself, because it is a *rational* conception for which no empirical perception can be

furnished; but it follows as an immediate consequence from the Postulate that has been enunciated.
For, if it is necessary to act according to that
juridical Principle, the rational or intelligible condition of a purely juridical possession must also be
possible.   It need astonish no one, then, that the
theoretical aspect of the Principles of the external
Mine and Thine, is lost from view in the rational
sphere of pure Intelligence, and presents no extension
of Knowledge; for the conception of Freedom upon
which they rest does not admit of any *theoretical*
Deduction of its possibility, and it can only be
inferred from the practical Law of Reason, called the
Categorical Imperative, viewed as a fact.

7.

Application of the Principle of the Possibility of an external Mine and Thine to Objects of Experience.

The conception of a purely juridical Possession, is
not an empirical conception dependent on conditions of
Space and Time, and yet it has practical reality.   As
such it must be applicable to objects of experience, the
knowledge of which is independent of the conditions
of Space and Time.   The rational process by which the
conception of Right is brought into relation to such
objects so as to constitute a possible external Mine and
Thine, is as follows.   The Conception of Right, being
contained merely in Reason, cannot be *immediately*
applied to objects of experience, so as to give the conception of an empirical *Possession*, but must be applied
directly to the mediating conception in the Understanding, of *Possession* in general ; so that, instead of
physical holding (*Detentio*) as an empirical representation
of possession, the formal conception or thought of

'*Having*,' abstracted from all conditions of Space and
Time, is conceived by the mind, and only as implying
that an object is in my power and at my disposal (*in
potestate mea positum esse*). In this relation, the term
'external' does not signify existence in *another place*
than where I am, nor my resolution and acceptance at
another time than the moment in which I have the offer
of a thing: it signifies only an object *different* from or
other than myself. Now the practical Reason by its
Law of Right wills, that I shall think the Mine and
Thine in application to objects, not according to sensible
conditions, but apart from these and from the Possession
they indicate; because they refer to determinations of
the activity of the Will that are in accordance with the
Laws of Freedom. For it is only a *conception of the
Understanding* that can be brought under the rational
Conception of Right. I may therefore say that I possess
a field, although it is in quite a different place from that
on which I actually find myself. For the question here
is not concerning an intellectual relation to the object,
but I have the thing practically *in my power* and at my
disposal, which is a conception of Possession realized by
the Understanding and independent of relations of space;
and it is *mine*, because my Will in determining itself to
any particular use of it, is not in conflict with the Law
of external Freedom. Now it is just in abstraction from
physical possession of the object of my free-will in the
sphere of sense, that the Practical Reason wills that a
rational possession of it shall be thought, according to
intellectual conceptions which are not empirical, but
contain *à priori* the conditions of rational possession.
Hence it is in this fact, that we found the ground of the
validity of such a rational conception of possession

be annulled by the fact that the promiser having said at one time, 'This thing shall be yours,' again at a subsequent time says, 'My will now is that the thing shall not be yours.' In such relations of rational Right the conditions hold just the same as if the promiser had, without any interval of time between them, made the two declarations of his Will, 'This shall be yours,' and also 'This shall not be yours;' which manifestly contradicts itself.

The same thing holds, in like manner, of the Conception of the juridical possession of a Person as belonging to the 'Having' of a subject, whether it be a Wife, a Child, or a Servant. The relations of Right involved in a household, and the reciprocal possession of all its members, are not annulled by the capability of separating from each other *in space;* because it is by *juridical* relations that they are connected, and the external 'Mine' and 'Thine,' as in the former cases, rests entirely upon the assumption of the possibility of a purely rational possession, without the accompaniment of physical detention or holding of the object.

Reason is forced to a Critique of its juridically Practical Function in special reference to the conception of the external Mine and Thine, by the Antinomy of the propositions enunciated regarding the possibility of such a form of Possession. For these give rise to an inevitable Dialectic, in which a Thesis and an Antithesis set up equal claims to the validity of two conflicting Conditions. Reason is thus compelled, in its practical function in relation to Right,— as it was in its theoretical function,—to make a distinction between Possession as a phenomenal appearance presented to the senses, and that Possession which is rational and thinkable only by the Understanding.

THESIS.—The Thesis, in this case, is, '*It is possible to have* something external as mine, although I am not in possession of it.'

ANTITHESIS.—The Antithesis is, '*It is not possible to have* anything external as mine, if I am not in possession of it.'

SOLUTION.— The Solution is, 'Both Propositions are true;' the former when I mean empirical Possession (*possessio phœnomenon*), the latter when I understand by the same term, a purely rational Possession (*possessio noumenon*).

But the possibility of a rational possession, and consequently of an external Mine and Thine, cannot be comprehended by direct insight, but must be deduced from the Practical Reason. And in this relation it is specially noteworthy that the Practical Reason without intuitional perceptions, and even without requiring such an element *à priori*, can *extend* its range by the mere *elimination* of empirical conditions, as justified by the law of Freedom, and can thus establish *synthetical* Propositions *à priori*. The proof of this in the practical connection, as will be shown afterwards, can be adduced in an analytical manner.

8.

To have anything External as one's own is only possible in a Juridical or Civil State of Society under the regulation of a public legislative Power.

If, by word or deed, I declare my Will that some external thing shall be mine, I make a declaration that every other person is obliged to abstain from the use of this object of my exercise of Will; and this imposes an Obligation which no one would be under, without such a juridical act on my part. But the assumption of this

Act, at the same time involves the admission that I am obliged reciprocally to observe a similar abstention towards every other in respect of what is externally theirs ; for the Obligation in question arises from a universal Rule regulating the external juridical relations. Hence I am not obliged to let alone what another person declares to be externally his, unless every other person likewise secures me by a guarantee that he will act in relation to what is mine, upon the same Principle. This guarantee of reciprocal and mutual abstention from what belongs to others, does not require a special juridical act for its establishment, but is already involved in the Conception of an external Obligation of Right, on account of the universality and consequently the reciprocity of the obligatoriness arising from a universal Rule.—Now a single Will, in relation to an external and consequently contingent Possession, cannot serve as a compulsory Law for all, because that would be to do violence to the Freedom which is in accordance with universal Laws. Therefore it is only a Will that binds every one, and as such a common, collective, and authoritative Will, that can furnish a guarantee of security to all. But the state of men under a universal, external, and public Legislation, conjoined with authority and power, is called the Civil state. There can therefore be an external Mine and Thine only in the Civil state of Society.

CONSEQUENCE.—It follows, as a Corollary, that if it is juridically possible to have an external object as one's own, the individual Subject of possession must be allowed *to compel* or constrain every person, with whom a dispute as to the Mine or Thine of such a possession may arise, to enter along with himself into the relations of a Civil Constitution.

9.

There may, however, be an external **Mine** and **Thine** found as a fact in the state of Nature, but it is only provisory.

Natural Right in the state of a Civil Constitution, means the forms of Right which may be deduced from Principles *à priori* as the conditions of such a Constitution. It is therefore not to be infringed by the statutory laws of such a Constitution; and accordingly the juridical Principle remains in force, that, 'Whoever proceeds upon a Maxim by which it becomes *impossible* for me to have an object of the exercise of my Will as Mine, does me a lesion or injury.' For a Civil Constitution is only the juridical condition under which every one has what is his own merely secured to him, as distinguised from its being specially assigned and determined to him.—All Guarantee, therefore, assumes that every one to whom a thing is secured, is already in possesion of it as his own. Hence, prior to the Civil Constitution—or *apart* from it — an external Mine and Thine must be assumed as possible, and along with it a Right to compel every one with whom we could come into any kind of intercourse, to enter with us into a constitution in which what is Mine or Thine can be secured.—There may thus be a Possession in expectation or in preparation for such a state of security, as can only be established on the Law of the Common Will; and as it is therefore in accordance with the *possibility* of such a state, it constitutes a *provisory* or temporary juridical Possession; whereas that Possession which is found in reality in the Civil state of Society will be a *peremptory* or guaranteed Possession.—Prior to entering into this state, for which he is naturally prepared, the individual rightfully resists those who will not adapt themselves to it, and who would disturb him in his provisory possession; because if the Will of all except himself were imposing upon him an obligation to withdraw from a certain possession, it would still be only a one-sided or *unilateral* Will, and consequently it would have just as little *legal* Title—which can be properly based only on the universalized Will—to contest a claim of Right; as he would have to *assert* it. Yet he has the advantage on his side, of being in accord with the conditions requisite to the introduction and institution of a civil form of Society. In a word, the mode in which anything external may be held as one's own in the *state of Nature,* is just *physical* possession with a *presumption* of Right thus far in its favour, that by union of the Wills of all in a public Legislation, it will be made *juridical ;* and in this expectation it holds *comparatively,* as a kind of potential juridical Possession.

This Prerogative of Right, as arising from the fact of empirical possession, is in accordance with the Formula, 'It is well for those who are in possession' (*Beati possidentes*). It does not consist in the fact that because the Possessor has the presumption of being a *rightful man,* it is unnecessary for him to bring forward proof that he possesses a certain thing rightfully, for this position applies only to a case of disputed Right. But it is because it accords with the Postulate of the Practical Reason, that every one is invested with the faculty of having as his own any external object upon which he has exerted his Will; and, consequently, all actual possession is a state whose rightfulness is established upon that Postulate

PRIVATE RIGHT

CHAPTER SECOND.

THE MODE OF ACQUIRING ANYTHING EXTERNAL.

10.

The general Principle of External Acquisition.

I ACQUIRE a thing when I act (*efficio*) so that it becomes *mine.*—An external thing is *originally* mine, when it is mine even without the intervention of a juridical Act. An Acquisition is *original* and *primary*, when it is not derived from what another had already made his own.

There is nothing External that is as such originally mine ; but anything external may be originally *acquired* when it is an object that no other person has yet made his. — A state in which the Mine and Thine are in common, cannot be conceived as having been at any time original. Such a state of things would have to be acquired by an external juridical Act, although there may be an original and common possession of an external object. Even if we think hypothetically of a state in which the Mine and Thine would be *originally* in common as a ' *Communio mei et tui originaria,*' it would still have to be distinguished from a *primeval* communion (*Com-*

munio primœva) with things in common, sometimes supposed to be founded in the first period of the relations of Right among men, and which could not be regarded as based upon Principles like the former, but only upon History. Even under that condition the historic *Communio*, as a supposed primeval Community, would always have to be viewed as acquired and derivative (*Communio derivativa*).

The Principle of external Acquisition, then, may be expressed thus : 'Whatever I bring under my power according to the Law of external Freedom, of which as an object of my free activity of Will I have the capability of making use according to the Postulate of the Practical Reason, and which I will to become mine in conformity with the Idea of a possible united common Will, *is* mine.'

The practical Elements (*Momenta attendenda*) constitutive of the process of *original* Acquisition are :—

1. PREHENSION or Seizure of an object which belongs to no one ; for if it belonged already to some one the act would conflict with the Freedom of others that is according to universal Laws. This is the *taking possession* of an object of my free activity of Will in Space and Time ; the Possession, therefore, into which I thus put myself is sensible or physical possession (*possessio phenomenon*) ;

2. DECLARATION of the possession of this object by formal designation and the act of my free-will in interdicting every other person from using it as his ;

3. APPROPRIATION, as the act, in Idea, of an externally legislative common Will, by which all and each are obliged to respect and act in conformity with my act of Will.

The validity of the last element in the process of

Acquisition, as that on which the conclusion that 'the external object is mine' rests, is what makes the possession valid as a purely rational and *juridical* possession (*possessio noumenon*).   It is founded upon the fact that as all these Acts are *juridical*, they consequently proceed from the Practical Reason, and therefore in the question as to what is Right, abstraction may be made of the empirical conditions involved, and the conclusion 'the external object is mine' thus becomes a correct inference from the external fact of sensible possession to the internal Right of rational Possession.

The original *primary* Acquisition of an external object of the action of the Will, is called OCCUPANCY. It can only take place in reference to Substances or Corporeal Things.   Now when this Occupation of an external object does take place, the Act presupposes as a condition of such empirical possession, its Priority in time before the act of any other who may also be willing to enter upon occupation of it.   Hence the legal maxim, '*qui prior tempore, potior jure.*'   Such Occupation as original or primary is, further, the effect only of a single or *unilateral* Will; for were a bilateral or twofold Will requisite for it, it would be derived from a Contract of two or more persons with each other, and consequently it would be based upon what another or others had already made their own.—It is not easy to see how such an act of free-will as this would be, could really form a foundation for every one having his own.—However, the *first* Acquisition of a thing is on that account not quite exactly the same as the *original* Acquisition of it.   For the Acquisition of a public juridical state by union of the Wills of all in a universal Legislation, would be such an original Acquisition, seeing that no other of the kind could precede it, and yet it would be *derived* from the particular Wills of all the individuals, and consequently become all-sided or *omnilateral;* for a properly *primary Acquisition* can only proceed from an individual or uni-lateral Will.

DIVISION OF THE SUBJECT OF THE ACQUISITION OF THE EXTERNAL MINE AND THINE.

I. In respect of the MATTER or Object of Acquisition, I acquire either a Corporeal THING (Substance), or the PERFORMANCE of something by another (Causality), or this other as a PERSON in respect of his state, so far as I have a Right to dispose of the same (in a relation of Reciprocity with him).

II. In respect of the FORM or Mode of Acquisition, it is either a REAL RIGHT (*jus reale*), or a PERSONAL RIGHT (*jus personale*), or a REAL-PERSONAL RIGHT (*jus realiter personale*), to the possession, although not to the use, of another Person as if he were a Thing.

III. In respect of the Ground of Right or THE TITLE (*titulus*) of Acquisition—which, properly, is not a par-ticular member of the Division of Rights, but rather a constituent element of the mode of exercising them—any thing External is acquired by a certain free Exercise of Will that is either *unilateral,* as the act of a single Will (*facto*), or *bilateral,* as the act of two Wills (*pacto*), or *omnilateral,* as the act of all the Wills of a Community together (*lege*).

FIRST SECTION.

PRINCIPLES OF REAL RIGHT.

11.

What is a Real Right?

The usual Definition of Real Right, or ' Right in a
Thing ' (*jus reale, jus in re*), is that ' it is a Right as
against every possessor of it.' This is a correct Nominal
Definition. But what is it that entitles me to claim an
external object from any one who may appear as its
possessor, and to compel him, *per vindicationem*, to put
me again, in place of himself, into possession of it ? Is
this external juridical relation of my Will a kind of
immediate relation to an external thing ?—If so, whoever
might think of his Right as referring not immediately
to Persons but to Things, would have to represent it,
although only in an obscure way, somewhat thus. A
Right on one side has always a Duty corresponding to it
on the other, so that an external thing, although away
from the hands of its first Possessor, continues to be
still connected with him by a continuing obligation ; and
thus it refuses to fall under the claim of any other
possessor, because it is already bound to another. In
this way my Right, viewed as a kind of good Genius
accompanying a thing and preserving it from all external
attack, would refer an alien possessor always to me !
It is, however, absurd to think of an obligation of
Persons towards Things, and conversely ; although it may
be allowed in any particular case, to represent the

juridical relation by a sensible image of this kind, and
to express it in this way.

The Real Definition would run thus: ' RIGHT IN A
THING is a Right to the Private Use of a Thing, of
which I am in possession—original or derivative—in
common with all others.' For this is the one condition under which it is alone possible that I can exclude
every other possessor from the private use of the Thing
(*jus contra quemlibet hujus rei possessorem*). For, except
by presupposing such a common collective possession, it
cannot be conceived how, when I am not in actual possession of a thing, I could be injured or wronged by
others who are in possession of it and use it.—By an
individual act of my own Will I cannot oblige any other
person to abstain from the use of a thing in respect of
which he would otherwise be under no obligation; and,
accordingly, such an Obligation can only arise from the
collective Will of all united in a relation of common
possession. Otherwise, I would have to think of a Right
in a Thing, as if the *Thing* had an Obligation towards
me, and as if the Right as against every Possessor
of it had to be derived from this Obligation in the
Thing, which is an absurd way of representing the
subject.

Further, by the term ' Real Right ' (*jus reale*) is
meant not only the ' Right in a Thing ' (*jus in re*), but
also the *constitutive principle* of all the Laws which
relate to the real Mine and Thine.—It is, however,
evident that a man entirely alone upon the earth could
properly neither have nor acquire any external thing as
his own; because between him as a Person and all
external Things as material objects, there could be no
relations of Obligation. There is therefore, literally,

no *direct* Right in a Thing, but only that Right is to be properly called 'real' which belongs to any one as constituted against a Person, who is in common possession of things with all others in the Civil state of Society.

12.

The First Acquisition of a Thing can only be that of the Soil.

By the Soil is understood all habitable Land. In relation to everything that is moveable upon it, it is to be regarded as a *Substance,* and the mode of the existence of the Moveables is viewed as an *Inherence* in it. And just as, in the theoretical acceptation, Accidents cannot exist apart from their Substances, so, in the practical relation, Moveables upon the Soil cannot be regarded as belonging to any one unless he is supposed to have been previously in juridical possession of the Soil so that it is thus considered to be his.

For, let it be supposed that the Soil belongs to no one. Then I would be entitled to remove every moveable thing found upon it from its place, even to total loss of it, in order to occupy that place, without infringing thereby on the freedom of any other; there being, by the hypothesis, no possessor of it at all. But everything that can be destroyed, such as a Tree, a House, and such like —as regards its matter at least—is moveable ; and if we call a thing which cannot be moved without destruction of its form an *immoveable,* the Mine and Thine in it is not understood as applying to its substance, but to that which is adherent to it, and which does not essentially constitute the thing itself.

13.

Every part of the Soil may be originarily acquired; and the Principle of the possibility of such Acquisition is the original Community of the Soil generally.

The first Clause of this Proposition is founded upon the Postulate of the Practical Reason (§ 2); the second is established by the following Proof.

All Men are originally and before any juridical act of Will in rightful possession of the Soil; that is, they have a Right to be wherever Nature or Chance has placed them without their will. Possession (*possessio*), which is to be distinguished from residential settlement (*sedes*) as a voluntary, acquired, and *permanent* possession, becomes *common* possession, on account of the connection with each other of all the places on the surface of the Earth as a globe. For, had the surface of the earth been an infinite plain, men could have been so dispersed upon it that they might not have come into any necessary communion with each other, and a state of social Community would not have been a necessary consequence of their existence upon the Earth.—Now that Possession proper to all men upon the earth which is prior to all their particular juridical acts, constitutes *an original possession in common* (*Communio possessionis originaria*). The conception of such an original, common Possession of things is not derived from experience, nor is it dependent on conditions of time, as is the case with the imaginary and indemonstrable fiction of *a primœval Community of possession* in actual history. Hence it is a practical conception of Reason, involving in itself the only Principle according to which Men may use the place they happen to occupy on the surface of the Earth, in accordance with Laws of Right.

14.

The juridical Act of this original Acquisition is Occupancy.

The Act of taking possession (*apprehensio*), as being at its beginning the physical appropriation of a corporeal thing in space (*possessionis physicæ*), can accord with the Law of the external Freedom of all, under no other condition than that of its *Priority* in respect of Time. In this relation it must have the characteristic of a first act in the way of taking possession, as a free exercise of Will. The activity of Will, however, as determining that the thing—in this case a definite separate place on the surface of the Earth—shall be mine, being an act of Appropriation, cannot be otherwise in the case of original Acquisition than individual or *unilateral* (*voluntas unilateralis s. propria*). Now, OCCUPANCY is the Acquisition of an external object by an individual act of Will. The original Acquisition of such an object as a limited portion of the Soil, can therefore only be accomplished by an act of Occupation.

The possibility of this mode of Acquisition cannot be intuitively apprehended by pure Reason in any way, nor established by its Principles, but is an immediate consequence from the Postulate of the Practical Reason. The Will as practical Reason, however, cannot justify external Acquisition otherwise than only in so far as it is itself included in an absolutely authoritative Will, with which it is united by implication ; or, in other words, only in so far as it is contained within a union of the Wills of all who come into practical relation with each

other.   For an individual, unilateral Will — and the
same applies to a Dual or other particular Will—cannot
impose on all an Obligation which is contingent in itself.
This requires an *omnilateral* or universal Will, which is
not contingent, but *à priori*, and which is therefore
necessarily united and legislative.   Only in accordance
with such a Principle can there be agreement of the
active free-will of each individual with the freedom of
all, and consequently Rights in general, or even the
possibility of an external Mine and Thine.

15.

It is only within a Civil Constitution that anything can be acquired peremptorily, whereas in the State of Nature Acquisition can only be provisory.

A Civil Constitution is objectively necessary as a
Duty, although subjectively its reality is contingent.
Hence, there is connected with it a real natural Law
of Right, to which all external Acquisition is subjected.

The *empirical Title of Acquisition* has been shown to
be constituted by the taking physical possession (*Apprehensio physica*) as founded upon an original community of
Right in all to the Soil.   And because a possession in
the phenomenal sphere of sense, can only be subordinated
to that Possession which is in accordance with rational
conceptions of right, there must correspond to this
physical act of possession a rational mode of taking
possession by elimination of all the empirical conditions
in Space and Time.   This rational form of possession
establishes the proposition, that ' whatever I bring under
my power in accordance with Laws of external Freedom,
and will that it shall be mine, becomes mine.'

The *rational Title of Acquisition* can therefore only lie originally in the Idea of the Will of all united implicitly, or necessarily to be united, which is here tacitly assumed as an indispensable Condition (*Conditio sine qua non*). For by a single Will there cannot be imposed upon others an obligation by which they would not have been otherwise bound.—But the fact formed by Wills actually and universally united in a Legislation, constitutes the Civil state of Society. Hence, it is only in conformity with the idea of a Civil state of Society, or in reference to it and its realization, that anything External can be acquired. Before such a state is realized, and in anticipation of it, Acquisition, which would otherwise be derived, is consequently only *provisory*. The Acquisition, which is *peremptory*, finds place only in the Civil state.

Nevertheless, such provisory Acquisition is real Acquisition. For, according to the Postulate of the juridically Practical Reason, the possibility of Acquisition in whatever state men may happen to be living beside one another, and therefore in the State of Nature as well, is a Principle of Private Right. And in accordance with this Principle, every one is justified or entitled to exercise that compulsion by which it alone becomes possible to pass out of the state of Nature, and to enter into that state of Civil Society which alone can make all Acquisition peremptory.

It is a question as to how far the right of taking possession of the Soil extends? The answer is, So far as the capability of having it under one's power extends, that is, just as far as he who wills to appropriate it can defend it, as if the Soil were to say, 'If you cannot protect me, neither can you command me.' In this way the controversy about what con-

stitutes a *free* or *closed* Sea must be decided. Thus,
within the range of a cannon-shot no one has a right
to intrude on the coast of a country that already
belongs to a certain State, in order to fish or gather
amber on the shore, or such like. — Further, the
question is put, 'Is Cultivation of the Soil, by building, agriculture, drainage, etc., necessary in order to
its Acquisition?' *No.* For, as these processes as
forms of specification are only Accidents, they do not
constitute objects of immediate possession, and can
only belong to the Subject in so far as the substance
of them has been already recognised as his. When it
is a question of the first Acquisition of a thing, the
cultivation or modification of it by labour forms
nothing more than an external sign of the fact that it.
has been taken into possession, and this can be indicated by many other signs that cost less trouble.—
Again, 'May any one be hindered in the *Act* of
taking possession, so that neither one nor other of
two Competitors shall acquire the Right of Priority,
and the Soil in consequence may remain for all time
free as belonging to no one?' *Not at all.* Such a
hindrance cannot be allowed to take place, because
the second of the two, in order to be enabled to do
this, would himself have to be upon some neighbouring Soil, where he also, in this manner, could be
hindered from being, and such *absolute Hindering*
would involve a Contradiction. It would, however,
be quite consistent with the Right of Occupation, in
the case of a certain intervening piece of the Soil, to
let it lie unused as a *neutral* ground for the separation of two neighbouring States; but under such a
condition, that ground would actually belong to them
both in common, and would not be without an owner
(*res nullius*), just because it would be *used* by both in
order to form a separation between them.—Again,
'May one have a thing as his, on a Soil of which no
one has appropriated any part as his own?' *Yes.* In

Mongolia, for example, any one may let lie whatever
baggage he has, or bring back the horse that has run
away from him into his possession as his own, because
the whole Soil belongs to the people generally, and
the use of it accordingly belongs to every individual.
But that any one can have a moveable thing on the
soil of another as his own, is only possible by *Contract*.
—Finally, there is the question: 'May one of two
neighbouring Nations or Tribes resist another when
attempting to impose upon them a certain mode of
using a particular Soil; as, for instance, a tribe of
hunters making such an attempt in relation to a
pastoral people, or the latter to agriculturists and
such like?' *Certainly*. For the mode in which such
peoples or tribes may *settle* themselves upon the
surface of the earth, provided they keep within their
own boundaries, is a matter of mere pleasure and
choice on their own part (*res meræ facultatis*).

As a further question, it may be asked: Whether,
when neither Nature nor Chance, but merely our own
Will, brings us into the neighbourhood of a people
that gives no promise of a prospect of entering into
Civil Union with us, we are to be considered entitled
in any case to proceed with force in the intention of
founding such a Union, and bringing into a juridical
state such men as the savage American Indians, the
Hottentots, and the New Hollanders; Or—and the
case is not much better—whether we may establish
Colonies by deceptive purchase, and so become owners
of their soil, and, in general, without regard to their
first possession, make use at will of our superiority in
relation to them? Further, may it not be held that
Nature herself, as abhorring a vacuum, seems to
demand such a procedure, and that large regions in
other Continents, that are now magnificently peopled,
would otherwise have remained unpossessed by civilised inhabitants, and might have for ever remained
thus, so that the end of Creation would have so far

been frustrated ? It is almost unnecessary to answer ;
for it is easy to see through all this flimsy veil of
injustice, which just amounts to the Jesuitism of
making a good End justify any Means. This mode
of acquiring the Soil is, therefore, to be repudiated.

The Indefiniteness of external acquirable objects in
respect of their Quantity, as well as their Quality,
makes the problem of the sole primary external
Acquisition of them one of the most difficult to solve.
There must, however, be some one first Acquisition
of an external object; for every Acquisition cannot
be derivative. Hence, the problem is not to be given
up as insoluble, or in itself as impossible. If it is
solved by reference to the Original Contract, unless
this Contract is extended so as to include the whole
human race, Acquisition under it would still remain
but provisional.

16.

Exposition of the Conception of a Primary Acquisition of the Soil.

All men are originally in a *common collective possession*
of the Soil of the whole Earth (*Communio fundi originaria*), and they have naturally each a Will to use it
(*lex justi*). But on account of the opposition of the free
Will of one to that of the other in the sphere of action,
which is inevitable by nature, all use of the soil would
be prevented did not every will contain at the same
time a Law for the regulation of the relation of all Wills
in action, according to which a *particular possession* can
be determined to every one upon the common soil. This
is the juridical Law (*lex juridica*). But the distributive
Law of the Mine and Thine, as applicable to each individual on the soil, according to the Axiom of external
Freedom, cannot proceed otherwise than from a *primarily*

united Will *à priori*—which does not presuppose any
juridical act as requisite for this union.   This Law can
only take form in the Civil State (*lex justitiæ distributivæ*); as it is in this state alone that the united
common Will determines what is *right*, what is *rightful*, and
what is the constitution of *Right*.   In reference to this state,
however,—and prior to its establishment and in view of it,
—it is *provisorily* a *Duty* for every one to proceed according to the Law of external Acquisition; and accordingly it
is a juridical procedure on the part of the Will to lay every
one under Obligation to recognise the act of possessing
and appropriating, although it be only unilaterally.   Hence
a provisory Acquisition of the Soil, with all its juridical
consequences, is possible in the state of Nature.

Such an Acquisition, however, requires and also
obtains the *favour* of a Permissive Law (*Lex permissiva*),
in respect of the determination of the limits of juridically possible Possession.   For it precedes the juridical
state, and as merely introductory to it is not yet
peremptory; and this favour does not extend farther
than the date of the consent of the *other* co-operators
in the establishment of the Civil State.   But if they
are opposed to entering into the Civil State, as long as
this opposition lasts it carries all the effect of a guaranteed juridical Acquisition with it, because the advance
from the state of nature to the Civil State is founded
upon a Duty.

17.

Deduction of the Conception of the original Primary Acquisition.

We have found the *Title* of Acquisition in a universal
original community of the Soil, under the conditions of

an external Acquisition in space; and the *Mode* of
Acquisition is contained in the empirical fact of taking
possession (*Apprehensio*), conjoined with the Will to have
an external object as one's own.   It is further necessary
to unfold from the Principles of the pure juridically
Practical Reason involved in the conception, the juridical
Acquisition proper of an object,—that is, the external
Mine and Thine that follows from the two previous
conditions, as Rational Possession (*possessio noumenon*).

The *juridical Conception* of the *external* Mine and
Thine, so far as it involves the category of *Substance*,
cannot by 'that which is *external* to me' mean merely
'*in a place* other than that in which I am;' for it is a
rational conception.   As under the conceptions of the
Reason only intellectual conceptions can be embraced, the
expression in question can only signify 'something that
is different and distinct from me' according to the idea
of a non-empirical Possession through, as it were, a continuous activity in taking possession of an external object;
and it involves only the notion of '*having something in
my power*,' which indicates the connection of an object
with myself, as a subjective condition of the possibility
of making use of it.   This forms a purely intellectual
conception of the Understanding.   Now we can leave
out or abstract from the sensible conditions of Possession, as relations of a Person to *objects* which have no
obligation.   This process of elimination just gives the
rational relation of a Person to *Persons;* and it is such
that he can bind them all by an obligation in reference
to the use of things through his act of Will, so far as it
is conformable to the *Axiom* of Freedom, the *Postulate*
of Right, and the universal *Legislation* of the common
Will conceived as united *à priori*.   This is therefore the

rational intelligible *possession* of things as by pure Right, although they are objects of sense.

It is evident that the first modification, limitation, or *transformation* generally of a portion of the Soil cannot of itself furnish a Title to its Acquisition, since possession of an Accident does not form a ground for legal possession of the Substance. Rather, conversely, the inference as to the Mine and Thine must be drawn from ownership of the Substance according to the rule, '*Accessarium sequitur suum principale.*' Hence one who has spent labour on a piece of ground that was not already his own, has lost his effort and work to the former Owner. This position is so evident of itself, that the old opinion to the opposite effect, that is still spread far and wide, can hardly be ascribed to any other than the prevailing illusion which unconsciously leads to the Personification of things; and, then, as if they could be bound under an obligation by the labour bestowed upon them to be at the service of the person who does the labour, to regard them as his by *immediate* Right. Otherwise it is probable that the natural question—already discussed—would not have been passed over with so light a tread, namely, 'How is a Right in a *thing* possible ?' For, Right as against every possible possessor of a Thing, means only the claim of a particular Will to the use of an object so far as it may be included in the All-comprehending universal Will, and can be thought as in harmony with its law.

As regards bodies situated upon a piece of ground which is already mine, if they otherwise belong to no other Person, they belong to me without my requiring any particular juridical act for the purpose of this Acquisition ; they are mine not *facto*, but *lege*. For they may be regarded as Accidents inhering in the Substance of the Soil, and they are thus mine *jure rei meæ*. To this Category also belongs everything which is so connected with anything of mine, that it cannot be separated from what is mine without altering it substantially. Examples of this are Gilding on an object, Mixture of a material belonging to me with other things, Alluvial deposit, or even Alteration of the adjoining bed of a stream or river in my favour so as to produce an increase of my land, etc. By the same principles the question must also be decided as to whether the acquirable Soil may extend farther than the existing land, so as even to include part of the bed of the Sea, with the Right to fish on my own shores, to gather Amber and such like. So far as I have the mechanical *capability* from my own *Site*, as the place I occupy, to secure my Soil from the attack of others—and, therefore, as far as Cannon can carry from the shore—all is included in my *possession*, and the sea is thus far closed (*mare clausum*). But as there is no *Site* for Occupation upon the wide sea itself, possible possession cannot be extended so far, and the open sea is free (*mare liberum*). But in the case of men, or things that belong to them, becoming *stranded* on the Shore, since the fact is not voluntary, it cannot be regarded by the owner of the shore as giving him a Right of Acquisition. For shipwreck is not an act of Will, nor is its result a lesion to him; and things which may have come thus upon his Soil, as still belonging to some one, are not to be treated as being without an Owner or *Res nullius*. On the other hand, a River, so far as possession of the bank reaches, may be originally acquired, like any other piece of ground, under the above restrictions, by one who is in possession of both its banks.

PROPERTY.

An external Object, which, in respect of its Substance, can be claimed by some one as his own, is called the

PROPERTY (*dominium*) of that Person to whom all the Rights in it as a thing belong, like the Accidents inhering in a Substance, and which, therefore, he as the Proprietor (*dominus*) can dispose of at will (*jus disponendi de re sua*). But from this it follows at once, that such an object can only be a Corporeal Thing towards which there is no direct personal Obligation. Hence a man may be HIS OWN MASTER (*sui juris*) but not the Proprietor *of himself* (*sui dominus*), so as to be able to dispose of himself at will, to say nothing of the possibility of such a relation to other men; because he is responsible to Humanity in his own person. This point, however, as belonging to the Right of Humanity as such, rather than to that of individual men, would not be discussed at its proper place here, but is only mentioned incidentally for the better elucidation of what has just been said. It may be further observed that there may be two full Proprietors of one and the same thing, without there being a Mine and Thine in common, but only in so far as they are common Possessors of what belongs only to *one* of them as *his own*. In such a case the whole Possession without the Use of the thing, belongs to one only of the Co-proprietors (*condomini*); while to the other belongs all the Use of the thing along with its Possession. The former as the direct Proprietor (*dominus directus*), therefore, restricts the latter as the Proprietor in use (*dominus utilis*) to the condition of a certain continuous performance, with reference to the thing itself, without limiting him in the use of it.

SECOND SECTION.

PRINCIPLES OF PERSONAL RIGHT.

18.

Nature and Acquisition of Personal Right.

The possession of the active free - will of another person, as the power to determine it by my Will to a certain action, according to Laws of Freedom, is a form of Right relating to the external Mine and Thine, as affected by the Causality of another. It is possible to have several such Rights in reference to the same Person or to different persons. The Principle of the System of Laws, according to which I can be in such possession, is that of Personal Right, and there is only one such Principle.

The Acquisition of a Personal Right can never be primary or arbitrary; for such a mode of acquiring it would not be in accordance with the Principle of the harmony of the freedom of my will with the freedom of every other, and it would therefore be wrong. Nor can such a Right be acquired by means of any *unjust* act of another (*facto injusti alterius*), as being itself contrary to Right; for if such a wrong as it implies were perpetrated on me, and I could demand satisfaction from the other, in accordance with Right, yet in such a case I would only be entitled to maintain undiminished what was mine, and not to acquire anything more than what I formerly had.

Acquisition by means of the action of another, to

which I determine his Will according to Laws of Right, is therefore always derived from what that other has as his own. This derivation, as a Juridical act, cannot be effected by a mere *negative relinquishment* or *renunciation* of what is his (*per derelictionem aut renunciationem*); because such a negative Act would only amount to a cessation of *his* Right, and not to the acquirement of a Right on the part of another. It is therefore only by positive TRANSFERENCE (*translatio*), or CONVEYANCE, that a Personal Right can be acquired; and this is only possible by means of a common Will, through which objects come into the power of one or other, so that as one renounces a particular thing which he holds under the common Right, the same object when accepted by another, in consequence of a positive act of Will, becomes his. Such transference of the *Property* of one to another is termed its ALIENATION. The act of the united Wills of two Persons, by which what belonged to one passes to the other, constitutes CONTRACT.

19.

Acquisition by Contract.

In every CONTRACT there are *four Juridical Acts* of Will involved; *two* of them being *preparatory Acts,* and *two* of them *constitutive Acts.* The two Preparatory Acts, as forms of treating in the Transaction, are OFFER (*oblatio*) and APPROVAL (*approbatio*); the two Constitutive Acts, as the forms of *concluding* the transaction, are PROMISE (*promissum*) and ACCEPTANCE (*acceptatio*). For an offer cannot constitute a Promise before it can be judged that the thing offered (*oblatum*) is something that is *agreeable* to the Party to whom it is offered, and this much is shown by the first two declarations; but by them alone there is nothing as yet acquired.

Further, it is neither by the *particular* Will of the Promiser nor that of the Acceptor that the property of the former passes over to the latter. This is effected only by the *combined* or united Wills of both, and consequently so far only as the Will of both is declared at the same time or simultaneously. Now, such simultaneousness is impossible by empirical acts of declaration, which can only *follow* each other in time, and are never actually simultaneous. For if I have promised, and another person is now merely willing to accept, during the interval before actual Acceptance, however short it may be, I may retract my offer, because I am thus far still free; and, on the other side, the Acceptor, for the same reason, may likewise hold himself not to be bound, up till the moment of Acceptance, by his counter-declaration following upon the Promise. — The external Formalities or Solemnities (*solemnia*) on the conclusion of a Contract,— such as shaking hands or breaking a straw (*stipula*) laid hold of by two persons,— and all the various modes of confirming the Declarations on either side, prove in fact the embarrassment of the contracting parties as to how and in what way they may represent Declarations, which are always *successive*, as existing *simultaneously* at the same moment; and these forms fail to do this. They are, by their very nature, Acts necessarily following each other in time, so that when the one Act is, the other either is *not yet* or is *no longer*.

It is only the philosophical Transcendental Deduction of the Conception of Acquisition by Contract, that can remove all these difficulties. In a *juridical* external relation, my taking possession of the free-will of another, as the cause that determined it to a certain Act, is conceived at first empirically by means of the declaration and counter-declaration of the free-will of each of us in time, as the sensible conditions of taking possession ; and the two juridical Acts must necessarily be regarded as following one another in time.   But because this relation, viewed as juridical, is purely Rational in itself, the Will as a law-giving faculty of Reason represents this possession as intelligible or rational (*possessio noumenon*), in accordance with conceptions of Freedom and under abstraction of those empirical conditions.   And now, the two Acts of Promise and Acceptance are not regarded as *following* one another in time, but, in the manner of a *pactum re initum,* as proceeding from a *common* Will, which is expressed by the term ' at the same time,' or ' simultaneous,' and the object promised (*promissum*) is represented, under elimination of empirical conditions, as acquired according to the Law of the pure Practical Reason.

That this is the true and only possible Deduction of the idea of Acquisition by Contract, is sufficiently attested by the laborious yet always futile striving of writers on Jurisprudence—such as Moses Mendelssohn in his *Jerusalem* — to adduce a proof of its rational possibility.—The question is put thus : ' Why *ought* I to keep my Promise ? ' for it is assumed as understood by all that I *ought* to do so.   It is, however, absolutely impossible to give any further proof of the Categorical Imperative implied ; just as it is impossible for the Geometrician to prove by rational Syllogisms that in order to construct a Triangle, I must take three Lines — so far an Analytical Proposition—of which three Lines any two together must be greater than the third—a Synthetical Proposition, and like the former *à priori*. It is a Postulate of the Pure Reason that we ought to abstract from all the sensible conditions of Space and Time in reference to the conception of Right; and the theory of the possibility of such Abstraction from these conditions without taking away the reality of the Possession, just constitutes the Transcendental Deduction of the Conception of Acquisition by Contract. It is quite akin to what was presented under the last Title, as the Theory of Acquisition by Occupation of the external object.

20.

What is acquired by Contract ?

But what is that, designated as 'External,' which I acquire by Contract ? As it is only the Causality of the active Will of another, in respect of the Performance of something promised to me, I do not immediately acquire thereby an external Thing, but an Act of the Will in question, whereby a Thing is brought under my power so that I make it mine.—By the Contract, therefore, I acquire the Promise of another, as distinguished from the Thing promised; and yet something is thereby added to my Having and Possession. I have become the *richer in possession* (*locupletior*) by the Acquisition of an active Obligation that I can bring to bear upon the Freedom and Capability of another. — This my *Right*, however, is only a *personal* Right, valid only to the effect of acting upon a *particular* physical Person and specially upon the Causality of his Will, so that he shall *perform* something for me. It is not a *Real* Right upon that *Moral Person*, which is identified with the Idea of the united *Will of All* viewed *à priori*, and through which alone I can acquire a *Right valid against every Possessor of the Thing*.   For, it is in this that all Right *in a Thing* consists.

The Transfer or transmission of what is mine to another by Contract, takes place according to the Law of Continuity (*Lex Continui*).   Possession of the object is not interrupted for a moment during this Act; for, otherwise, I would acquire an object in this state as a Thing that had no Possessor, and it would thus be acquired originally; which is contrary to the idea of a Contract.—This Continuity, however, implies that it is not the particular Will of either the Promiser or the Acceptor, but their united Will in common, that transfers what is mine to another.   And hence it is not accomplished in such a manner that the Promiser first relinquishes (*derelinquit*) his Possession for the benefit of another, or renounces his Right (*renunciat*), and thereupon the other at the same time enters upon it ; or conversely.   The Transfer (*translatio*) is therefore an Act in which the object belongs for a moment *at the same time* to both, just as in the parabolic path of a projectile the object on reaching its highest point may be regarded for a moment as *at the same time* both rising and falling, and as thus passing in fact from the ascending to the falling motion.

21.

Acceptance and Delivery.

A thing is not acquired in a case of Contract by the ACCEPTANCE (*acceptatio*) of the Promise, but only by the DELIVERY (*traditio*) of the object promised.   For all Promise is relative to *Performance ;* and if what was promised is a Thing, the Performance cannot be executed otherwise than by an act whereby the Acceptor

is put by the Promiser into possession of the Thing; and
this is Delivery.   Before the Delivery and the Reception
of the Thing, the Performance of the act required has
not yet taken place ; the Thing has not yet passed from
the one person to the other, and consequently has not
been acquired by that other.   Hence the Right arising
from a Contract, is only a Personal Right ; and it only
becomes a Real Right by Delivery.

A Contract upon which Delivery immediately
follows (*pactum re initum*) excludes any interval of
time between its conclusion and its execution ; and as
such it requires no further particular act in the future
by which one person may transfer to another what is
his.   But if there is a time—definite or indefinite—
agreed upon between them for the Delivery, the
question then arises, Whether the Thing has already
before that time become the Acceptor's by the Contract, so that his Right is a Right in the Thing ; *or*
whether a further special Contract regarding the
Delivery alone must be entered upon, so that the
Right that is acquired by mere Acceptance is only
a Personal Right, and thus it does not become a Right
in the Thing until Delivery ?   That the relation must
be determined according to the latter alternative, will
be clear from what follows.
Suppose I conclude a Contract about a Thing that
I wish to acquire,—such as a Horse,—and that I take
it immediately into my Stable, or otherwise into my
possession ; then it is mine (*vi pacti re initi*), and my
Right is a Right in the Thing.   But if I leave it in
the hands of the Seller without arranging with him
specially in whose physical possession or holding
(*detentio*) this Thing shall be before my taking possession of it (*apprehensio*), and consequently before
the actual change of possession, the Horse is not yet
mine ; and the Right which I acquire is only a Right

against a particular Person—namely, the Seller of the Horse—*to be put into possession* of the object (*poscendi traditionem*) as the subjective condition of any use of it at my will. My Right is thus only a Personal Right to demand from the Seller the *performance* of his promise (*præstatio*) to put me into possession of the thing. Now, if the Contract does not contain the condition of Delivery *at the same time*,—as a *pactum re initum*,—and consequently an interval of time intervenes between the conclusion of the Contract and the taking possession of the object of acquisition, I cannot obtain possession of it during this interval otherwise than by exercising the particular juridical activity called *a possessory Act* (*actum possessorium*) which constitutes a special Contract. This Act consists in my saying, ' I will send to fetch the horse,' to which the Seller has to agree. For it is not self-evident or universally reasonable, that any one will take a Thing destined for the use of another into his charge at his own risk. On the contrary, a special Contract is necessary for this arrangement, according to which the Alienator of a thing continues to be its owner during a certain *definite* time, and must bear the risk of whatever may happen to it; while the Acquirer can only be regarded by the Seller as the Owner, when he has delayed to enter into possession beyond the date at which he agreed to take delivery. Prior to the Possessory Act, therefore, all that is acquired by the Contract is only a Personal Right; and the Acceptor can acquire an external Thing only by Delivery.

THIRD SECTION.

PRINCIPLES OF PERSONAL RIGHT THAT IS REAL IN KIND.

(Jus realiter personale.)

22.

Nature of Personal Right of a Real Kind.

Personal Right of a real kind is the Right to the
possession of an external object AS A THING, and to the
use of it AS A PERSON.—The Mine and Thine embraced
under this Right relate specially to the Family and
Household; and the relations involved are those of free
beings in reciprocal real interaction with each other.
Through their relations and influence as Persons upon
one another, in accordance with the principle of external
Freedom as the *cause* of it, they form a Society composed as a whole of members standing in community
with each other as Persons; and this constitutes the
HOUSEHOLD.—The mode in which this social status is
acquired by individuals, and the functions which prevail
within it, proceed neither by arbitrary individual action
(*facto*), nor by mere Contract (*pacto*), but by Law (*lege*).
And this Law as being not only a Right, but also as constituting Possession in reference to a Person, is a Right
rising above all *mere* Real and Personal Right. It must,
in fact, form the Right of Humanity in our own Person;
and, as such, it has as its consequence a natural Permissive Law, by the favour of which such Acquisition
becomes possible to us.

23.

What is acquired in the Household?

The Acquisition that is founded upon this Law is, as regards its objects, threefold. The Man acquires a WIFE; the Husband and Wife acquire CHILDREN, constituting a Family; and the Family acquire DOMESTICS. All these objects, while acquirable, are inalienable; and the Right of Possession in these objects is *the most strictly personal of all Rights.*

THE RIGHTS OF THE FAMILY AS A DOMESTIC SOCIETY.

TITLE FIRST.

CONJUGAL RIGHT.
(Husband and Wife.)

24.

The Natural Basis of Marriage.

The domestic Relations are founded on Marriage, and Marriage is founded upon the natural Reciprocity or intercommunity (*commercium*) of the Sexes.[1] This natural

---

[1] *Commercium sexuale est usus membrorum et facultatum sexualium alterius.* This '*usus*' is either natural, by which human beings may reproduce their own kind, or unnatural, which, again, refers either to a person of the same sex or to an animal of another species than man. These transgressions of all Law, as '*crimina carnis contra naturam,*' are even 'not to be named;' and as wrongs against all Humanity in the Person they cannot be saved, by any limitation or exception whatever, from entire reprobation.

union of the sexes proceeds either according to the mere
animal Nature (*vaga libido, venus vulgivaga, fornicatio*),
or according to Law. The latter is MARRIAGE (*matri-
monium*), which is the Union of two Persons of different
sex for life - long reciprocal possession of their sexual
faculties.—The End of producing and educating children
may be regarded as always the End of Nature in im-
planting mutual desire and inclination in the sexes; but
it is not necessary for the rightfulness of marriage that
those who marry should set this before themselves as
the End of their Union, otherwise the Marriage would
be dissolved of itself when the production of children
ceased.

And even assuming that enjoyment in the reciprocal
use of the sexual endowments is an end of marriage,
yet the Contract of Marriage is not on that account a
matter of arbitrary will, but is a Contract necessary in
its nature by the Law of Humanity. In other words,
if a man and a woman have the will to enter on
reciprocal enjoyment in accordance with their sexual
nature, they *must* necessarily marry each other; and
this necessity is in accordance with the juridical Laws
of Pure Reason.

25.

The Rational Right of Marriage.

For, this natural ' *Commercium* '—as a ' *usus membrorum sexualium alterius* '—is an enjoyment for which
the one person is given up to the other. In this relation the human individual makes himself a ' *res*,' which
is contrary to the Right of Humanity in his own Person.
This, however, is only possible under the one condition,

that as the one Person is acquired by the other as a *res*, that same Person also equally acquires the other reciprocally, and thus regains and re-establishes the rational Personality. The Acquisition of a part of the human organism being, on account of its unity, at the same time the acquisition of the whole Person, it follows that the surrender and acceptation of, or by, one sex in relation to the other, is not only *permissible* under the condition of Marriage, but is further *only* really possible under that condition. But the Personal Right thus acquired is at the same time, *real in kind ;* and this characteristic of it is established by the fact that if one of the married Persons run away or enter into the possession of another, the other is entitled, at any time, and incontestably, to bring such a one back to the former relation, as if that Person were a Thing.

26.

Monogamy and Equality in Marriage.

For the same reasons, the relation of the Married Persons to each other is a relation of EQUALITY as regards the mutual possession of their Persons, as well as of their Goods. Consequently Marriage is only truly realized in MONOGAMY; for in the relation of Polygamy the Person who is given away on the one side, gains only a part of the one to whom that Person is given up, and therefore becomes a mere *res*. But in respect of their Goods, they have severally the Right to renounce the use of any part of them, although only by a special Contract.

From the Principle thus stated, it also follows that Concubinage is as little capable of being brought

under a Contract of Right, as the hiring of a person
on any one occasion, in the way of a *pactum forni-
cationis*. For, as regards such a Contract as this
latter relation would imply, it must be admitted by
all that any one who might enter into it could not be
legally held to the fulfilment of their promise if they
wished to resile from it. And as regards the former,
a Contract of Concubinage would also fall as a
pactum turpe; because as a Contract of the *hire*
(*locatio, conductio*), of a part for the use of another,
on account of the inseparable unity of the members
of a Person, any one entering into such a Contract
would be actually surrendering as a *res* to the arbitrary Will of another. Hence any party may annul
a Contract like this if entered into with any other,
at any time and at pleasure; and that other would
have no ground, in the circumstances, to complain of
a lesion of his Right. The same holds likewise of a
morganatic or 'left-hand' Marriage contracted in
order to turn the inequality in the social status of the
two parties to advantage in the way of establishing
the social supremacy of the one over the other; for,
in fact, such a relation is not really different from
Concubinage, according to the principles of Natural
Right, and therefore does not constitute a real
Marriage. Hence the question may be raised as to
whether it is not contrary to the Equality of married
Persons when the Law says in any way of the Husband in relation to the Wife, 'he shall be thy master,'
so that he is represented as the one who commands,
and she as the one who obeys. This, however, cannot
be regarded as contrary to the natural Equality of a
human pair, if such legal Supremacy is based only
upon the natural superiority of the faculties of the
Husband compared with the Wife, in the effectuation
of the common interest of the household; and if the
Right to command, is based merely upon this fact.
For this Right may thus be deduced from the very

duty of Unity and Equality in relation to the *End* involved.

27.

Fulfilment of the Contract of Marriage.

The Contract of Marriage is completed only by conjugal cohabitation. A Contract of two Persons of different sex, with the secret understanding either to abstain from conjugal cohabitation or with the consciousness on either side of incapacity for it, is a *simulated Contract;* it does not constitute a marriage, and it may be dissolved by either of the parties at will. But if the incapacity only arises after marriage, the Right of the Contract is not annulled or diminished by a contingency that cannot be legally blamed.

The Acquisition of a Spouse either as a Husband or as a Wife, is therefore not constituted *facto*—that is, by Cohabitation—without a preceding Contract; nor even *pacto*—by a mere Contract of Marriage, without subsequent Cohabitation; but only *lege,* that is, as a juridical consequence of the obligation that is formed by two Persons entering into a sexual Union solely on the basis of a reciprocal *Possession* of each other, which Possession at the same time is only effected in reality by the reciprocal ' usus facultatum sexualium alterius.'

RIGHTS OF THE FAMILY AS A DOMESTIC SOCIETY.

TITLE SECOND.

PARENTAL RIGHT.

(Parent and Child.)

28.

The Relation of Parent and Child.

From the Duty of Man towards himself—that is, towards the Humanity in his own Person—there thus arises a personal Right on the part of the Members of the opposite sexes, as Persons, to acquire one another really and reciprocally by Marriage. In like manner, from the fact of *Procreation* in the union thus constituted, there follows the Duty of preserving and rearing *Children* as the Products of this Union. Accordingly Children, as Persons, have, at the same time, an original congenital Right—distinguished from mere hereditary Right—to be reared by the care of their Parents till they are capable of maintaining themselves ; and this provision becomes immediately theirs by Law, without any particular juridical Act being required to determine it.

For what is thus produced is a *Person*, and it is impossible to think of a Being endowed with personal Freedom as produced merely by a physical process. And hence, *in the practical relation*, it is quite a correct and even a necessary Idea to regard the act of generation as a process by which a Person is brought without his

consent into the world, and placed in it by the responsible free will of others.   This Act, therefore, attaches an
obligation to the Parents to make their Children—as far
as their power goes—contented with the condition thus
acquired.   Hence Parents cannot regard their Child as,
in a manner, a Thing *of their own making*, for a Being
endowed with Freedom cannot be so regarded.   Nor,
consequently, have they a Right to destroy it as if it
were their own property, or even to leave it to chance;
because they have brought a Being into the world who
becomes in fact a Citizen of the world, and they have
placed that Being in a state which they cannot be left to
treat with indifference, even according to the natural
conceptions of Right.

We cannot even conceive how it is possible that
GOD *can create* FREE Beings ; for it appears as if all
their future actions, being predetermined by that
first act, would be contained in the chain of natural
necessity, and that, therefore, they could not be free.
But as men we *are* free in fact, as is proved by the
Categorical Imperative in the moral and practical
relation as an authoritative decision of Reason ; yet
reason cannot make the possibility of such a relation
of Cause to Effect conceivable from the theoretical
point of view, because they are both suprasensible.
All that can be demanded of Reason under these
conditions, would merely be to prove that there is
no Contradiction involved in the conception of a
CREATION OF FREE BEINGS; and this may be done by
showing that Contradiction only arises when, along
with the Category of Causality, the *Condition of Time*
is transferred to the relation of suprasensible Things.
This condition, as implying that the cause of an effect
must precede the effect as its reason, is inevitable
in thinking the relation of objects of sense to one

another; and if this conception of Causality were to have objective reality given to it in the theoretical bearing, it would also have to be referred to the suprasensible sphere. But the Contradiction vanishes when the pure Category, apart from any sensible conditions, is applied from the moral and practical point of view, and consequently as in a non-sensible relation to the conception of Creation.

The philosophical Jurist will not regard this investigation, when thus carried back even to the ultimate Principles of the Transcendental Philosophy, as an unnecessary subtlety in a Metaphysic of Morals, or as losing itself in aimless obscurity, when he takes into consideration the difficulty of the problem to be solved, and also the necessity of doing justice in this inquiry to the ultimate relations of the Principles of Right.

29.

The Rights of the Parent.

From the Duty thus indicated, there further necessarily arises the Right of the Parents to THE MANAGEMENT AND TRAINING OF THE CHILD, so long as it is itself incapable of making proper use of its body as an Organism, and of its mind as an Understanding. This involves its nourishment and the care of its Education. This includes, in general, the function of forming and developing it *practically*, that it may be able in the future to maintain and advance itself, and also its moral Culture and Development, the guilt of neglecting it falling upon the Parents. All this training is to be continued till the Child reaches the period of Emancipation (*emancipatio*), as the age of practicable self-support. The Parents then virtually renounce the parental Right to command, as well as all claim to repayment for their previous care and trouble ; for which care and trouble, after the process of Education is complete, they can only appeal to the Children by way of any claim, on the ground of the Obligation of Gratitude as a Duty of Virtue.

From the fact of Personality in the Children, it further follows that they can never be regarded as the Property of the Parents, but only as belonging to them by way of being in their *possession*, like other things that are held apart from the possession of all others and that can be brought back even against the will of the Subjects. Hence the Right of the Parents is not a purely Real Right, and it is not alienable (*jus personalissimum*).   But neither is it a *merely* Personal Right ; it is a Personal Right of a *real* kind, that is, a Personal Right that is constituted and exercised after the *manner* of a Real Right.

It is therefore evident that the Title of *a Personal Right of a Real Kind* must necessarily be added, in the Science of Right, to the Titles of Real Right and Personal Right, the Division of Rights into these two being not complete.   For, if the Right of the Parents to the Children were treated as if it were merely a Real Right to a part of what belongs to their house, they could not found only upon the Duty of the Children to return to them in claiming them when they run away, but they would be then entitled to seize them and to impound them like things or runaway cattle.

RIGHTS OF THE FAMILY AS A DOMESTIC SOCIETY.

TITLE THIRD.

HOUSEHOLD RIGHT.
(Master and Servant.)

30.

Relation and Right of the Master of a Household.

The Children of the House, who, along with the
Parents, constitute a Family, attain *majority*, and become
MASTERS OF THEMSELVES (*majorennes, sui juris*), even
without a Contract of release from their previous state of
Dependence, by their actually attaining to the capability
of self-maintenance.   This attainment arises, on the one
hand, as a state of natural Majority, with the advance of
years in the general course of Nature ; and, on the other
hand, it takes form, as a state in accordance with their
own natural condition.   They thus acquire the Right of
being their own Masters, without the interposition of any
special juridical act, and therefore merely by Law (*lege*);
and they owe their Parents nothing by way of legal debt
for their Education, just as the parents, on their side, are
now released from their Obligations to the Children in
the same way.   Parents and Children thus gain or regain
their natural Freedom ; and the domestic society, which
was necessary according to the Law of Right, is thus
naturally dissolved.

Both Parties, however, may resolve to continue the

Household, but under another mode of Obligation.   It may assume the form of a relation between the Head of the House as its Master, and the other members as domestic Servants, male or female; and the connection between them in this new *regulated* domestic economy (*societas herilis*) may be determined by Contract.   The Master of the House, actually or virtually, enters into Contract with the Children, now become major and masters of themselves; or, if there be no Children in the Family, with other free Persons constituting the membership of the Household; and thus there is established a domestic relationship not founded on social equality, but such that one *commands* as Master, and another *obeys* as Servant (*Imperantis et subjecti Domestici*).

The Domestics or Servants may then be regarded by the Master of the household, as thus far his.   As regards the *form* or mode of his Possession of them, they belong to him as if by a Real Right; for if any of them run away, he is entitled to bring them again under his power by a unilateral act of his will.   But as regards the *matter* of his Right, or the *use* he is entitled to make of such persons as his Domestics, he is not entitled to conduct himself towards them as if he was their proprietor or owner (*dominus servi*); because they are only subjected to his power by Contract, and by a Contract under certain definite restrictions.   For a Contract by which the one party renounced his *whole* freedom for the advantage of the other, ceasing thereby to be a person and consequently having no duty even to observe a Contract, is self-contradictory, and is therefore of itself null and void.   The question as to the Right of Property in relation to one who has lost his legal personality by a Crime, does not concern us here.

This Contract, then, of the Master of a Household with his Domestics, cannot be of such a nature that the *use* of them could ever rightly become an *abuse* of them; and the judgment as to what constitutes *use* or *abuse* in such circumstances is not left merely to the Master, but is also competent to the Servants, who ought never to be held in bondage or bodily servitude as Slaves or Serfs. Such a Contract cannot, therefore, be concluded for life, but in all cases only for a definite period, within which one party may intimate to the other a termination of their connection. Children, however, including even the children of one who has become enslaved owing to a Crime, are always free. For every man is born free, because he has at birth as yet broken no Law; and even the cost of his education till his maturity, cannot be reckoned as a debt which he is bound to pay. Even a Slave, if it were in his power, would be bound to educate his children without being entitled to count and reckon with them for the cost; and in view of his own incapacity for discharging this function, the Possessor of a Slave, therefore, enters upon the Obligation which he has rendered the Slave himself unable to fulfil.

Here, again, as under the first two Titles, it is clear that there is a Personal Right of a *Real* kind, in the relation of the Master of a House to his Domestics. For he can legally demand them as belonging to what is externally his, from any other possessor of them; and he is entitled to fetch them back to his house, even before the reasons that may have led them to run away, and their particular Right in the circumstances, have been judicially investigated. [See *Supplementary Explanations*, I. II. III.]

SYSTEMATIC DIVISION

Of all the Rights capable of being acquired by
Contract.

31.

Division of Contracts.   Juridical Conceptions of Money and A Book.

It is reasonable to demand that a metaphysical Science of Right shall completely and definitely determine the members of a logical Division of its Conceptions *à priori*, and thus establish them in a genuine System.   All *empirical* Division, on the other hand, is merely *fragmentary Partition*, and it leaves us in uncertainty as to whether there may not be more members still required to complete the whole sphere of the divided Conception. A Division that is made according to a Principle *à priori* may be called, in contrast to all empirical Partitions, a *dogmatic* Division.

Every Contract, regarded in itself *objectively*, consists of two juridical Acts : the Promise and its Acceptance. Acquisition by the latter, unless it be a *pactum re initum* which requires Delivery, is not a *part*, but the juridically necessary *Consequence* of the Contract.   Considered again *subjectively*, or as to whether the *Acquisition*, which *ought* to happen as a necessary Consequence according to Reason, will also follow, in fact, as a *physical* Consequence, it is evident that I have no *Security* or Guarantee that this will happen by the mere Acceptance of a Promise.   There is therefore something externally required

connected with the mode of the Contract, in reference to
the *certainty* of Acquisition by it; and this can only be
some element completing and determining the Means
necessary to the attainment of Acquisition as realizing
the purpose of the Contract.   And in his connection
and behoof, three Persons are required to intervene—the
PROMISER, the ACCEPTOR, and the CAUTIONER or Surety.
The importance of the Cautioner is evident; but by his
intervention and his special Contract with the Promiser,
the Acceptor gains nothing in respect of the Object, but
the means of Compulsion that enable him to obtain what
is his own.

According to these rational Principles of logical Division, there are properly only *three* pure and simple *Modes
of Contract.*   There are, however, innumerable mixed
and empirical Modes, adding statutory and conventional
Forms to the Principles of the Mine and Thine that are
in accordance with rational Laws.   But they lie outside
of the circle of the Metaphysical Science of Right, whose
Rational Modes of Contract can alone be indicated here.

All Contracts are founded upon a purpose of Acquisition, and are either

A. GRATUITOUS CONTRACTS, *with unilateral Acquisition; or*

B. ONEROUS CONTRACTS, *with reciprocal Acquisition; or*

C. CAUTIONARY CONTRACTS, *with no Acquisition,
but only Guarantee of what has been already
acquired.*   These Contracts may be *gratuitous*
on the one side, and yet, at the same time,
onerous on the other.

A. THE GRATUITOUS CONTRACTS (*pacta gratuita*) are—

1. **Deposition** (*depositum*), involving the Preservation of some valuable deposited in Trust.

2. **Commodate** (*commodatum*), a Loan of the *use* of a Thing.

3. **Donation** (*donatio*), a free Gift.

B. THE ONEROUS CONTRACTS, are Contracts either of Permutation or of Hiring.

 I. CONTRACTS OF PERMUTATION OR RECIPROCAL EXCHANGE (*permutatio late sic dicta*):

  1. **Barter,** or strictly real Exchange (*permutatio stricte sic dicta*). Goods exchanged for Goods.

  2. **Purchase and Sale** (*emptio venditio*). Goods exchanged for Money.

  3. **Loan** (*mutuum*). Loan of a fungible under condition of its being returned in kind: Corn for Corn, or Money for Money.

 II. CONTRACTS OF LETTING AND HIRING (*locatio conductio*):

  1. **Letting of a Thing on Hire** to another person who is to make use of it (*locatio rei*). If the Thing can only be restored *in specie*, it may be the subject of an Onerous Contract combining the consideration of *Interest* with it (*pactum usurarium*).

  2. **Letting of Work on Hire** (*locatio operæ*). Consent to the use of my Powers by another for a certain Price (*merces*). The Worker under this Contract is a hired Servant (*mercenarius*).

  3. **Mandate** (*mandatum*). The Contract of Mandate is an engagement to perform or execute a certain business in place and in *name* of another person. If the action is merely done in the place of another, but

not, at the same time, in his *name*, it is *performance without Commission* (*gestio negotii*); but if it is (rightfully) performed in name of the other, it constitutes *Mandate*, which as a Contract of Procuration is an *onerous* Contract (*mandatum onerosum*).

C. THE CAUTIONARY CONTRACTS (*cautiones*) are :—

1. **Pledge** (*pignus*).   Caution by a Moveable deposited as security.
2. **Suretyship** (*fidejussio*).   Caution for the fulfilment of the promise of another.
3. **Personal Security** (*præstatio obsidis*).   Guarantee of Personal Performance.

This List of all the modes in which the property of one Person may be transferred or conveyed to another, includes conceptions of certain objects or Instruments required for such transference (*translatio*).   These appear to be entirely empirical, and it may therefore seem questionable whether they are entitled to a place in a *Metaphysical* Science of Right.   For, in such a Science the Divisions must be made according to Principles *à priori;* and hence the *matter* of the juridical relation, which may be *conventional,* ought to be left out of account, and only its Form should be taken into consideration.

Such conceptions may be illustrated by taking the instance of *Money,* in contradistinction from all other exchangeable things as Wares and Merchandise; or by the case of a *Book.*   And considering these as illustrative examples in this connection, it will be shown that the conception of MONEY as the *greatest* and *most useable* of all the Means of human intercommunication through Things, in the way of **Purchase and Sale** in commerce,

as well as that of Books as the greatest Means of carrying on the interchange of Thought, resolve themselves
into relations that are purely intellectual and rational.
And hence it will be made evident that such Conceptions
do not really detract from the purity of the given Scheme
of pure Rational Contracts, by empirical admixture.

ILLUSTRATION OF RELATIONS OF CONTRACT BY THE CONCEPTIONS OF MONEY AND A BOOK.

I. What is Money?

MONEY is a thing which can only be made *use* of, by
being *alienated* or exchanged. This is a good *Nominal*
Definition, as given by Achenwall ; and it is sufficient to
distinguish objects of the Will of this kind from all
other objects.   But it gives us no information regarding
the rational possibility of such a thing as money is.
Yet we see thus much by the Definition : (1) that the
Alienation in this mode of human intercommunication
and exchange is not viewed as a Gift, but is intended as
a mode of *reciprocal* Acquisition by an Onerous Contract ;
and (2) that it is regarded as a mere means of carrying
on *Commerce*, universally adopted by the people, but
having no value as such of itself, in contrast to other
Things as mercantile Goods or Wares which have a
particular value in relation to special wants existing
among the people.   It therefore *represents* all exchangeable things.

A bushel of Corn has the greatest direct value as a
means of satisfying human wants.   Cattle may be fed
by it ; and these again are subservient to our nourishment and locomotion, and they even labour in our stead.
Thus by means of corn men are multiplied and sup-

ported, who not only act again in reproducing such
natural products, but also by other artificial products
they can come to the relief of all our proper wants.
Thus are men enabled to build dwellings, to prepare
clothing, and to supply all the ingenious comforts and
enjoyments which make up the products of industry.—
On the other hand, the value of Money is only indirect.
It cannot be itself enjoyed, nor be used directly for
enjoyment; it is, however, a Means towards this, and of
all outward things it is of the highest utility.

We may found a *Real* Definition of Money provisionally upon these considerations. It may thus
be defined as *the universal means of carrying on the*
INDUSTRY *of men in exchanging intercommunications with
each other.* Hence national Wealth, in so far as it can
be acquired by means of Money, is properly only the
sum of the Industry or applied Labour with which men
pay each other, and which is represented by the Money
in circulation among the people.

The Thing which is to be called *Money* must, therefore, have cost as much Industry to produce it, or even
to put it into the hands of others, as may be equivalent
to the Industry or Labour required for the acquisition
of the Goods or Wares or Merchandise, as natural or
artificial products, for which it is exchanged. For if
it were easier to procure the material which is called
Money than the goods that are required, there would be
more Money in the market than goods to be sold; and
because the Seller would then have to expend more
labour upon his goods than the Buyer on the equivalent,
the Money coming in to him more rapidly, the Labour
applied to the preparation of goods and Industry generally,
with the industrial productivity which is the source of the

public Wealth, would at the same time dwindle and be cut down. — Hence Bank Notes and Assignations are not to be regarded as Money although they may take its place by way of representing it for a time; because it costs almost no Labour to prepare them, and their value is based merely upon the opinion prevailing as to the further continuance of the previous possibility of changing them into Ready Money. But on its being in any way found out that there is not Ready Money in sufficient quantity for easy and safe conversion of such Notes or Assignations, the opinion gives way, and a fall in their value becomes inevitable. Thus the industrial Labour of those who work the Gold and Silver Mines in Peru and Mexico—especially on account of the frequent failures in the application of fruitless efforts to discover new veins of these precious metals—is probably even greater than what is expended in the manufacture of Goods in Europe. Hence such mining Labour, as unrewarded in the circumstances, would be abandoned of itself, and the countries mentioned would in consequence soon sink into poverty, did not the Industry of Europe, stimulated in turn by these very metals, proportionally expand at the same time so as constantly to keep up the zeal of the Miners in their work by the articles of luxury thereby offered to them. It is thus that the concurrence of Industry with Industry, and of Labour with Labour, is always maintained.

But how is it possible that what at the beginning constituted only Goods or Wares, at length became Money? This has happened wherever a Sovereign as a great and powerful consumer of a particular substance, which he at first used merely for the adornment and decoration of his servants and court, has enforced the tribute of his subjects in this kind of material. Thus it may have been Gold, or Silver, or Copper, or a species of beautiful shells called *Cowries*, or even a sort of mat called *Makutes*, as in Congo; or Ingots of Iron, as in Senegal; or Negro Slaves, as on the Guinea Coast. When the Ruler of the country demanded such things as imposts, those whose Labour had to be put in motion to procure them were also paid by means of them, according to certain regulations of commerce then established, as. in a Market or Exchange. As it appears to me, it is only thus that a particular species of goods came to be made a legal means of carrying on the industrial labour of the Subjects in their commerce with each other, and thereby forming the medium of the national Wealth. And thus it practically became MONEY.

The Rational Conception of Money, under which the empirical conception is embraced, is therefore that of a thing which, in the course of the public permutation or Exchange of possessions (*permutatio publica*), determines the *Price* of all the other things that form products or Goods — under which term even the Sciences are included, in so far as they are not taught *gratis* to others. The quantity of it among a people constitutes their Wealth (*opulentia*). For Price (*pretium*) is the public judgment about the *Value* of a thing, in relation to the proportionate abundance of what forms the universal representative means in circulation for carrying on the reciprocal interchange of the products of Industry or Labour.[1] The precious metals, when they are not merely

---

[1] Hence where Commerce is extensive neither Gold nor Copper is specially used as Money, but only as constituting wares; because there is too little of the first and too much of the second for them to be easily brought into circulation, so as at once to have the former in such small

weighed but also stamped or provided with a sign indicating how much they are worth, form legal Money, and are called *Coin*.

According to Adam Smith, 'Money has become, in all civilised nations, the universal instrument of Commerce, by the intervention of which Goods of all kinds are bought and sold or exchanged for one another.'—This Definition expands the empirical conception of Money to the rational idea of it, by taking regard only to the implied *form* of the Reciprocal Performances in the Onerous Contracts, and thus abstracting from their matter. It is thus conformable to the conception of Right in the Permutation and Exchange of the Mine and Thine generally (*commutatio late sic dicta*). The Definition, therefore, accords with the representation in the above Synopsis of a Dogmatic Division of Contracts *à priori*, and consequently with the Metaphysical Principle of Right in general.

II. What is a Book?

A Book is a Writing which contains a Discourse addressed by some one to the Public, through visible signs of Speech. It is a matter of indifference to the present considerations whether it is written by a pen or imprinted by types, and on few or many pages. He who speaks to the Public in his own name, is the AUTHOR.

pieces as are necessary in payment for particular goods and not to have the latter in great quantity in case of the smallest acquisitions. Hence SILVER — more or less alloyed with Copper — is taken as the proper material of Money, and the Measure of the calculation of all Prices in the great commercial intercommunications of the world ; and the other Metals —and still more non-metallic substances—can only take its place in the case of a people of limited commerce.

130 KANT'S PHILOSOPHY OF LAW.

He who addresses the writing to the Public in the name of the Author, is the PUBLISHER. When a Publisher does this with the permission or authority of the Author, the act is in accordance with Right, and he is the rightful Publisher; but if this is done without such permission or authority, the act is contrary to Right, and the Publisher is a counterfeiter or unlawful Publisher. The whole of a set of Copies of the original Document, is called an Edition.

The unauthorized Publishing of Books is contrary to the Principles of Right, and is rightly prohibited.

A *Writing* is not an immediate direct presentation of a conception, as is the case, for instance, with an Engraving that exhibits a Portrait, or a Bust or Caste by a Sculptor. It is a *Discourse* addressed in a particular form to the Public; and the Author may be said to *speak* publicly by means of his Publisher. The Publisher, again, speaks by the aid of the Printer as his workman (*operarius*), yet not in his own name,—for otherwise he would be the Author,—but in the name of the Author; and he is only entitled to do so in virtue of a MANDATE given him to that effect by the Author.—Now the unauthorized Printer and Publisher speaks by an assumed authority in his Publication; in the name indeed of the Author, but without a Mandate to that effect (*gerit se mandatarium absque mandato*). Consequently such an unauthorized Publication is a wrong committed upon the authorized and only lawful Publisher, as it amounts to a pilfering of the Profits which the latter was entitled and able to draw from the use of his proper Right (*furtum usus*). Unauthorized Printing and Publication of Books

is therefore forbidden—as an act Counterfeit and Piracy
—on the ground of Right.

There seems, however, to be an impression that there
is a sort of common Right to print and publish Books;
but the slightest reflection must convince any one that
this would be a great injustice. The ·reason of it is found
simply in the fact that a Book, regarded from *one* point
of view, is an external product of mechanical art (*opus
mechanicum*), that can be imitated by any one who may
be in rightful possession of a Copy; and it is therefore
his by a *Real Right*. But from *another* point of view, a
Book is not merely an external Thing, but is a *Discourse*
of the Publisher to the public, and he is only entitled to
do this publicly under the Mandate of the Author (*præstatio operæ*); and this constitutes a *Personal Right*. The
error underlying the impression referred to, therefore,
arises from an interchange and confusion of these two
kinds of Right in relation to Books.

Confusion of Personal Right and Real Right.

The confusion of Personal Right with Real Right may
be likewise shown by reference to a difference of view
in connection with another Contract, falling under the
head of Contracts of Hiring (B. II. 1), namely, the Contract of LEASE (*jus incolatus*). The question is raised as
to whether a Proprietor when he has sold a house or a
piece of ground held on lease, before the expiry of the
period of Lease, was bound to add the condition of the
continuance of the Lease to the Contract of Purchase; *or*
whether it should be held that 'Purchase breaks Hire,'
of course under reservation of a period of warning determined by the nature of the subject in use.—In the

former view, a house or farm would be regarded as having
a *Burden* lying upon it, constituting a Real Right acquired
in it by the Lessee; and this might well enough be
carried out by a clause merely indorsing or ingrossing
the Contract of Lease in the Deed of Sale.   But as it
would no longer then be a simple Lease, another Contract
would properly be required to be conjoined, a matter
which few Lessors would be disposed to grant.   The
proposition, then, that 'Purchase breaks Hire' holds in
principle; for the full Right in a Thing as a Property,
overbears all Personal Right which is inconsistent with
it.   But there remains a Right of Action to the Lessee,
on the ground of a Personal Right for indemnification
on account of any loss arising from breaking of the
Contract.   [See *Supplementary Explanations*, IV.]

EPISODICAL SECTION.

THE IDEAL ACQUISITION OF EXTERNAL OBJECTS OF THE WILL.

32.

The Nature and Modes of Ideal Acquisition.

I call that mode of Acquisition *ideal* which involves
no Causality in time, and which is founded upon a mere
Idea of pure reason.   It is nevertheless *actual*, and not
merely imaginary Acquisition; and it is not called *real*
only because the Act of Acquisition is not empirical.
This character of the Act arises from the peculiarity that
the Person acquiring, acquires from another who either is
not yet, and who can only be regarded as a *possible* Being,

or who *is just ceasing to be,* or who *no longer* is. Hence such a mode of attaining to Possession is to be regarded as a mere practical Idea of Reason.

There are three Modes of Ideal Acquisition :—

I. Acquisition by USUCAPION ;

II. Acquisition by INHERITANCE or SUCCESSION ;

III. Acquisition by UNDYING MERIT (*meritum immortale*), or the Claim by Right to a good name at Death.

These three Modes of Acquisition can, as a matter of fact, only have effect in a public juridical state of existence, but they are *not founded* merely upon the Civil Constitution or upon arbitrary Statutes ; they are already contained *à priori* in the conception of the state of Nature, and are thus necessarily conceivable prior to their empirical manifestation. The Laws regarding them in the Civil Constitution ought to be regulated by that rational Conception.

33.

I. Acquisition by Usucapion.

(Acquisitio per Usucapionem.)

I may acquire the Property of another merely by *long possession* and use of it (*Usucapio*). Such Property is not acquired, because I may legitimately *presume* that his Consent is given to this effect (*per consensum præsumptum*) ; nor because I can assume that as he does not oppose my Acquisition of it, he has *relinquished* or abandoned it as his (*rem derelictam*). But I acquire it thus, because even if there were any one actually raising a claim to this Property as its true Owner, I may *exclude* him on the ground of my long Possession of it, ignore his previous existence, and proceed as if he existed during the time of my Possession as a mere abstraction, although I may have been subsequently apprized of his reality as well as of his claim. This Mode of Acquisition is not quite correctly designated Acquisition by *Prescription* (*per præscriptionem*); for the exclusion of all other claimants is to be regarded as only the Consequence of the Usucapion; and the process of Acquisition must have gone before the Right of Exclusion. The rational possibility of such a Mode of Acquisition, has now to be proved.

Any one who does not exercise a continuous *possessory activity* (*actus possessorius*) in relation to a Thing as his, is regarded with good Right as one who does not at all exist as its Possessor. For he cannot complain of lesion so long as he does not qualify himself with a Title as its Possessor. And even if he should afterwards lay claim to the Thing when another has already taken possession of it, he only says he was once on a time Owner of it, but not that he is so still, or that his Possession has continued without interruption as a juridical fact. It can, therefore, only be by a juridical process of Possession, that has been maintained without interruption and is proveable by documentary fact, that any one can secure for himself what is his own after ceasing for a long time to make use of it.

For, suppose that the neglect to exercise this possessory activity had not the effect of enabling another to found upon his hitherto lawful, undisputed and *bona fide* Possession, an irrefragable Right to continue in its possession so that he may regard the thing that is thus in his Possession as acquired by him. Then no Acquisition would ever become peremptory and secured, but all Acquisition would only be provisory and temporary. This is evident on the ground that there are no historical Records available to carry the investigation of a Title back to the first Possessor and his act of Acquisition.— The Presumption upon which Acquisition by Usucapion is founded is, therefore, not merely its conformity to *Right* as allowed and just, but also the presumption of its *being* Right (*præsumtio juris et de jure*), and its being assumed to be in accordance with compulsory Laws (*suppositio legalis*). Any one who has neglected to embody his possessory Act in a documentary Title, has lost his Claim to the Right of being Possessor for the time; and the length of the period of his neglecting to do so—which need not necessarily be particularly defined —can be referred to only as establishing the certainty of this neglect. And it would contradict the Postulate of the Juridically Practical Reason to maintain that one hitherto unknown as a Possessor, and whose possessory activity has at least been interrupted, whether by or without fault of his own, could always at any time re-acquire a Property; for this would be to make all Ownership uncertain (*Dominia rerum incerta facere*).

But if he is a member of the Commonwealth or Civil Union, the State may maintain his Possession for him vicariously, although it may be interrupted as private Possession; and in that case the actual Possessor will not be able to prove a Title of Acquisition even from a first occupation, nor to found upon a Title of Usucapion. But in the state of Nature Usucapion is universally a rightful ground of holding, not properly as a juridical mode of requiring a Thing, but as a ground for maintaining oneself in possession of it where there are no Juridical Acts. A release from juridical claims is commonly also called Acquisition. The Prescriptive Title of

the older Possessor, therefore, belongs to the sphere of
Natural Right (*est juris naturæ*). [See *Supplementary
Explanations*, VI.]

34.

II. Acquisition by Inheritance.

(Acquisitio hæreditatis.)

INHERITANCE is constituted by the transfer (*translatio*)
of the Property or goods of one who is dying to a
Survivor, through the consent of the Will of both. The
Acquisition of the HEIR who takes the Estate (*hæredis
instituti*) and the Relinquishment of the TESTATOR who
leaves it, being the acts that constitute the Exchange
of the Mine and Thine, take place in the same moment
of time—*in articulo mortis*—and just when the Testator
ceases to be.   There is therefore no special Act of
Transfer (*translatio*) in the empirical sense; for that
would involve two successive acts, by which the one
would first divest himself of his Possession, and the other
would thereupon enter into it.   Inheritance as constituted by a simultaneous double Act is, therefore, an
ideal Mode of Acquisition.   Inheritance is inconceivable
in the State of Nature without a Testamentary Disposition (*dispositio ultimæ voluntatis*); and the question
arises as to whether this mode of Acquisition is to be
regarded as a *Contract of Succession,* or a *unilateral Act
instituting an Heir by a Will* (*testamentum*).   The determination of this question depends on the further question,
Whether and How, in the very same moment in which
one individual ceases to be, there can be a transition of
his Property to another Person.   Hence the problem as
to how a mode of Acquisition by Inheritance is *possible,*

must be investigated independently of the various possible forms in which it is practically carried out, and which can have place only in a Commonwealth.

'It is *possible* to acquire by being instituted or appointed Heir in a Testamentary Disposition.' For the Testator *Caius* promises and declares in his last Will to *Titius*, who knows nothing of this Promise, to transfer to him his Estate in case of death, but thus continuing as long as he lives sole Owner of it. Now by a mere unilateral act of Will, nothing can in fact be transmitted to another person, as in addition to the Promise of the one party there is required Acceptance (*acceptatio*) on the part of the other, and a simultaneous bilateral act of Will (*voluntas simultanea*) which, however, is here awanting. So long as Caius lives, Titius cannot expressly accept in order to enter on Acquisition, because Caius has only promised in case of death; otherwise the Property would be for a moment at least in common possession, which is not the Will of the Testator.—However, Titius acquires *tacitly* a special Right to the Inheritance as a Real Right. This is constituted by the sole and exclusive Right to *accept* the Estate (*jus in re jacente*), which is therefore called at that point of time a *hœreditas jacens.* Now as every man—because he must always gain and never lose by it—necessarily, although tacitly, accepts such a Right, and as Titius after the death of Caius is in this position, he may acquire the succession as Heir by Acceptance of the Promise. And the Estate is not in the meantime entirely without an Owner (*res nullius*), but is only *in abeyance* or vacant (*vacua*); because he has exclusively the Right of Choice as to whether he will actually make the Estate bequeathed to him, his own or not.

Hence Testaments are valid according to mere Natural Right (*sunt juris naturæ*). This assertion, however, is to be understood in the sense that they are capable and worthy of being introduced and sanctioned in the Civil state, whenever it is instituted. For it is only the Common Will in the Civil state that maintains the possession of the Inheritance or Succession, while it hangs between Acceptance or Rejection and specially belongs to no particular individual. [See *Supplementary Explanations*, VII.]

35.

III. The continuing Right of a good Name after Death.

(Bona fama Defuncti.)

It would be absurd to think that a dead Person could possess anything after his death, when he no longer exists in the eye of the Law, if the matter in question were a mere Thing. But a good Name is a congenital and external, although merely ideal possession, which attaches inseparably to the individual as a Person. Now we can and must abstract here from all consideration as to whether the Persons cease to be after death or still continue as such to exist; because in considering their juridical relation to others, we regard Persons merely according to their humanity and as rational Beings (*homo noumenon*). Hence any attempt to bring the Reputation or good Name of a Person into evil and false repute after death, is always questionable, even although a well-founded charge may be allowed—for to that extent the brocard '*De mortuis nil nisi bene*' is wrong. Yet to spread charges against one who is absent and cannot defend himself, shows at least a want of magnanimity.

By a blameless life and a death that worthily ends it,

it is admitted that a man may acquire a (negatively) good reputation constituting something that is his own, even when he no longer exists in the world of sense as a visible Person (*homo phænomenon*). It is further held that his Survivors and Successors—whether relatives or strangers—are entitled to defend his good Name as a matter of Right, on the ground that unproved accusations subject them all to the danger of similar treatment after death. Now that a Man when dead can yet acquire such a Right is a peculiar and, nevertheless, an undeniable manifestation in fact, of the *à priori* law-giving Reason thus extending its Law of Command or Prohibition beyond the limits of the present life. If some one then spreads a charge regarding a dead person that would have dishonoured him when living, or even made him despicable, any one who can adduce a proof that this accusation is intentionally false and untrue, may publicly declare him who thus brings the dead person into ill repute to be a Calumniator, and affix dishonour to him in turn. This would not be allowable unless it were legitimate to assume that the dead person was injured by the accusation, although he is dead, and that a certain just satisfaction was done to him by an Apology, although he no longer sensibly exists. A Title to act the part of the Vindicator of the dead person does not require to be established; for every one necessarily claims this of himself, not merely as a Duty of Virtue regarded ethically, but as a Right belonging to him in virtue of his Humanity. Nor does the Vindicator require to show any special personal damage, accruing to him as a friend or relative, from a stain on the character of the Deceased, to justify him in proceeding to censure it. That such a form of ideal Acquisition, and even a

Right in an individual after death against survivors, is thus actually founded, cannot, therefore, be disputed, although the possibility of such a Right is not capable of logical Deduction.

There is no ground for drawing visionary inferences from what has just been stated, to the presentiment of a future life and invisible relations to departed souls. For the considerations connected with this Right, turn on nothing more than the purely moral and juridical Relation which subsists among men even in the present life, as Rational Beings. Abstraction is, however, made from all that belongs physically to their existence in Space and Time; that is, men are considered logically apart from these physical concomitants of their nature, not as to their state when actually deprived of them, but only in so far as being spirits they are in a condition that might realize the injury done them by Calumniators. Any one who may falsely say something against me a hundred years hence, injures me even now. For in the pure juridical Relation, which is entirely rational and suprasensible, abstraction is made from the physical conditions of Time, and the Calumniator is as culpable as if he had committed the offence in my lifetime; only this will not be tried by a Criminal Process, but he will only be punished with that loss of honour he would have caused to another, and this is inflicted upon him by Public Opinion according to the *Lex talionis.* Even a *Plagiarism* from a dead Author, although it does not tarnish the honour of the Deceased, but only deprives him of a part of his property, is yet properly regarded as a lesion of his human Right.

PRIVATE RIGHT.

CHAPTER THIRD.

ACQUISITION CONDITIONED BY THE SENTENCE OF A PUBLIC JUDICATORY.

36.

How and what Acquisition is subjectively conditioned by the Principle of a Public Court.

NATURAL RIGHT, understood simply as that Right which is not statutory, and which is knowable purely *à priori*, by every man's Reason, will include Distributive Justice as well as Commutative Justice. It is manifest that the latter as constituting the Justice that is valid between Persons in their reciprocal relations of intercourse with one another, must belong to Natural Right. But this holds also of Distributive Justice, in so far as it can be known *à priori;* and Decisions or Sentences regarding it, must be regulated by the Law of Natural Right.

The Moral Person who presides in the sphere of Justice and administers it, is called the COURT of Justice, and as engaged in the process of official duty, the Judicatory; the Sentence delivered in a case, is the Judgment

(*judicium*).   All this is to be here viewed *à priori*,
according to the rational Conditions of Right, without
taking into consideration how such a Constitution is to
be actually established or organized, for which particular
Statutes, and consequently empirical Principles, are
requisite.

The question, then, in this connection, is not merely
'What is *right in itself?* in the sense in which every
man must determine it by the Judgment of Reason;
but 'What is Right as applied to this case?' that is,
what is right and just as viewed by a Court? The
rational and the judicial points of view, are therefore to be
distinguished; and there are *four Cases* in which the two
forms of Judgment have a different and opposite issue.
And yet they may coexist with each other, because
they are delivered from two different, yet respectively
true points of view: the one from regard to Private
Right, the other from the Idea of Public Right.   They
are: I. THE CONTRACT OF DONATION (*pactum donationis*), II. THE CONTRACT OF LOAN (*commodatum*), III.
THE ACTION OF REAL REVINDICATION (*vindicatio*), and
IV. GUARANTEE BY OATH (*juramentum*).

> It is a common error on the part of the Jurist to
> fall here into the fallacy of begging the question, by
> a tacit assumption (*vitium subreptionis*). This is done
> by assuming as objective and absolute the juridical
> Principle which a Public Court of Justice is entitled
> and even bound to adopt in its own behoof, and only
> from the *subjective* purpose of qualifying itself to
> decide and judge upon all the Rights pertaining to
> individuals. It is therefore of no small importance
> to make this specific difference intelligible, and to
> draw attention to it.

37.

I. The Contract of Donation.

(Pactum donationis.)

The Contract of Donation signifies the *gratuitous* alienation (*gratis*) of a Thing or Right that is Mine. It involves a relation between me as the Donor (*donans*), and another Person as the Donatory (*donatarius*), in accordance with the Principle of Private Right, by which what is mine is transferred to the latter, on his acceptance of it, as a Gift (*donum*). However, it is not to be presumed that I have voluntarily bound myself thereby so as to be *compelled* to keep my Promise, and that I have thus given away my *Freedom* gratuitously, and, as it were, to that extent thrown myself away. *Nemo suum jactare præsumitur.* But this is what would happen, under such circumstances, according to the principle of Right in the Civil state; for in this sphere the Donatory can *compel* me, under certain conditions, to perform my Promise. If, then, the case comes before a Court, according to the conditions of Public Right, it must either be presumed that the Donor has consented to such Compulsion, or the Court would give no regard, in the Sentence, to the consideration as to whether he intended to reserve the Right to resile from his Promise or not; but would only refer to what is certain, namely, the condition of the Promise and the Acceptance of the Donatory. Although the Promiser, therefore, thought— as may easily be supposed—that he could not be bound by his Promise in any case, if he ' rued ' it before it was actually carried out, yet the Court assumes that he ought *expressly* to have reserved this condition if such was his

mind ; and if he did not make such an express reservation, it will be held that he can be compelled to imple-
ment his Promise.   And this Principle is assumed by
the Court, because the administration of Justice would
otherwise be endlessly impeded, or even made entirely
impossible.

38.

II. The Contract of Loan.
(Commodatum.)

In the Contract of Commodate-Loan (*commodatum*) I
give some one the gratuitous *use* of something that is
mine.   If it is a Thing that is given on Loan, the contracting Parties agree that the Borrower will restore *the
very same thing* to the power of the Lender.   But the
Receiver of the Loan (*commodatarius*) cannot, at the
same time, assume that the Owner of the Thing lent
(*commodans*) will take upon himself all risk (*casus*) of
any possible loss of it, or of its useful quality, that may
arise from having given it into the possession of the
Receiver.   For it is not to be understood of itself, that
the Owner, besides the *use* of the Thing, which he has
granted to the Receiver, and the detriment that is
inseparable from such use, also gives a *Guarantee* or
Warrandice against all damage that may arise from such
use.   On the contrary, a special Accessory Contract
would have to be entered into for this purpose.   The
only question, then, that can be raised is this : Is it
incumbent on the Lender or the Borrower to add
expressly the condition of undertaking the risk that may
accrue to the Thing lent ; *or*, if this is not done, which
of the Parties is to be presumed to have *consented and
agreed* to guarantee the property of the Lender, up to

restoration of the very same Thing or its equivalent? Certainly not the Lender; because it cannot be presumed that he has gratuitously agreed to give more than the mere use of the Thing, so that he cannot be supposed to have also undertaken the risk of loss of his property. But this may be assumed on the side of the Borrower; because he thereby undertakes and performs nothing more than what is implied in the Contract.

For example, I enter a house when overtaken by a shower of rain, and ask the Loan of a cloak. But through accidental contact with colouring matter, it becomes entirely spoiled while in my possession; or on entering another house, I lay it aside and it is stolen. Under such circumstances, everybody would think it absurd for me to assert that I had no further concern with the cloak but to return it as it was, or, in the latter case, only to mention the fact of the theft; and that, in any case, anything more required would be but an act of Courtesy in expressing sympathy with the Owner on account of his loss, seeing he can claim nothing on the ground of Right.—It would be otherwise, however, if on asking the use of an article, I discharged myself beforehand from all responsibility, in case of its coming to grief among my hands, on the ground of my being poor, and unable to compensate any incidental loss. No one could find such a condition superfluous or ludicrous, unless the Borrower were, in fact, known to be a well-to-do and well-disposed man; because in such a case it would almost be an insult not to act on the presumption of generous compensation for any loss sustained.

.   .   .   .

Now by the very nature of this Contract, the possible

damage (*casus*) which the Thing lent may undergo cannot be exactly determined in any Agreement. Commodate is therefore an uncertain Contract (*pactum incertum*), because the consent can only be so far presumed. The Judgment, in any case, deciding upon whom the incidence of any loss must fall, cannot therefore be determined from the conditions of the Contract in itself, but only *by the Principle of the Court* before which it comes, and which can only consider what is certain in the Contract; and the only thing certain is always the fact as to the possession of the Thing as property. Hence the Judgment passed in the state of Nature, will be different from that given by a Court of Justice in the Civil state. The Judgment from the standpoint of Natural Right will be determined by regard to the inner rational quality of the Thing, and will run thus: 'Loss arising from damage accruing to a Thing lent falls upon the *Borrower*' (*casum sentit commodatarius*); whereas the Sentence of a Court of Justice in the Civil state will run thus: 'The Loss falls upon the *Lender*' (*casum sentit dominus*). The latter Judgment turns out differently from the former as the Sentence of the mere sound Reason, because a Public Judge cannot found upon presumptions as to what either party may have thought; and thus the one who has not obtained release from all loss in the Thing by a special Accessory Contract, must bear the loss.—Hence the difference between the Judgment as the Court must deliver it, and the form in which each individual is entitled to hold it for himself by his private Reason, is a matter of importance, and is not to be overlooked in the consideration of Juridical Judgments.

39.

III. The Revindication of what has been Lost.
(Vindicatio.)

It is clear from what has been already said that a Thing of mine which continues to exist, remains mine although I may not be in continuous occupation of it ; and that it does not cease to be mine without a Juridical Act of dereliction or alienation.   Further, it is evident that a Right in this Thing (*jus reale*) belongs in consequence to me (*jus personale*), against *every* holder of it, and not merely against some Particular Person.   But the question now arises as to whether this Right must be regarded by *every* other person as a continuous Right of Property *per se*, if I have not in any way *renounced* it, although the Thing is in the possession of another.

A Thing may be lost (*res amissa*), and thus come into other hands in an honourable *bonâ fide* way as a supposed ' Find ; ' or it may come to me by formal transfer on the part of one who is in possession of it, and who professes to be its Owner, although he is not so.   Taking the latter case, the question arises, Whether, since I cannot acquire a Thing from one who is not its Owner (*a non domino*), I am excluded by the fact from all Right in the Thing itself, and have merely a personal Right against a wrongful Possessor ?   This is manifestly so, if the Acquisition is judged purely according to its inner justifying grounds and viewed according to the State of Nature, and not according to the convenience of a Court of Justice.

For everything alienable must be capable of being acquired by any one.   The Rightfulness of Acquisition, however, rests entirely upon the form in accordance with which what is in possession of another, is transferred to me and accepted by me. In other words, rightful Acquisition depends upon the formality of the juridical act of commutation or interchange between the Possessor of the Thing and the Acquirer of it, without its being required to ask how the former came by it; because this would itself be an injury, on the ground that *Quilibet præsumitur bonus*. Now suppose it turned out that the said Possessor was not the real Owner, I cannot admit that the real Owner is entitled to hold me directly responsible, or so entitled with regard to any one who might be holding the Thing. For I have myself taken nothing away from him, when, for example, I bought his horse according to the Law (*titulo empti venditi*) when it was offered for sale in the public market. The Title of Acquisition is therefore unimpeachable on my side; and as Buyer I am not bound, nor even have I the Right, to investigate the Title of the Seller; for this process of investigation would have to go on in an ascending series *ad infinitum*. Hence on such grounds I ought to be regarded, in virtue of a regular and formal purchase, as not merely the *putative*, but the *real* Owner of the horse.

But against this position, there immediately start up the following juridical Principles. Any Acquisition derived from one who is not the Owner of the Thing in question, is null and void. I cannot derive from another anything more than what he himself rightfully has; and although as regards the form of the Acquisition—the *modus acquirendi*—I may proceed in accordance with all the conditions of Right when I deal in a stolen horse exposed for sale in the market, yet a real Title warranting

the Acquisition was awanting ; for the horse was not really
the property of the Seller in question.   However I may
be a *bonâ fide* Possessor of a Thing under such conditions,
I am still only a *putative* Owner, and the real Owner has
the Right *of Vindication* against me (*rem suam vindi-
candi*).

Now, it may be again asked, what is right and just *in
itself* regarding the Acquisition of external things among
men in their intercourse with one another—viewed in the
state of Nature—according to the Principles of Commutative Justice ?   And it must be admitted in this
connection, that whoever has a purpose of acquiring
anything, must regard it as absolutely necessary to investigate whether the Thing which he wishes to acquire
does not already belong to another person.   For although
he may carefully observe the formal conditions required
for appropriating what may belong to the property of
another, as in buying a horse according to the usual
terms in a market, yet he can, at the most, acquire only
a *Personal Right* in relation to a Thing (*jus ad rem*) so
long as it is still unknown to him whether another than
the Seller may not be the real Owner.   Hence, if some
other person were to come forward, and prove by
documentary evidence a prior Right of property in the
Thing, nothing would remain for the putative new Owner
but the advantage which he has drawn as a *bonâ fide*
Possessor of it up to that moment.   Now it is frequently
impossible to discover the absolutely first original Owner
of a Thing in the series of putative Owners, who derive
their Rights from one another.   Hence no mere exchange
of external things, however well it may agree with the
formal conditions of Commutative Justice, can ever
guarantee an absolutely certain Acquisition.

.   .   .   .

Here, however, the juridically law-giving Reason comes in again with the Principle of *Distributive Justice;* and it adopts as a criterion of the Rightfulness of Possession, not what it is *in itself* in reference to the Private Will of each individual in the state of Nature, but only the consideration of how it would be adjudged by a *Court of Justice* in a Civil state, constituted by the united Will of all. In this connection, fulfilment of the formal conditions of Acquisition that in themselves only establish a Personal Right, is postulated as sufficient; and they stand as an equivalent for the material conditions which properly establish the derivation of Property from a prior putative Owner, to the extent of making what is *in itself* only a Personal Right, valid *before a Court*, as a Real Right. Thus the horse which I bought when exposed for sale in the public market under conditions regulated by the Municipal Law, becomes my property if all the conditions of Purchase and Sale have been exactly observed in the transaction; but always under the reservation that the real Owner continues to have the Right of a claim against the Seller, on the ground of his prior unalienated possession. My otherwise Personal Right is thus transmuted into a Real Right, according to which I may take and vindicate the object as mine wherever I may find it, without being responsible for the way in which the Seller had come into possession of it.

It is therefore only in behoof of the requirements of juridical decision in a Court (*in favorem justitiæ distributivæ*) that the Right in respect of a Thing is regarded, not as Personal, which it is *in itself*, but as Real, because it can thus be *most easily and certainly adjudged;* and it is thus accepted and dealt with according to a pure Principle *à priori*. Upon this Principle various Statutory Laws come to be founded which specially aim at laying down the conditions under which alone a mode of Acquisition shall be legitimate, so that the Judge may be able to assign every one his own as *easily* and *certainly* as possible.   Thus, in the brocard, 'Purchase breaks Hire,' what by the nature of the subject is a Real Right— namely the Hire—is taken to hold as a merely Personal Right; and, conversely, as in the case referred to above, what is in itself merely a Personal Right is held to be valid as a Real Right.   And this is done only when the question arises as to the Principles by which a Court of Justice in the Civil state is to be guided, in order to proceed with all possible safety in delivering judgment on the Rights of individuals.

40.

IV. Acquisition of Security by the taking of an Oath.
(Cautio juratoria.)

Only one ground can be assigned on which it could be held that men are bound in the juridical relation, to *believe* and to confess that there are Gods, or that there is a God.   It is that they may be able to swear an Oath; and that thus by the fear of an all-seeing Supreme Power, whose revenge they must solemnly invoke upon themselves in case their utterance should be false, they may be constrained to be truthful in statement and faithful in promising.   It is not Morality but merely blind Superstition that is reckoned upon in this process; for it is evident it implies that no certainty is to be expected from a mere *solemn* declaration in matters of

Right before a Court, although the duty of truthfulness must have always appeared self-evident to all, in a matter which concerns the Holiest that can be among men— namely, the Right of Man. Hence recourse has been had to a motive founded on mere myths and fables as imaginary guarantees. Thus among the *Rejangs*, a heathen people in Sumatra, it is the custom—according to the testimony of Marsden—to swear by the bones of their dead relatives, although they have no belief in a life after death. In like manner the negroes of *Guinea* swear by their *Fetish*, a bird's feather, which they imprecate under the belief that it will break their neck. And so in other cases. The belief underlying these oaths is that an invisible Power—whether it has Understanding or not—by its very nature possesses magical power that can be put into action by such invocations. Such a belief—which is commonly called Religion, but which ought to be called Superstition—is, however, indispensable for the administration of Justice; because, without referring to it, a Court of Justice would not have adequate means to ascertain facts otherwise kept secret, and to determine rights. A Law making an Oath obligatory, is therefore only given in behoof of the judicial Authority.

But then the question arises as to what the obligation could be founded upon, that would bind any one in a Court of Justice to accept the Oath of another person, as a right and valid proof of the truth of his statements which are to put an end to all dispute. In other words, What obliges me juridically to believe that another person when taking an Oath has any Religion at all, so that I should subordinate or entrust my Right to his Oath? And, on like grounds, conversely, Can I be bound at all to take an Oath ?   It is evident that both these questions point to what is in itself morally wrong.

But in relation to a Court of Justice—and generally in the Civil state—if it be assumed there are no other means of getting to the truth in certain cases than by an Oath, it must be adopted.   In regard to Religion, under the supposition that every one has it, it may be utilized as a necessary means (*in causu necessitatis*), in behoof of the legitimate procedure of a Court of Justice.   The Court uses this form of spiritual compulsion (*tortura spiritualis*) as an available means, in conformity with the superstitious propensity of mankind, for the ascertainment of what is concealed ; and therefore holds itself justified in so doing.   The Legislative Power, however, is fundamentally wrong in assigning this authority to the Judicial Power, because even in the Civil state any compulsion with regard to the taking of Oaths is contrary to the inalienable Freedom of Man.

OFFICIAL OATHS, which are usually *promissory*, being taken on entering upon an Office to the effect that the individual has sincere *intention* to administer his functions dutifully, might well be changed into *assertory* Oaths, to be taken at the end of a year or more of actual administration, the official swearing to the faithfulness of his discharge of duty during that time.   This would bring the Conscience . more into action than the Promissory Oath, which always gives room for the internal pretext that, with the best intention, the difficulties that arose during the administration of the official function were not foreseen. And, further, violations of Duty, under the prospect of their being summed up by future Censors, would give rise to more anxiety as to censure than when they are merely represented, one after the other, and forgotten.

TRANSITION

FROM THE MINE AND THINE IN THE STATE OF NATURE
TO THE MINE AND THINE IN THE JURIDICAL STATE
GENERALLY.

41.

Public Justice as related to the Natural and the Civil state.

The Juridical state is that relation of men to one another which contains the conditions, under which it is alone possible for every one to obtain the Right that is his due.   The formal Principle of the possibility of actually *participating* in such Right, viewed in accordance with the Idea of a universally legislative Will, is PUBLIC JUSTICE.   Public Justice may be considered in relation either to the Possibility, or Actuality, or Necessity of the Possession of objects — regarded as the matter of the activity of the Will—according to laws.   It may thus be divided into *Protective Justice* (*justitia testatrix*), *Commutative Justice* (*justitia commutativa*), and *Distributive Justice* (*justitia distributiva*).   In the *first* mode of Justice, the Law declares merely what Relation is internally *right* in respect of Form (*lex justi*) ; in the *second*, it declares what is likewise externally in accord with a Law in respect of the Object, and what Possession is rightful (*lex juridica*) ; and in the *third*, it declares what is right, and what is *just*, and to what extent, by the Judgment of a Court in any particular case coming under the given Law.   In this latter relation, the Public

Court is called the *Justice* of the Country ; and the question whether there actually is or is not such an administration of Public Justice, may be regarded as the most important of all juridical interests.

The non-juridical state is that condition of Society in which there is no Distributive Justice. It is commonly called the *Natural* state (*status naturalis*), or the state of Nature. It is not the '*Social* State,' as Achenwall puts it, for this may be in itself an *artificial* state (*status artificialis*), that is to be contradistinguished from the 'Natural' state. The opposite of the state of Nature is the *Civil* state (*status civilis*) as the condition of a Society standing under a Distributive Justice. In the state of Nature there may even be juridical forms of Society— such as Marriage, Parental Authority, the Household, and such like. For none of these, however, does any Law *à priori* lay it down as an incumbent obligation, ' Thou *shalt* enter into this state.' But it may be said of the *Juridical* state that 'all men who *may* even involuntarily come into Relations of Right with one another, *ought* to enter into this state.'

The Natural or non-juridical Social state may be viewed as the sphere of PRIVATE RIGHT, and the Civil state may be specially regarded as the sphere of PUBLIC RIGHT. The latter state contains no more and no other Duties of men towards each other than what may be conceived in connection with the former state ; the Matter of Private Right is, in short, the very same in both. The Laws of the Civil state, therefore, only turn upon the juridical Form of the co-existence of men under a common Constitution ; and in this respect these Laws must necessarily be regarded and conceived as Public Laws.

The Civil Union (*Unio civilis*) cannot, in the strict sense, be properly called a *Society;* for there is no sociality in common between the Ruler (*imperans*) and the Subject (*subditus*) under a Civil Constitution. They are not co-ordinated as Associates in a Society with each other, but the one is *subordinated* to the other. Those who may be co-ordinated with one another must consider themselves as mutually equal, in so far as they stand under common Laws. The Civil Union may therefore be regarded not so much as *being*, but rather as *making* a Society.

42.

The Postulate of Public Right.

From the conditions of Private Right in the Natural state, there arises the Postulate of Public Right. It may be thus expressed : ' In the relation of unavoidable co-existence with others, thou shalt pass from the state of Nature into a juridical Union constituted under the condition of a Distributive Justice.' The Principle of this Postulate may be unfolded analytically from the conception of *Right* in the external relation, contradistinguished from mere *Might* as Violence.

No one is under obligation to abstain from interfering with the Possession of others, unless they give him a reciprocal guarantee for the observance of a similar abstention from interference with his Possession. Nor does he require to wait for proof by experience of the need of this guarantee, in view of the antagonistic disposition of others. He is therefore under no obligation to wait till he acquires practical prudence at his own cost ; for he can perceive in himself evidence of the natural Inclination of men to play the master over others, and to disregard the claims of the Right of others, when they feel themselves their superiors by Might or Fraud. And thus it is not necessary to wait for the melancholy experience of actual hostility; the individual is from the first entitled to exercise a rightful compulsion towards those who already threaten him by their very nature. *Quilibet præsumitur malus, donec securitatem dederit oppositi.*

So long as the intention to live and continue in this state of externally lawless Freedom prevails, men may be said to do no wrong or injustice at all *to one another*, even when they wage war against each other. For what seems competent as good for the one, is equally valid for the other, as if it were so by mutual agreement. *Uti partes de jure suo disponunt, ita jus est.* But generally they must be considered as being in the highest state of Wrong, as being and willing to be in a condition which is not juridical; and in which, therefore, no one can be secured against Violence, in the possession of his own.

> The distinction between what is only *formally* and what is also *materially* wrong and unjust, finds frequent application in the Science of Right. An enemy who, on occupying a besieged fortress, instead of honourably fulfilling the conditions of a Capitulation, maltreats the garrison on marching out, or otherwise violates the agreement, cannot complain of injury or wrong if on another occasion the same treatment is inflicted upon themselves. But, in fact, all such actions fundamentally involve the commission of wrong and injustice, in the highest degree; because they take all validity away from the conception of Right, and give up everything, as it were by law itself, to savage Violence, and thus overthrow the Rights of Men generally.

THE SCIENCE OF RIGHT.

———o———

PART SECOND.

PUBLIC RIGHT.

THE SYSTEM OF THOSE LAWS WHICH REQUIRE
PUBLIC PROMULGATION.

PUBLIC RIGHT.

THE PRINCIPLES OF RIGHT IN CIVIL SOCIETY.

43.

Definition and Division of Public Right.

PUBLIC RIGHT embraces the whole of the Laws that
require to be universally promulgated in order to produce
a juridical state of Society. It is therefore a System of
those Laws that are requisite for a People as a multitude
of men forming a Nation, or for a number of Nations, in
their relations to each other. Men and Nations, on
account of their mutual influence on one another, require
a juridical *Constitution* uniting them under one Will, in
order that they may participate in what is right.—This
relation of the Individuals of a Nation to each other,
constitutes THE CIVIL UNION in the social state; and,
viewed as a whole in relation to its constituent members,
it forms THE POLITICAL STATE (*Civitas*).

1. The State, as constituted by the common interest of
all to live in a juridical union, is called, in view of its
form, the COMMONWEALTH or the REPUBLIC in the wider
sense of the term (*Res publica latius sic dicta*). The
Principles of Right in this sphere, thus constitute the
first department of Public Right as the RIGHT OF THE
STATE (*jus Civitatis*) or National Right.—2. The State,
again, viewed in relation to other peoples, is called a

Power (*potentia*), whence arises the idea of Potentates. Viewed in relation to the supposed hereditary unity of the people composing it, the State constitutes a Nation (*gens*).   Under the general conception of Public Right, in addition to the Right of the individual State, there thus arises another department of Right, constituting the RIGHT OF NATIONS (*jus gentium*) or International Right.— 3. Further, as the surface of the earth is not unlimited in extent, but is circumscribed into a unity, National Right and International Right necessarily culminate in the idea of a UNIVERSAL RIGHT OF MANKIND, which may be called 'Cosmopolitical Right' (*jus cosmopoliticum*). And National, International, and Cosmopolitical Right are so interconnected, that if any one of these three possible forms of the juridical Relation fails to embody the essential Principles that ought to regulate external freedom by law, the structure of Legislation reared by the others will also be undermined, and the whole System would at last fall to pieces.

is to be renounced, the first thing incumbent on men is to accept the Principle that it is necessary to leave the state of Nature, in which every one follows his own inclinations, and to form a union of all those who cannot avoid coming into reciprocal communication, and thus subject themselves in common to the external restraint of public compulsory Laws.   Men thus enter into a Civil Union, in which every one has it determined by Law what shall be recognised as his; and this is secured to him by a competent external Power distinct from his own individuality.   Such is the primary Obligation, on the part of all men, to enter into the relations of a Civil State of Society.

The natural condition of mankind need not, on this ground, be represented as a state of absolute *Injustice*, as if there could have been no other relation originally among men but what was merely determined by force. But this natural condition must be regarded, if it ever existed, as a state of society that was void of regulation by Right (*status justitiæ vacuus*), so that if a matter of Right came to be *in dispute* (*jus controversum*), no competent judge was found to give an authorized legal decision upon it.   It is therefore reasonable that any one should constrain another by force, to pass from such a non - juridical state of life and enter within the jurisdiction of a civil state of Society.   For, although on the basis of the *ideas of Right* held by individuals as such, external things may be acquired by Occupancy or Contract, yet such acquisition is only *provisory* so long as it has not yet obtained the sanction of a Public Law. Till this sanction is reached, the condition of possession is not determined by any public Distributive Justice, nor is it secured by any Power exercising Public Right.

If men were not disposed to recognise any Acquisition at all as rightful—even in a provisional way—prior to entering into the Civil state, this state of Society would itself be impossible. For the Laws regarding the Mine and Thine in the state of Nature, contain formally the very same thing as they prescribe in the Civil state, when it is viewed merely according to rational conceptions : only that in the forms of the Civil state the conditions are laid down under which the formal prescriptions of the state of Nature attain realization conformable to Distributive Justice. — Were there, then, not even *provisionally*, an external Meum and Tuum in the state of Nature, neither would there be any juridical Duties in relation to them ; and, consequently, there would be no obligation to pass out of that state into another.

45.

The Form of the State and its Three Powers.

A State (*Civitas*) is the union of a number of men under juridical Laws. These Laws, as such, are to be regarded as necessary *à priori*,—that is, as following of themselves from the conceptions of external Right generally,—and not as merely established by Statute. The FORM of the State is thus involved in the *Idea* of the State, viewed as it ought to be according to pure principles of Right; and this ideal Form furnishes the normal criterion of every real union that constitutes a Commonwealth.

Every State contains in itself THREE POWERS, the universal united Will of the People being thus personified in a political triad. These are *the Legislative Power, the Executive Power,* and *the Judiciary Power.*—1. The *Legislative* Power of the Sovereignty in the State, is embodied in the person of the Lawgiver; 2. the Executive Power is embodied in the person of the Ruler who administers the Law; and 3. the Judiciary Power, embodied in the person of the Judge, is the function of assigning every one what is his own, according to the Law (*Potestas legislatoria, rectoria et judiciaria*). These three Powers may be compared to the three propositions in a practical Syllogism:—the Major as the sumption laying down the universal *Law* of a Will, the Minor presenting the *command* applicable to an action according to the Law as the principle of the subsumption, and the Conclusion containing the Sentence or judgment of Right in the particular case under consideration.

46.

The Legislative Power and the Members of the State.

The Legislative Power, viewed in its rational Principle, can only belong to the united Will of the People. For, as all Right ought to proceed from this Power, it is necessary that its Laws should be unable to do wrong to any one whatever. Now, if any *one* individual determines anything in the State in contradistinction to *another*, it is always possible that he may perpetrate a wrong on that other; but this is never possible when *all* determine and decree what is to be Law to themselves. '*Volenti non fit injuria.*' Hence it is only the united and consenting Will of all the People—in so far as Each of them determines the same thing about all, and All determine the same thing about each—that ought to have the power of enacting Law in the State.

The Members of a Civil Society thus united for the purpose of Legislation, and thereby constituting a State,

are called its CITIZENS; and there are three juridical
attributes that inseparably belong to them by Right. These
are—1. Constitutional FREEDOM, as the Right of every
Citizen to have to obey no other Law than that to which
he has given his consent or approval; 2. Civil EQUALITY,
as the Right of the Citizen to recognise no one as a
Superior among the people in relation to himself, except
in so far as such a one is as subject to *his* moral power
to impose obligations, as that other has power to impose
obligations upon him; and 3. Political INDEPENDENCE, as
the Right to owe his existence and continuance in Society
not to the arbitrary Will of another, but to his own
Rights and Powers as a Member of the Commonwealth;
and, consequently, the possession of a Civil Personality,
which cannot be represented by any other than himself.

The capability of Voting by possession of the
Suffrage, properly constitutes the political qualification of a Citizen as a Member of the State.   But this,
again, presupposes the Independence or Self-sufficiency
of the individual Citizen among the people, as one who
is not a mere incidental part of the Commonwealth,
but a Member of it acting of his own Will in community with others.   The last of the three qualities
involved, necessarily constitutes the distinction between *active* and *passive* Citizenship; although the
latter conception appears to stand in contradiction to
the definition of a Citizen as such.   The following
examples may serve to remove this difficulty.   The
Apprentice of a Merchant or Tradesman, a Servant
who is not in the employ of the State, a Minor
(*naturaliter vel civiliter*), all Women, and, generally,
every one who is compelled to maintain himself not
according to his own industry, but as it is arranged
by others (the State excepted), are without Civil
Personality, and their existence is only, as it were,

incidentally included in the State. The Woodcutter whom I employ on my estate; the Smith in India who carries his hammer, anvil, and bellows into the houses where he is engaged to work in iron, as distinguished from the European Carpenter or Smith, who can offer the independent products of his labour as wares for public sale; the resident Tutor as distinguished from the Schoolmaster; the Ploughman as distinguished from the Farmer and such like, illustrate the distinction in question. In all these cases, the former members of the contrast are distinguished from the latter by being mere subsidiaries of the Commonwealth and not active independent Members of it, because they are of necessity commanded and protected by others, and consequently possess no political Self-sufficiency in themselves. Such Dependence on the Will of others and the consequent Inequality are, however, not inconsistent with the Freedom and Equality of the individuals *as Men* helping to constitute the people. Much rather is it the case that it is only under such conditions, that a People can become a State and enter into a Civil Constitution. But all are not equally qualified to exercise the Right of the Suffrage under the Constitution, and to be full Citizens of the State, and not mere passive Subjects under its protection. For, although they are entitled to demand to be treated by all the other Citizens according to laws of natural Freedom and Equality, as *passive* parts of the State, it does not follow that they ought themselves to have the Right to deal with the State as active Members of it, to reorganize it, or to take action by way of introducing certain laws. All they have a right in their circumstances to claim, may be no more than that whatever be the mode in which the positive laws are enacted, these laws must not be contrary to the natural Laws that demand the Freedom of all the people and the Equality that is conformable thereto; and it must therefore be made possible for them to raise themselves from this passive condition in the State, to the condition of active Citizenship.

47.

Dignities in the State and the Original Contract.

All these three Powers in the State are DIGNITIES ; and as necessarily arising out of the Idea of the State and essential generally to the foundation of its Constitution, they are to be regarded as POLITICAL Dignities. They imply the relation between a universal SOVEREIGN as Head of the State—which according to the laws of freedom can be none other than the People itself united into a Nation —and the mass of the individuals of the Nation as SUBJECTS. The former member of the relation is the *ruling* Power, whose function is to govern (*imperans*) ; the latter is the *ruled* Constituents of the State, whose function is to obey (*subditi*).

The act by which a People is represented as constituting itself into a State, is termed THE ORIGINAL CONTRACT. This is properly only an outward mode of representing the idea by which the rightfulness of the process of organizing the Constitution, may be made conceivable. According to this representation, all and each of the people give up their external Freedom in order to receive it immediately again as Members of a Commonwealth. The Commonwealth is the people viewed as united altogether into a State. And thus it is not to be said that the individual in the State has sacrificed *a part* of his inborn external Freedom for a particular purpose ; but he has abandoned his wild lawless Freedom wholly, in order to find all his proper Freedom again entire and undiminished, but in the form of a regulated order of dependence, that is, in a Civil state regulated by laws of Right. This relation of Dependence thus arises out of his own regulative law-giving Will.

48.

Mutual Relations and Characteristics of the Three Powers.

The three Powers in the State, as regards their relations to each other, are, therefore—(1) *co-ordinate* with one another as so many Moral Persons, and the one is thus the Complement of the other in the way of completing the Constitution of the State ; (2) they are likewise *subordinate* to one another, so that the one cannot at the same time usurp the function of the other by whose side it moves, each having its own Principle, and maintaining its authority in a particular person, but under the condition of the Will of a Superior ; and, further, (3) by the *union* of both these relations, they assign distributively to every subject in the State his own Rights.

Considered as to their respective Dignity, the three Powers may be thus described. The Will of the *Sovereign Legislator*, in respect of what constitutes the external Mine and Thine, is to be regarded as *irreprehensible ;* the executive Function of the *supreme Ruler* is to be regarded as *irresistible ;* and the judicial Sentence of the *Supreme Judge* is to be regarded as *irreversible*, being beyond appeal.

49.

Distinct Functions of the Three Powers. Autonomy of the State.

1. The Executive Power belongs to the *Governor* or *Regent* of the State, whether it assumes the form of a Moral or Individual Person, as the King or Prince (*rex, princeps*). This Executive Authority, as the Supreme *Agent* of the State, appoints the Magistrates, and prescribes the Rules to the people, in accordance with which individuals may acquire anything or maintain what is their own conformably to the Law, each case being brought under its application. Regarded as a Moral Person, this Executive Authority constitutes the Government. The Orders issued by the Government to the People and the Magistrates as well as to the higher Ministerial *Administrators* of the State (*gubernatio*), are Rescripts or *Decrees*, and not Laws ; for they terminate in the decision of particular cases, and are given forth as unchangeable. A Government acting as an Executive, and at the same time laying down the Law as the Legislative Power, would be a *Despotic* Government, and would have to be contradistinguished from a *patriotic* Government. A *patriotic* Government, again, is to be distinguished from a *paternal* Government (*regimen paternale*) which is the most despotic Government of all, the Citizens being dealt with by it as mere children. A patriotic Government, however, is one in which the State, while dealing with the Subjects as if they were Members of a Family, still treats them likewise as Citizens, and according to Laws that recognise their independence, each individual possessing himself and not being depen-

dent on the absolute Will of another beside him or above him.

2. The Legislative Authority ought not at the same time to be the Executive or Governor; for the Governor, as Administrator, should stand under the authority of the Law, and is bound by it under the supreme control of the Legislator. The Legislative Authority may therefore deprive the Governor of his power, depose him, or reform his administration, but not *punish* him. This is the proper and only meaning of the common saying in England, ' The King—as the Supreme Executive Power—can do no wrong.' For any such application of Punishment would necessarily be an act of that very Executive Power to which the supreme Right to *compel* according to Law pertains, and which would itself be thus subjected to coercion; which is self-contradictory.

3. Further, neither the Legislative Power nor the Executive Power ought to exercise the *judicial* Function, but only appoint Judges as Magistrates. It is the People who ought to judge themselves, through those of the Citizens who are elected by free Choice as their Representatives for this purpose, and even specially for every process or cause. For the judicial Sentence is a special act of public Distributive Justice performed by a Judge or Court as a constitutional Administrator of the Law, to a Subject as one of the People. Such an act is not invested inherently with the power to determine and assign to any one what is his. Every individual among the people being merely passive in this relation to the Supreme Power, either the Executive or the Legislative Authority might do him wrong in their determinations in cases of dispute regarding the property of individuals. It would not be the people themselves who thus deter-

mined, or who pronounced the judgments of 'guilty' or
'not guilty' regarding their fellow-citizens. For it is
to the determination of this issue in a cause, that the
Court has to apply the Law; and it is by means of
the Executive Authority, that the Judge holds power to
assign to every one his own. Hence it is only the
People that properly can judge in a cause—although
indirectly—by Representatives elected and deputed by
themselves, as in a Jury.—It would even be beneath the
dignity of the Sovereign Head of the State to play the
Judge; for this would be to put himself into a position
in which it would be possible to do Wrong, and thus to
subject himself to the demand for an appeal to a still
higher Power (*a rege male informato ad regem melius
informandum*).

It is by the co-operation of these three Powers—the
Legislative, the Executive, and the Judicial—that the
State realizes its *Autonomy.* This Autonomy consists in
its organizing, forming, and maintaining itself in accordance with the Laws of Freedom. In their union the
Welfare of the State is realized. *Salus reipublicæ suprema
lex.* By this is not to be understood merely the individual *well-being* and *happiness* of the Citizens of the
State; for—as Rousseau asserts—this End may perhaps
be more agreeably and more desirably attained in the
state of Nature, or even under a despotic Government.
But the Welfare of the State as its own Highest Good,
signifies that condition in which the greatest harmony
is attained between its Constitution and the Principles
of Right,—a condition of the State which Reason by
a Categorical Imperative makes it obligatory upon us to
strive after.

CONSTITUTIONAL AND JURIDICAL CONSEQUENCES ARISING
FROM THE NATURE OF THE CIVIL UNION.

A. Right of the Supreme Power, Treason ; Dethronement ;
Revolution ; Reform.

The Origin of the Supreme Power is *practically in-
scrutable* by the People who are placed under its
authority. In other words, the Subject need not *reason
too curiously* in regard to its origin in the practical
relation, as if the Right of the obedience due to it were
to be doubted (*jus controversum*). For as the People, in
order to be able to adjudicate with a title of Right
regarding the Supreme Power in the State, must be
regarded as already united under one common legislative
Will, it cannot judge otherwise than as the present
Supreme Head of the State (*summus imperans*) wills.
The question has been raised as to whether an actual
Contract of Subjection (*pactum subjectionis civilis*)
originally preceded the Civil Government as a fact ; or
whether the Power arose first, and the Law only followed
afterwards, or may have followed in this order. But
such questions, as regards the People already actually
living under the Civil Law, are either entirely aimless,
or even fraught with subtle danger to the State. For,
should the Subject, after having dug down to the
ultimate origin of the State, rise in opposition to the
present ruling Authority, he would expose himself as a
Citizen, according to the Law and with full Right, to be
punished, destroyed, or outlawed. A Law which is so
holy and inviolable that it is *practically* a crime even
to cast doubt upon it, or to suspend its operation for a
moment, is represented of itself as necessarily derived

from some Supreme, unblameable Lawgiver. And this is the meaning of the maxim, 'All Authority is from God;' which proposition does not express the *historical foundation* of the Civil Constitution, but an ideal Principle of the Practical Reason. It may be otherwise rendered thus, 'It is a Duty to obey the Law of the existing Legislative Power, be its origin what it may.'

Hence it follows, that the Supreme Power in the State has only Rights, and no (compulsory) Duties towards the Subject.—Further, if the Ruler or Regent, as the organ of the Supreme Power, proceeds in violation of the Laws, as in imposing taxes, recruiting soldiers, and so on, contrary to the Law of Equality in the distribution of the political burdens, the Subject may oppose *complaints* and *objections* (*gravamina*) to this injustice, but not active resistance.

There cannot even be an Article contained in the political Constitution that would make it possible for a Power in the State, in case of the transgression of the Constitutional Laws by the Supreme Authority, to resist or even to restrict it in so doing. For, whoever would restrict the Supreme Power of the State must have more, or at least equal power as compared with the Power that is so restricted; and if competent to command the subjects to resist, such a one would also have to be able to *protect* them, and if he is to be considered capable of judging what is right in every case, he may also publicly order Resistance. But such a one, and not the actual Authority, would then be the Supreme Power; which is contradictory. The Supreme Sovereign Power, then, in proceeding by a Minister who is at the same time the Ruler of the State, consequently becomes despotic; and the expedient of giving the People to imagine — when they have properly only Legislative influence—that they act by their Deputies by way of limiting the Sovereign Authority, cannot so mask and disguise the actual Despotism of such a Government that it will not appear in the measures and means adopted by the Minister to carry out his function. The People, while represented by their Deputies in Parliament, under such conditions, may have in these warrantors of their Freedom and Rights, persons who are keenly interested on their own account and their families, and who look to such a Minister for the benefit of his influence in the Army, Navy, and Public Offices. And hence, instead of offering resistance to the undue pretensions of the Government—whose public declarations ought to carry a prior accord on the part of the people, which, however, cannot be allowed in peace,—they are rather always ready to play into the hands of the Government. Hence the so-called limited political Constitution, as a Constitution of the internal Rights of the State, is an unreality; and instead of being consistent with Right, it is only a Principle of Expediency. And its aim is not so much to throw all possible obstacles in the way of a powerful violator of popular Rights by his arbitrary influence upon the Government, as rather to cloak it over under the illusion of a Right of opposition conceded to the People.

Resistance on the part of the People to the Supreme Legislative Power of the State, is in no case legitimate ; for it is only by submission to the universal Legislative Will, that a condition of law and order is possible. Hence there is no Right of Sedition, and still less of Rebellion, belonging to the People. And least of all, when the Supreme Power is embodied in an individual

Monarch, is there any justification, under the pretext of his abuse of power, for seizing his Person or taking away his Life (*monarchomachismus sub specie tyrannicidii*). The slightest attempt of this kind is *High Treason (proditio eminens)*; and a Traitor of this sort who aims at the *overthrow* of his country may be punished, as a political parricide, even with Death. It is the duty of the People to bear any abuse of the Supreme Power, even then though it should be considered to be unbearable. And the reason is, that any Resistance of the highest Legislative Authority can never but be contrary to the Law, and must even be regarded as tending to destroy the whole legal Constitution. In order to be entitled to offer such Resistance, a Public Law would be required to permit it. But the Supreme Legislation would by such a Law cease to be supreme, and the People as Subjects would be made sovereign over that to which they are subject; which is a contradiction. And the contradiction becomes more apparent when the question is put: Who is to be the Judge in a controversy between the People and the Sovereign? For the People and the Sovereign are to be constitutionally or juridically regarded as two different Moral Persons; but the question shows that the People would then have to be the Judge in their own cause.—See *Supplementary Explanations*, IX.

The *Dethronement* of a Monarch may be also conceived as a *voluntary* abdication of the Crown, and a resignation of his power into the hands of the People; or it might be a deliberate surrender of these without any assault on the royal person, in order that the Monarch may be relegated into private life. But, however it happen, forcible compulsion of it, on the part of the People, cannot be justified under the pretext of a 'Right of Necessity' (*casus necessitatis*); and least of all can the slightest Right be shown for punishing the Sovereign on the ground of previous maladministration. For all that has been already done in the quality of a Sovereign, must be regarded as done outwardly by Right; and, considered as the source of the Laws, the. Sovereign himself can do no wrong. Of all the abominations in the overthrow of a State by Revolution, even the murder or *assassination* of the Monarch is not the worst. For that may be done by the People out of fear, lest if he is allowed to live, he may again acquire power and inflict punishment upon them; and so it may be done, not as an act of punitive Justice, but merely from regard to self-preservation. It is the formal *Execution* of a Monarch that horrifies a soul filled with ideas of human right; and this feeling occurs again and again as often as the mind realizes the scenes that terminated the fate of Charles I. or Louis XVI. Now how is this Feeling to be explained? It is not a mere æsthetic feeling, arising from the working of the Imagination, nor from Sympathy, produced by fancying ourselves in the place of the sufferer. On the contrary, it is a *moral* feeling arising from the entire subversion of all our notions of Right. Regicide, in short, is regarded as a Crime which always remains such, and can never be expiated (*crimen immortale, inexpiabile*); and it appears to resemble that Sin which the Theologians declare can neither be forgiven in this world nor in the next. The explanation of this phenomenon in the human mind appears to be furnished by the following reflections upon it; and they even shed some light upon the Principles of Political Right.

Every Transgression of a Law only can and must be explained as arising from a Maxim of the transgressor making such wrong-doing his rule of action; for were it not committed by him as a *free* Being, it

could not be imputed to him.   But it is absolutely
impossible to explain how any rational individual
forms such a Maxim against the clear prohibition of
the lawgiving Reason; for it is only events which
happen according to the mechanical laws of Nature
that are capable of explanation.   Now a transgressor
or criminal may commit his wrong-doing either according to the Maxim of a Rule supposed to be valid
objectively and universally, or only as an Exception
from the Rule by dispensing with its obligation for
the occasion.   In the *latter* case, he only *diverges* from
the Law, although intentionally.   He may, at the
same time, abhor his own transgression, and without
formally renouncing his obedience to the Law only
wish to avoid it.   In the *former* case, however, he
rejects the authority of the Law itself, the validity of
which, however, he cannot repudiate before his own
Reason, even while he makes it his Rule to act
against it.   His Maxim is therefore not merely
defective as being *negatively* contrary to the Law, but
it is even positively illegal, as being *diametrically*
contrary and in hostile opposition to it.   So far as we
can see into and understand the relation, it would
appear as if it were impossible for men to commit
wrongs and crimes of a wholly useless form of wickedness, and yet the idea of such extreme perversity
cannot be overlooked in a System of Moral Philosophy.

There is thus a feeling of horror at the thought of
the formal Execution of a Monarch *by his People.*
And the reason of it is, that whereas an act of Assassination must be considered as only an *exception* from
the Rule which has been constituted a Maxim, such
an *Execution* must be regarded as a complete *perversion* of the Principles that should regulate the
relation between a Sovereign and his People.   For it
makes the People, who owe their constitutional existence to the Legislation that issued from the Sovereign,

to be the Ruler over him.   Hence mere violence is thus
elevated with bold brow, and as it were by principle,
above the holiest Right; and, appearing like an abyss
to swallow up everything without recall, it seems like
suicide committed by the State upon itself, and a crime
that is capable of no atonement.   There is therefore
reason to assume that the consent that is accorded to
such executions is not really based upon a supposed
Principle of Right, but only springs from fear of the
vengeance that would be taken upon the People were
the same Power to revive again in the State.   And
hence it may be held that the formalities accompanying them, have only been put forward in order to give
these deeds a look of Punishment from the accompaniment of a *judicial process*, such as could not go
along with a mere Murder or Assassination.   But
such a cloaking of the deed entirely fails of its purpose, because this pretension on the part of the People
is even worse than Murder itself, as it implies a
principle which would necessarily make the restoration of a State, when once overthrown, an impossibility.

An alteration of the still defective Constitution of the
State may sometimes be quite necessary.   But all such
changes ought only to proceed from the Sovereign Power
in the way of *Reform*, and are not to be brought about
by the people in the way of *Revolution ;* and when they
take place, they should only affect the *Executive*, and not
the *Legislative* Power.   A political Constitution which is
so modified that the People by their Representatives in
Parliament can legally *resist* the Executive Power and
its representative Minister, is called a Limited Constitution.   Yet even under such a Constitution there is no
Right of *active* Resistance, as by an arbitrary combination
of the People to coerce the Government into a certain
active procedure ; for this would be to assume to perform

an act of the Executive itself. All that can rightly be allowed, is only a *negative* Resistance, amounting to an act of *Refusal* on the part of the People to concede all the demands which the Executive may deem it necessary to make in behoof of the political Administration. And if this Right were never exercised, it would be a sure sign that the People were corrupted, their Representatives venal, the Supreme Head of the Government despotic, and his Ministers practically betrayers of the People.

Further, when on the success of a Revolution a new Constitution has been founded, the unlawfulness of its beginning and of its institution cannot release the Subjects from the obligation of adapting themselves, as good Citizens, to the new order of things; and they are not entitled to refuse honourably to obey the authority that has thus attained the power in the State. A dethroned Monarch, who has survived such a Revolution, is not to be called to account on the ground of his former administration; and still less may he be punished for it, when withdrawing into the private life of a citizen he prefers his own quiet and the peace of the State to the uncertainty of exile, with the intention of maintaining his claims for restoration at all hazards, and pushing these either by secret counter-revolution or by the assistance of other Powers. However, if he prefers to follow the latter course, his Rights remain, because the Rebellion that drove him from his position was inherently unjust. But the question then emerges as to whether other Powers have the Right to form themselves into an alliance in behalf of such a dethroned Monarch merely in order not to leave the crime committed by the People unavenged, or to do away with it as a scandal to all the States; and whether they are therefore justified and called upon to

ciple of a Division of the Soil according to conceptions of Right. In accordance with this Principle, the Supreme Universal Proprietor cannot have any private property in any part of the Soil; for otherwise he would make himself a private Person. Private property in the Soil belongs only to the People, taken distributively and not collectively;—from which condition, however, a nomadic people must be excepted as having no private property at all in the Soil. The Supreme Proprietor accordingly ought not to hold private *Estates*, either for private use or for the support of the Court. For, as it would depend upon his own pleasure how far these should extend, the State would be in danger of seeing all property in the Land taken into the hands of the Government, and all the Subjects treated as *bondsmen of the Soil (glebæ adscripti)*. As possessors only of what was the private property of another, they might thus be deprived of all freedom and regarded as Serfs or Slaves. Of the Supreme Proprietor of the Land, it may be said that *he possesses nothing* as his own, except himself; for if he possessed things in the State alongside of others, dispute and litigation would be possible with these others regarding those things, and there would be no independent Judge to settle the cause. But it may be also said that *he possesses everything;* for he has the Supreme Right of Sovereignty over the whole People, to whom all external things severally (*divisim*) belong; and as such he assigns distributively to every one what is to be his.

Hence there cannot be any Corporation in the State, nor any Class or Order, that as Proprietors can transmit the Land for a sole exclusive use to the following generations for all time (*ad infinitum*), according to certain fixed Statutes. The State may annul and abrogate all

such Statutes at any time, only under the condition of
indemnifying survivors for their interests.   The Order of
Knights, constituting the nobility regarded as a mere
rank or class of specially titled individuals, as well as
the Order of the *Clergy*, called the Church, are both
subject to this relation.   They can never be entitled by
any hereditary privileges with which they may be
favoured, to acquire an absolute property in the soil
transmissible to their successors.   They can only acquire
the use of such property for the time being.   If Public
Opinion has ceased, on account of other arrangements, to
impel the State to protect itself from negligence in the
national defence by appeal to the *military honour* of the
knightly order, the Estates granted on that condition
may be recalled.   And, in like manner, the Church Lands
or Spiritualities may be reclaimed by the State without
scruple, if Public Opinion has ceased to impel the
members of the State to maintain Masses for the Souls of
the Dead, Prayers for the Living, and a multitude of
Clergy, as means to protect themselves from eternal fire.
But in both cases, the condition of indemnifying existing
interests must be observed.   Those who in this connection fall under the movement of Reform, are not entitled
to complain that their property is taken from them ; for
the foundation of their previous possession lay only in
the *Opinion of the People,* and it can be valid only so
long as this opinion lasts.   As soon as this Public
Opinion in favour of such institutions dies out, or is even
extinguished in the judgment of those who have the greatest
claim by their acknowledged merit to lead and represent it,
the putative proprietorship in question must cease, as if
by a public appeal made regarding it to the State (*a rege
male informato ad regem melius informandum*).

On this primarily acquired Supreme Proprietorship in the Land, rests the Right of the Sovereign, as universal Proprietor of the country, to *assess* the private proprietors of the Soil, and to demand Taxes, Excise, and Dues, or the performance of Service to the State such as may be required in War. But this is to be done so that it is actually the People that assess themselves, this being the only mode of proceeding according to Laws of Right. This may be effected through the medium of the Body of Deputies who represent the People. It is also permissible, in circumstances in which the State is in imminent danger, to proceed by a forced Loan, as a Right vested in the Sovereign, although this may be a divergence from the existing Law.

Upon this Principle is also founded the Right of administering the National Economy, including the Finance and the Police. The Police has specially to care for the Public *Safety, Convenience,* and *Decency.* As regards the last of these,—the feeling or negative taste for public Propriety,—it is important that it be not deadened by such influences as Begging, disorderly Noises, offensive Smells, public Prostitution (*Venus vulgi-vaga*), or other offences against the Moral Sense, as it greatly facilitates the Government in the task of regulating the life of the People by law.

For the preservation of the State there further belongs to it a Right of *Inspection* (*jus inspectionis*), which entitles the public Authority to see that no secret Society, political or religious, exists among the people that can exert a prejudicial influence upon the *public* Weal. Accordingly, when it is required by the Police, no such secret Society may refuse to lay open its constitution. But the visitation and search of private houses by the

Police, can only be justified in a case of Necessity; and in every particular instance, it must be authorized by a higher Authority.

C. Relief of the Poor. Foundling Hospitals. The Church.

The Sovereign, as undertaker of the duty of the People, has the Right to tax them for purposes essentially connected with their own preservation. Such are, in particular, the Relief of the Poor, Foundling Asylums, and Ecclesiastical Establishments, otherwise designated charitable or pious Foundations.

1. The People have in fact united themselves by their common Will into a Society, which has to be perpetually maintained; and for this purpose they have subjected themselves to the internal Power of the State, in order to preserve the members of this Society even when they are not able to support themselves. By the fundamental principle of the State, the Government is justified and entitled to compel those who are able, to furnish the means necessary to preserve those who are not themselves capable of providing for the most necessary wants of Nature. For the existence of persons with property in the State, implies their submission under it for protection and the provision by the State of what is necessary for their existence; and accordingly the State founds a Right upon an obligation on their part to contribute of their means for the preservation of their fellow-citizens. This may be carried out by taxing the Property or the commercial industry of the Citizens, or by establishing Funds and drawing interest from them, not for the wants of the State as such, which is rich, but

for those of the People. And this is not to be done merely by *voluntary* contributions, but by *compulsory* exactions as State-burdens, for we are here considering only the *Right* of the State in relation to the People. Among the *voluntary* modes of raising such contributions *Lotteries* ought not to be allowed, because they increase the number of those who are poor, and involve danger to the public property.—It may be asked whether the Relief of the Poor ought to be administered out of *current contributions*, so that every age should maintain its own Poor ; or whether this were better done by means of *permanent funds* and charitable institutions, such as Widows' Homes, Hospitals, etc. ? And if the former method is the better, it may also be considered whether the means necessary are to be raised by a legal Assessment rather than by Begging, which is generally nigh akin to robbing. The former method must in reality be regarded as the only one that is conformable to the Right of the State, which cannot withdraw its connection from any one who has to live. For a legal current provision does not make the profession of poverty a means of gain for the indolent, as is to be feared is the case with pious Foundations when they grow with the number of the poor ; nor can it be charged with being an unjust or unrighteous burden imposed by the Government on the people.

2. The State has also a Right to impose upon the People the duty of preserving Children exposed from want or shame, and who would otherwise perish ; for it cannot knowingly allow this increase of its power to be destroyed, however unwelcome in some respects it may be. But it is a difficult question to determine how this may most justly be carried out. It might be considered

whether it would not be right to exact contributions for
this purpose from the unmarried persons of both sexes
who are possessed of means, as being in part responsible
for the evil; and further, whether the end in view would
be best carried out by Foundling Hospitals, or in what
other way consistent with Right.   But this is a problem
of which no solution has yet been offered that does not
in some measure offend against Right or Morality.

3. The *Church* is here regarded as an Ecclesiastical
Establishment merely, and as such it must be carefully
distinguished from Religion, which as an internal mode
of feeling lies wholly beyond the sphere of the action of
the Civil Power.   Viewed as an Institution for public
Worship founded for the people,—to whose opinion or
conviction it owes its origin,—the Church Establishment
responds to a real want in the State.   This is the need
felt by the people to regard themselves as also Subjects
of a Supreme *Invisible* Power to which they must pay
homage, and which may often be brought into a very
undesirable collision with the Civil Power.   The State
has therefore a Right in this relation; but it is not to be
regarded as the Right of Constitutional Legislation in the
Church, so as to organize it as may seem most advan-
tageous for itself, or to prescribe and command its faith and
ritual forms of worship (*ritus*); for all this must be left
entirely to the teachers and rulers which the Church has
chosen for itself.   The function of the State in this connection, only includes the *negative* Right of regulating the
influence of these public teachers upon the *visible* political
Commonwealth, that it may not be prejudicial to the
public peace and tranquillity.   Consequently the State
has to take measures, on occasion of any internal conflict
in the Church, or on occasion of any collision of the

several Churches with each other, that Civil concord is not endangered; and this Right falls within the province of the Police. It is *beneath the dignity* of the Supreme Power to interpose in determining what particular faith the Church shall profess, or to decree that a certain faith shall be unalterably held, and that the Church may not reform itself. For in doing so, the Supreme Power would be mixing itself up in a scholastic wrangle, on a footing of equality with its subjects; the Monarch would be making himself a priest; and the Churchmen might even reproach the Supreme Power with understanding nothing about matters of faith. Especially would this hold in respect of any prohibition of internal Reform in the Church; for what the People as a whole cannot determine upon for themselves, cannot be determined for the People by the Legislator. But no People can ever rationally determine that they will never advance farther in their insight into matters of faith, or resolve that they will never reform the institutions of the Church; because this would be opposed to the humanity in their own persons, and to their highest Rights. And therefore the Supreme Power cannot of itself resolve and decree in these matters for the People.—As regards the cost of maintaining the Ecclesiastical Establishment, for similar reasons this must be derived not from the public funds of the State, but from the section of the People who profess the particular faith of the Church; and thus only ought it to fall as a burden on the Community.—See *Supplementary Explanations*, VIII.

D. The Right of assigning Offices and Dignities in the State.

The Right of the Supreme Authority in the State also includes :

1. The Distribution of *Offices*, as public and paid employments ;

2. The Conferring of *Dignities*, as unpaid distinctions of Rank, founded merely on honour, but establishing a gradation of higher and lower orders in the political scale; the latter, although free in themselves, being under obligation determined by the public law to obey the former so far as they are also entitled to command ;

3. Besides these relatively beneficent Rights, the Supreme Power in the State is also invested with the Right of administering *Punishment*.

As regards *Civil Offices*, the question arises as to whether the Sovereign has the Right, after bestowing an office on an individual, to take it again away at his mere pleasure, without any crime having been committed by the holder of the office. I say, *No*. For what the united Will of the People would never resolve regarding their Civil Officers, cannot (constitutionally) be determined by the Sovereign regarding them. The People have to bear the cost incurred by the appointment of an Official, and undoubtedly it must be their Will that any one in Office should be completely competent for its duties. But such competency can only be acquired by a long preparation and training, and this process would necessarily occupy the time that would be required for acquiring the means of support by a different occupation. Arbitrary and frequent changes would therefore, as a rule, have the effect of filling Offices with functionaries who have not acquired the skill required for their duties, and whose judgments had not attained maturity by practice.   All this is contrary to the purpose of the State.   And besides it is requisite in the interest of the People, that it should be possible for every individual to rise from a lower office to the higher offices, as these latter would otherwise fall into incompetent hands, and that competent officials generally should have some guarantee of life-long provision.

Civil Dignities include not only such as are connected with a public Office, but also those which make the possessors of them without any accompanying services to the State, members of a higher class or rank.   The latter constitute the *Nobility*, whose members are distinguished from the common citizens who form the mass of the People.   The rank of the Nobility is inherited by male descendants ; and these again communicate it to wives who are not nobly born.   Female descendants of noble families, however, do not communicate their rank to husbands who are not of noble birth, but they descend themselves into the common civil status of the People. This being so, the question then emerges as to whether the Sovereign has the Right to found a *hereditary* rank and class, intermediate between himself and the other Citizens ?   The import of this question does not turn on whether it is conformable to the prudence of the Sovereign, from regard to his own and the People's interests, to have such an institution ; but whether it is in accordance with the Right of the People that they should have a class of Persons above them, who, while being Subjects like themselves, are' yet born as their Commanders, or at

least as privileged Superiors ?   The answer to this
question, as in previous instances, is to be derived from
the Principle that 'what the People as constituting the
whole mass of the Subjects could not determine regarding themselves and their associated citizens, cannot be
constitutionally determined by the Sovereign regarding
the People.'   Now a *hereditary* Nobility is a Rank which
takes precedence of Merit and is hoped for without any
good reason,—a thing of the imagination without genuine
reality.   For if an Ancestor had merit, he could not
transmit it to his posterity, but they must always acquire
it for themselves.   Nature has in fact not so arranged
that the Talent and Will which give rise to merit in the
State, are hereditary.   And because it cannot be supposed
of any individual that he will throw away his *Freedom*,
it is impossible that the common Will of all the People
should agree to such a groundless Prerogative, and hence
the Sovereign cannot make it valid.—It may happen,
however, that such an anomaly as that of Subjects who
would be more than Citizens, in the manner of born
Officials or hereditary Professors, has slipped into the
mechanism of the Government in olden times, as in the
case of the Feudal System, which was almost entirely
organized with reference to War.   Under such circumstances, the State cannot deal otherwise with this error
of a wrongly instituted Rank in its midst, than by the
remedy of a gradual extinction through hereditary positions being left unfilled as they fall vacant.   The State
has therefore the Right provisorily to let a Dignity in
Title continue, until the Public Opinion matures on the
subject.   And this will thus pass from the threefold
division into Sovereign, Nobles, and People, to the twofold and only natural division into Sovereign and People.

No individual in the State can indeed be entirely without Dignity; for he has at least that of being a Citizen, except when he has lost his Civil Status by a Crime. As a Criminal he is still maintained in life, but he is made the mere instrument of the Will of another, whether it be the State or a particular Citizen. In the latter position, in which he could only be placed by a juridical judgment, he would practically become a *Slave*, and would belong as property (*dominium*) to another, who would be not merely his Master (*herus*) but his Owner (*dominus*). Such an Owner would be entitled to exchange or alienate him as a thing, to use him at will except for shameful purposes, and to *dispose of his Powers*, but not of his Life and Members. No one can bind himself to such a condition of dependence, as he would thereby cease to be a Person, and it is only as a Person that he can make a Contract. It may, however, appear that one man may bind himself to another by a Contract of Hire, to discharge a certain service that is permissible in its kind, but is left entirely *undetermined* as regards its measure or amount; and that as receiving wages or board or protection in return, he thus becomes only a Servant subject to the Will of a Master (*subditus*) and not a Slave (*servus*). But this is an illusion. For if Masters are entitled to use the powers of such subjects at will, they may exhaust these powers,—as has been done in the case of Negroes in the Sugar Islands,—and they may thus reduce their servants to despair and death. But this would imply that they had actually given themselves away to their Masters as property; which, in the case of persons is impossible. A Person can therefore only contract to perform work that is defined both in quality and quantity, either as a Day-labourer or as a domiciled Subject.

dealt with by a Civil Court ; Public Crimes by a Criminal Court.—Embezzlement or peculation of money or goods entrusted in trade, Fraud in purchase or sale, if done before the eyes of the party who suffers, are Private Crimes. On the other hand, Coining false money or forging Bills of Exchange, Theft, Robbery, etc., are Public Crimes, because the Commonwealth, and not merely some particular individual, is endangered thereby. Such Crimes may be divided into those of a *base* character (*indolis abjectæ*) and those of a *violent* character (*indolis violentiæ*).

Judicial or Juridical Punishment (*pœna forensis*) is to be distinguished from Natural Punishment (*pœna naturalis*), in which Crime as Vice punishes itself, and does not as such come within the cognizance of the Legislator. Juridical Punishment can never be administered merely as a means for promoting another Good either with regard to the Criminal himself or to Civil Society, but must in all cases be imposed only because the individual on whom it is inflicted *has committed a Crime.* For one man ought never to be dealt with merely as a means subservient to the purpose of another, nor be mixed up with the subjects of Real Right. Against such treatment his Inborn Personality has a Right to protect him, even although he may be condemned to lose his Civil Personality. He must first be found guilty and *punishable*, before there can be any thought of drawing from his Punishment any benefit for himself or his fellow-citizens. The Penal Law is a Categorical Imperative ; and woe to him who creeps through the serpent-windings of Utilitarianism to discover some advantage that may discharge him from the Justice of Punishment, or even from the due measure of it, according to the Pharisaic

maxim: 'It is better that *one* man should die than that
the whole people should perish.' For if Justice and
Righteousness perish, human life would no longer have
any value in the world.—What, then, is to be said of
such a proposal as to keep a Criminal alive who has
been condemned to death, on his being given to understand that if he agreed to certain dangerous experiments
being performed upon him, he would be allowed to sur-
vive if he came happily through them? It is argued
that Physicians might thus obtain new information that
would be of value to the Commonweal. But a Court
of Justice would repudiate with scorn any proposal of
this kind if made to it by the Medical Faculty; for
Justice would cease to be Justice, if it were bartered
away for any consideration whatever.

But what is the mode and measure of Punishment
which Public Justice takes as its Principle and Standard?
It is just the Principle of Equality, by which the
pointer of the Scale of Justice is made to incline no
more to the one side than the other. It may be rendered by saying that the undeserved evil which any one
commits on another, is to be regarded as perpetrated on
himself. Hence it may be said: 'If you slander
another, you slander yourself; if you steal from
another, you steal from yourself; if you strike another,
you strike yourself; if you kill another, you kill yourself.' This is the Right of RETALIATION (*jus talionis*);
and properly understood, it is the only Principle which
in regulating a Public Court, as distinguished from mere
private judgment, can definitely assign both the quality
and the quantity of a just penalty. All other standards
are wavering and uncertain; and on account of other
considerations involved in them, they contain no prin-

ciple conformable to the sentence of pure and strict
Justice. It may appear, however, that difference of
social status would not admit the application of the
Principle of Retaliation, which is that of 'Like with
Like.' But although the application may not in all
cases be possible according to the letter, yet as regards
the effect it may always be attained in practice, by due
regard being given to the disposition and sentiment of
the parties in the higher social sphere. Thus a pecuniary
penalty on account of a verbal injury, may have no
direct proportion to the injustice of slander; for one
who is wealthy may be able to indulge himself in this
offence for his own gratification. Yet the attack committed on the honour of the party aggrieved may have
its equivalent in the pain inflicted upon the pride of
the aggressor, especially if he is condemned by the
judgment of the Court, not only to retract and apologize,
but to submit to some meaner ordeal, as kissing the hand
of the injured person. In like manner, if a man of the
highest rank has violently assaulted an innocent citizen
of the lower orders, he may be condemned not only to
apologize but to undergo a solitary and painful imprison-
ment, whereby, in addition to the discomfort endured, the
vanity of the offender would be painfully affected, and
the very shame of his position would constitute an
adequate Retaliation after the principle of 'Like with
Like.' But how then would we render the statement:
'If you *steal* from another, you steal from yourself'?
In this way, that whoever steals anything makes the
property of all insecure; he therefore robs himself of
all security in property, according to the Right of
Retaliation. Such a one has nothing, and can acquire
nothing, but he has the Will to live; and this is only

possible by others supporting him. But as the State should not do this gratuitously, he must for this purpose yield his powers to the State to be used in penal labour; and thus he falls for a time, or it may be for life, into a condition of slavery.—But whoever has committed Murder, must *die.* There is, in this case, no juridical substitute or surrogate, that can be given or taken for the satisfaction of Justice. There is no *Likeness* or proportion between Life, however painful, and Death; and therefore there is no Equality between the crime of Murder and the retaliation of it but what is judicially accomplished by the execution of the Criminal. His death, however, must be kept free from all maltreatment that would make the humanity suffering in his Person loathsome or abominable. Even if a Civil Society resolved to dissolve itself with the consent of all its members—as might be supposed in the case of a People inhabiting an island resolving to separate and scatter themselves throughout the whole world—the last Murderer lying in the prison ought to be executed before the resolution was carried out. This ought to be done in order that every one may realize the desert of his deeds, and that bloodguiltiness may not remain upon the people; for otherwise they might all be regarded as participators in the murder as a public violation of Justice.

The Equalization of Punishment with Crime, is therefore only possible by the cognition of the Judge extending even to the penalty of Death, according to the Right of Retaliation. This is manifest from the fact that it is only thus that a Sentence can be pronounced over all criminals proportionate to their internal *wickedness;* as may be seen by considering the case when the

punishment of Death has to be inflicted, not on account
of a murder, but on account of a political crime that
can only be punished capitally. A hypothetical case,
founded on history, will illustrate this. In the last
Scottish Rebellion there were various participators in it
—such as Balmerino and others—who believed that in
taking part in the Rebellion they were only discharging
their duty to the House of Stuart; but there were also
others who were animated only by private motives and
interests. Now, suppose that the Judgment of the
Supreme Court regarding them had been this: that
every one should have liberty to choose between the
punishment of Death or Penal Servitude for life. In
view of such an alternative, I say that the Man of
Honour would choose Death, and the Knave would
choose servitude. This would be the effect of their
human nature as it is; for the honourable man values
his Honour more highly than even Life itself, whereas
a Knave regards a Life, although covered with shame,
as better in his eyes than not to be.[1] The former is,
without gainsaying, less guilty than the other; and they
can only be proportionately punished by death being
inflicted equally upon them both; yet to the one it is a
mild punishment when his nobler temperament is taken
into account, whereas it is a hard punishment to the
other in view of his baser temperament. But, on the
other hand, were they all equally condemned to Penal
Servitude for life, the honourable man would be too
severely punished, while the other, on account of his
baseness of nature, would be too mildly punished. In
the judgment to be pronounced over a number of
criminals united in such a conspiracy, the best Equalizer

[1] 'Animam præferre pudori, *Juven.*

of Punishment and Crime in the form of public Justice is Death. And besides all this, it has never been heard of, that a Criminal condemned to death on account of a murder has complained that the Sentence inflicted on him more than was right and just; and any one would treat him with scorn if he expressed himself to this effect against it. Otherwise it would be necessary to admit that although wrong and injustice are not done to the Criminal by the Law, yet the Legislative Power is not entitled to administer this mode of Punishment; and if it did so, it would be in contradiction with itself.

However many they may be who have committed a murder, or have even commanded it, or acted as art and part in it, they ought all to suffer death; for so Justice wills it, in accordance with the Idea of the juridical Power as founded on the universal Laws of Reason. But the number of the Accomplices (*correi*) in such a deed might happen to be so great that the State, in resolving to be without such criminals, would be in danger of soon also being deprived of subjects. But it will not thus dissolve itself, neither must it return to the much worse condition of Nature, in which there would be no external Justice. Nor, above all, should it deaden the sensibilities of the People by the spectacle of Justice being exhibited in the mere carnage of a slaughtering bench. In such circumstances the Sovereign must always be allowed to have it in his power to take the part of the Judge upon himself as a case of Necessity,—and to deliver a Judgment which, instead of the penalty of death, shall assign some other punishment to the Criminals, and thereby preserve a multitude of the People. The penalty of Deportation is relevant in this connection. Such a form of Judgment cannot

be carried out according to a public law, but only by
an authoritative act of the royal Prerogative, and it may
only be applied as an act of grace in individual cases.

Against these doctrines, the Marquis BECCARIA has
given forth a different view. Moved by the compas-
sionate sentimentality of a humane feeling, he has
asserted that all Capital Punishment is wrong in itself
and unjust. He has put forward this view on the
ground that the penalty of death could not be contained
in the original Civil Contract; for, in that case, every
one of the People would have had to consent to lose his
life if he murdered any of his fellow-citizens. But, it
is argued, such a consent is impossible, because no one
can thus dispose of his own life.—All this is mere
sophistry and perversion of Right. No one undergoes
Punishment because he has willed to be punished, but
because he has willed a *punishable Action ;* for it is in
fact no Punishment when any one experiences what he
wills, and it is impossible for any one to *will* to be
punished. To say, ' I *will* to be punished, if I murder
any one,' can mean nothing more than, ' I submit myself
along with all the other citizens to the Laws ; ' and if
there are any Criminals among the People, these Laws
will include Penal Laws. The individual who, as a
Co-legislator, enacts *Penal Law,* cannot possibly be the
same Person who, as a Subject, is punished according
to the Law ; for, *quâ* Criminal, he cannot possibly be
regarded as having a voice in the Legislation, the
Legislator being rationally viewed as just and holy. If
any one, then, enact a Penal Law against himself as a
Criminal, it must be the pure juridically law‑giving
Reason (*homo noumenon*), which subjects him as one
capable of crime, and consequently as another Person

(*homo phenomenon*), along with all the others in the Civil
Union, to this Penal Law.   In other words, it is not the
People taken distributively, but the Tribunal of public
Justice, as distinct from the Criminal, that prescribes
Capital Punishment; and it is not to be viewed as if
the Social Contract contained the Promise of all the
individuals to allow themselves to be punished, thus dis-
posing of themselves and their lives.   For if the Right
to punish must be grounded upon a promise of the
wrongdoer, whereby he is to be regarded as being willing
to be punished, it ought also to be left to him to find
himself deserving of the Punishment; and the Criminal
would thus be his own Judge.   The chief error (πρῶτον
ψεῦδος) of this sophistry consists in regarding the
judgment of the Criminal himself, necessarily determined by his Reason, that he is under obligation to
undergo the loss of his life, as a judgment that must
be grounded on a resolution of his *Will* to take it away
himself; and thus the execution of the Right in question
is represented as united in one and the same person with
the adjudication of the Right.

   There are, however, two crimes worthy of death, in
respect of which it still remains doubtful whether the
Legislature have the Right to deal with them capitally.
It is the sentiment of Honour that induces their perpetration.   The one originates in a regard for *womanly*
Honour, the other in a regard for *military* Honour;
and in both cases there is a genuine feeling of honour
incumbent on the individuals as a Duty.   The former is
the Crime of MATERNAL INFANTICIDE (*infanticidium
maternale*); the latter is the Crime of KILLING A FELLOW-
SOLDIER in a Duel (*Commilitonicidium*).   Now Legislation
cannot take away the shame of an illegitimate birth, nor

wipe off the stain attaching from a suspicion of cowardice, to an officer who does not resist an act that would bring him into contempt, by an effort of his own that is superior to the fear of death.   Hence it appears that in such circumstances, the individuals concerned are remitted to the State of Nature; and their acts in both cases must be called *Homicide*, and not *Murder*, which involves evil intent (*homicidium dolosum*).   In all instances the acts are undoubtedly punishable; but they cannot be punished by the Supreme Power with death.   An illegitimate child comes into the world outside of the Law which properly regulates Marriage, and it is thus born beyond the pale or constitutional protection of the Law. Such a child is introduced, as it were, like prohibited goods, into the Commonwealth, and as it has no legal right to existence in this way, its destruction might also be ignored; nor can the shame of the mother when her unmarried confinement is known, be removed by any legal ordinance.   A subordinate Officer, again, on whom an insult is inflicted, sees himself compelled by the public opinion of his associates to obtain satisfaction; and, as in the state of Nature, the punishment of the offender can only be effected by a Duel, in which his own life is exposed to danger, and not by means of the Law in a Court of Justice.   The Duel is therefore adopted as the means of demonstrating his courage as that characteristic upon which the Honour of his profession essentially rests; and this is done even if it should issue in the killing of his adversary.   But as such a result takes place publicly and under consent of both parties, although it may be done unwillingly, it cannot properly be called Murder (*homicidium dolosum*).—What then is the Right in both cases as relating to Criminal Justice?   Penal Justice is

here in fact brought into great straits, having apparently
either to declare the notion of Honour, which is certainly
no mere fancy here, to be nothing in the eye of the Law,
or to exempt the crime from its due punishment; and
thus it would become either remiss or cruel. The knot
thus tied is to be resolved in the following way. The
Categorical Imperative of Penal Justice, that the killing
of any person contrary to the Law must be punished
with death, remains in force; but the Legislation itself
and the Civil Constitution generally, so long as they are
still barbarous and incomplete, are at fault. And this is
the reason why the subjective motive-principles of Honour
among the People, do not coincide with the standards
which are objectively conformable to another purpose;
so that the public Justice issuing from the State becomes
Injustice relatively to that which is upheld among the
People themselves. [See *Supplementary Explanations*, v.]

II. The Right of Pardoning.

The Right of Pardoning (*Jus aggratiandi*), viewed in
relation to the Criminal, is the Right of mitigating or
entirely remitting his Punishment. On the side of the
Sovereign this is the most delicate of all Rights, as it
may be exercised so as to set forth the splendour of his
dignity, and yet so as to do a great wrong by it. It
ought not to be exercised in application to the crimes of
the subjects against each other; for exemption from
Punishment (*impunitas criminis*) would be the greatest
wrong that could be done to them. It is only on
occasion of some form of Treason (*crimen læsæ majes-
tatis*), as a lesion against himself, that the Sovereign
should make use of this Right. And it should not be

exercised even in this connection, if the safety of the
People would be endangered by remitting such Punishment. This Right is the only one which properly
deserves the name of a ' Right of Majesty.'

50.

Juridical Relations of the Citizen to his Country and to other Countries. Emigration; Immigration; Banishment; Exile.

The Land or Territory whose inhabitants—in virtue
of its political Constitution and without the necessary
intervention of a special juridical act—are, by birth,
fellow-citizens of one and the same Commonwealth, is
called their COUNTRY or Fatherland. A *Foreign* Country
is one in which they would not possess this condition,
but would be living *abroad*. If a Country abroad form
part of the territory under the same Government as at
home, it constitutes a *Province*, according to the Roman
usage of the term. It does not constitute an incorporated
portion of the Empire (*imperii*) so as to be the *abode*
of equal fellow-citizens, but is only a *possession* of the
Government, like a *lower House ;* and it must therefore
honour the domain of the ruling State as the ' Mother
Country ' (*regio domina*).

1. A Subject, even regarded as a Citizen, has the
Right of *Emigration ;* for the State cannot retain him as
if he were its property. But he may only carry away
with him his Moveables as distinguished from his fixed
possessions. However, he is entitled to sell his immov-
able property, and take the value of it in money with him.

2. The Supreme Power as Master of the Country, has
the Right to favour *Immigration*, and the settlement of

Strangers and Colonists. This will hold even although the natives of the Country may be unfavourably disposed to it, if their private property in the soil is not diminished or interfered with.

3. In the case of a Subject who has committed a Crime that renders all society of his fellow-citizens with him prejudicial to the State, the Supreme Power has also the Right of inflicting *Banishment* to a Country abroad. By such Deportation, he does not acquire any share in the Rights of the Citizens of the territory to which he is banished.

4. The Supreme Power has also the Right of imposing *Exile* generally (*Jus exilii*), by which a Citizen is sent abroad into the wide world as the 'Out-land.'[1] And because the Supreme Authority thus withdraws all legal protection from the Citizen, this amounts to making him an 'outlaw' within the territory of his own country.

51.

The Three Forms of the State. Autocracy; Aristocracy; Democracy.

The three Powers in the State, involved in the conception of a Public Government generally (*res publica latius dicta*), are only so many Relations of the united Will of the People which emanates from the *à priori* Reason; and viewed as such it is the objective practical realization of the pure Idea of a Supreme Head of the State. This Supreme Head is the Sovereign; but conceived only as a Representation of the whole People, the Idea still requires physical embodiment in a Person, who

[1] In the old German language '*Elend*,' which in its modern use means 'misery.'

may exhibit the Supreme Power of the State, and bring the idea actively to bear upon the popular Will. The relation of the Supreme Power to the People, is conceivable in three different forms: Either *One* in the State rules over all; or *Some*, united in a relation of Equality with each other, rule over all the others; or *All* together rule over each and all individually, including themselves. The Form of the State is therefore either *autocratic*, or *aristocratic*, or *democratic.*—The expression '*monarchic*' is not so suitable as 'autocratic' for the conception here intended; for a 'Monarch' is one who has the *highest* power, an 'Autocrat' is one who has *all* power, so that this latter *is* the Sovereign, whereas the former merely represents the Sovereignty.

It is evident that an Autocracy is the *simplest* form of Government in the State, being constituted by the relation of One, as King, to the People, so that there is one only who is the Lawgiver. An Aristocracy, as a form of Government, is, however, *compounded* of the union of two relations: that of the Nobles in relation to one another as the Lawgivers, thereby constituting the Sovereignty, and that of this Sovereign Power to the People. A Democracy, again, is the most *complex* of all the forms of the State, for it has to begin by uniting the will of all so as to form a People; and then it has to appoint a Sovereign over this common Union, which Sovereign is no other than the United Will itself.—The consideration of the ways in which these Forms are adulterated by the intrusion of violent and illegitimate usurpers of power, as in *Oligarchy* and *Ochlocracy*, as well as the discussion of the so-called *mixed* Constitutions, may be passed over here as not essential, and as leading into too much detail.

As regards the *Administration* of Right in the State, it may be said that the simplest mode is also the best; but as regards its bearing on Right itself, it is also the most dangerous for the People, in view of the Despotism to which simplicity of Administration so naturally gives rise. It is undoubtedly a rational maxim to aim at simplification in the machinery which is to unite the People under compulsory Laws, and this would be secured were all the People to be passive and to obey only one person over them; but the method would not give Subjects who were also Citizens of the State. It is sometimes said that the People should be satisfied with the reflection that Monarchy, regarded as an Autocracy, is the best political Constitution, *if the Monarch is good*, that is, if he has the judgment as well as the Will to do right. But this is a mere evasion, and belongs to the common class of wise tautological phrases. It only amounts to saying that 'the best Constitution is that by which the supreme administrator of the State is made the best Ruler;' that is, that the best Constitution *is* the best!

52.

Historical Origin and Changes. A Pure Republic. Representative Government.

It is vain to inquire into the historical Origin of the political Mechanism; for it is no longer possible to discover historically the point of time at which Civil Society took its beginning. Savages do not draw up a documentary Record of their having submitted themselves to Law; and it may be inferred from the nature of uncivilised men that they must have set out from a state of violence. To prosecute such an inquiry in the intention of finding a pretext for altering the existing Constitution by violence, is no less than penal. For such a mode of alteration would amount to a Revolution, that could only be carried out by an Insurrection of the People, and not by constitutional modes of Legislation. But Insurrection against an already existing Constitution, is an overthrow of all civil and juridical relations, and of Right generally; and hence it is not a mere alteration of the Civil Constitution, but a dissolution of it. It would thus form a mode of transition to a better Constitution by Palingenesis and not by mere Metamorphosis; and it would require a new Social Contract, upon which the former Original Contract, as then annulled, would have no influence.

It must, however, be possible for the Sovereign to change the existing Constitution, if it is not actually consistent with the Idea of the Original Contract. In doing so it is essential to give existence to that form of Government which will properly constitute the People into a State. Such a change cannot be made by the State deliberately altering its Constitution from one of the three Forms to one of the other two.—For example, political changes should not be carried out by the Aristocrats combining to subject themselves to an Autocracy, or resolving to fuse all into a Democracy, or conversely; as if it depended on the arbitrary choice and liking of the Sovereign what Constitution he may impose on the People. For, even if as Sovereign he resolved to alter the Constitution into a Democracy, he might be doing Wrong to the People, because they might hold such a Constitution in abhorrence, and regard either of the other two as more suitable to them in the circumstances.

The Forms of the State are only the *letter* (*littera*) of the original Constitution in the Civil Union; and they may therefore remain so long as they are considered, from ancient and long habit (and therefore only subjectively), to be necessary to the machinery of the political Constitution. But the *spirit* of that original Contract (*anima pacti originarii*) contains and imposes the obligation on the constituting Power to make the mode of the *Government* conformable to its Idea; and, if this cannot be effected at once, to change it gradually and continuously till it harmonize *in its working* with the only rightful Constitution, which is that of a *Pure Republic*. Thus the old empirical and statutory Forms, which serve only to effect the political *subjection* of the People, will be resolved into the original and rational Forms which alone take Freedom as their principle, and even as the condition of all compulsion and constraint. Compulsion is in fact requisite for the realization of a juridical Constitution, according to the proper idea of the State; and it will lead at last to the realization of that Idea, even according to the letter. This is the only enduring political Constitution, as in it the Law is itself Sovereign, and is no longer attached to a particular person. This is the ultimate End of all Public Right, and the state in which every citizen can have what is his own *peremptorily* assigned to him. But so long as the Form of the State has to be represented, according to the Letter, by many different Moral Persons invested with the Supreme Power, there can only be a *provisory* internal Right, and not an absolutely juridical state of Civil Society.

Every true Republic is and can only be constituted by a *Representative System* of the People. Such a Representative System is instituted in name of the People,

and is constituted by all the Citizens being united together,
in order, by means of their Deputies, to protect and secure
their Rights. But as soon as a Supreme Head of the
State in person—be it as King, or Nobility, or the
whole body of the People in a democratic Union—becomes also representative, the United People then does
not merely *represent* the Sovereignty, but they *are* themselves sovereign. It is in the People that the Supreme
Power originally resides, and it is accordingly from this
Power that all the Rights of individual Citizens as mere
Subjects, and especially as Officials of the State, must be
derived. When the Sovereignty of the People themselves
is thus realized, the Republic is established; and it is no
longer necessary to give up the reins of Government into
the hands of those by whom they have been hitherto held,
especially as they might again destroy all the new Institutions by their arbitrary and absolute Will.

It was therefore a great error in judgment on the
part of a powerful Ruler in our time, when he tried
to extricate himself from the embarrassment arising
from great public debts, by transferring this burden
to the People, and leaving them to undertake and dis-
tribute them among themselves as they might best
think fit. It thus became natural that the Legislative
Power, not only in respect of the Taxation of the
Subjects, but in respect of the Government, should
come into the hands of the People. It was requisite
that they should be able to prevent the incurring of
new Debts by extravagance or war; and in consequence, the Supreme Power of the Monarch entirely
disappeared, not by being merely suspended, but by
passing over in fact to the People, to whose legislative
Will the property of every Subject thus became subjected. Nor can it be said that a tacit and yet
obligatory promise must be assumed as having, under

PUBLIC RIGHT.

II.

The Right of Nations and International Law.

(Jus Gentium.)

53.

Nature and Division of the Right of Nations.

The individuals, who make up a People, may be regarded as Natives of the Country sprung by natural descent from a Common Ancestry (*congeniti*), although this may not hold entirely true in detail. Again, they may be viewed according to the intellectual and juridical relation, as born of a common political Mother, the Republic, so that they constitute, as it were, a public Family or NATION (*gens, natio*) whose Members are all related to each other as Citizens of the State. As members of a State, they do not mix with those who live beside them in the state of Nature, considering such to be ignoble. Yet these savages, on account of the lawless freedom they have chosen, regard themselves as superior to civilised peoples; and they constitute tribes and even races, but not States.—The public Right of *States* (*jus publicum Civitatum*) in their relations to one another, is what we have to consider under the designation of the 'Right of Nations.' Wherever a State, viewed as a Moral Person, acts in relation to another existing in the condition of natural freedom, and consequently in a state of continual war, such Right takes it rise.

The Right of Nations in relation to the State of War may be divided into: 1. The Right of *going to* War; 2. Right *during* War; and 3. Right *after* War, the object of which is to constrain the nations mutually to pass from this state of war, and to found a common Constitution establishing Perpetual Peace. The difference between the Right of individual men or families as related to each other in the state of Nature, and the Right of the Nations among themselves, consists in this, that in the Right of Nations we have to consider not merely a relation of one State to another as a whole, but also the relation of the individual persons in one State to the individuals of another State, as well as to that State as a whole. This difference, however, between the Right of Nations and the Right of Individuals in the mere State of Nature, requires to be determined by elements which can easily be deduced from the conception of the latter.

54.

Elements of the Right of Nations.

The elements of the Right of Nations are as follow:—

1. STATES, viewed as NATIONS, in their external relations to one another — like lawless savages — are naturally in a non-juridical condition;

2. This natural condition is a STATE OF WAR in which the Right of the stronger prevails; and although it may not in fact be always found as a state of actual

war and incessant hostility, and although no real wrong is done to any one therein, yet the condition is wrong in itself in the highest degree, and the Nations which form States contiguous to each other are bound mutually to pass out of it;

3. An ALLIANCE OF NATIONS, in accordance with the idea of an original Social Contract, is necessary to protect each other against external aggression and attack, but not involving interference with their several internal difficulties and disputes;

4. This mutual connection by Alliance must dispense with a distinct Sovereign Power, such as is set up in the Civil Constitution; it can only take the form of a FEDERATION, which as such may be revoked on any occasion, and must consequently be renewed from time to time.

This is therefore a Right which comes in as an accessory (*in subsidium*) of another original Right, in order to prevent the Nations from falling from Right, and lapsing into the state of actual war with each other. It thus issues in the idea of a *Fœdus Amphictyonum*.

55.

Right of Going to War as related to the Subjects of the State.

We have then to consider, in the first place, the original Right of free States *to go to War* with each other as being still in a state of Nature, but as exercising this Right in order to establish some condition of society approaching the juridical state. And, first of all, the question arises as to what Right the State has in *relation to its own Subjects*, to use them in order to make war against other States, to employ their property and even their lives for this purpose, or at least to expose them to hazard and danger; and all this in such a way that it does not depend upon their own personal judgment whether they will march into the field of war or not, but the Supreme Command of the Sovereign claims to settle and dispose of them thus.

This Right appears capable of being easily established. It may be grounded upon the Right which every one has to do with what is his own as he will. Whatever one has *made* substantially for himself, he holds as his incontestable property. The following, then, is such a deduction as a mere Jurist would put forward.

There are various *natural Products* in a country which, as regards the *number* and *quantity* in which they exist, must be considered as specially *produced* (*artefacta*) by the work of the State; for the country would not yield them to such extent were it not under the Constitution of the State and its regular administrative Government, or if the inhabitants were still living in the State of Nature. Sheep, cattle, domestic fowl,—the most useful of their kind,—swine, and such like, would either be used up as necessary food or destroyed by beasts of prey in the district in which I live, so that they would entirely disappear, or be found in very scant supplies, were it not for the Government securing to the inhabitants their acquisitions and property. This holds likewise of the population itself, as we see in the case of the American deserts; and even were the greatest industry applied in those regions—which is not yet done—there might be but a scanty population. The inhabitants of any country would be but sparsely sown here and there were it not for the protection of Government; because without it they could not spread themselves with their households upon a territory which was always in danger of being devastated by enemies or by wild beasts of prey ; and further, so great a multitude of men as now live in any one country could not otherwise obtain sufficient means of support. Hence, as it can be said of vegetable growths, such as potatoes, as well as of domesticated animals, that because the abundance in which they are found is a *product* of human labour, they may be used, destroyed, and consumed by man ; so it seems that it may be said of the Sovereign as the Supreme Power in the State, that he has the Right to lead his Subjects, as being for the most part productions of his own, to war, as if it were to the chase, and even to march them to the field of battle, as if it were on a pleasure excursion.

This principle of Right may be supposed to float dimly before the mind of the Monarch, and it certainly holds true at least of the lower animals which may become the property of man. But such a principle will not at all apply to men, especially when viewed as citizens who must be regarded as members of the State, with a share in the legislation, and not merely as means for others but as Ends in themselves. As such they must give their free consent, through their representatives, not only to the carrying on of war generally, but to every separate declaration of war ; and it is only under this limiting condition that the State has a Right to demand their services in undertakings so full of danger.

We would therefore deduce this Right rather from the duty of the Sovereign to the people than conversely.

Under this relation the people must be regarded as
having given their sanction; and, having the Right of
voting, they may be considered, although thus passive
in reference to themselves individually, to be active in
so far as they represent the Sovereignty itself.

56.

Right of Going to War in relation to Hostile States.

Viewed as in the state of Nature, the Right of
Nations *to go to War* and to carry on hostilities is the
legitimate way by which they prosecute their Rights by
their own power when they regard themselves as
injured; and this is done because in that state the
method of a juridical *Process*, although the only one
proper to settle such disputes, cannot be adopted.

The *threatening of War* is to be distinguished from
the active injury of a first Aggression, which again is
distinguished from the general outbreak of Hostilities.
A threat or menace may be given by the active preparation of *Armaments,* upon which a Right of Prevention (*jus præventionis*) is founded on the other side, or
merely by the *formidable increase* of the power of another
State (*potestas tremenda*) by acquisition of Territory. Lesion
of a less powerful country may be involved merely in
the condition of a more powerful neighbour *prior* to any
action at all; and in the State of Nature an attack
under such circumstances would be warrantable. This
international relation is the foundation of the Right of
Equilibrium, or of the 'balance of Power,' among all
the States that are in active contiguity to each other.

The *Right to go to War* is constituted by any overt
act of Injury. This includes any arbitrary Retaliation

or act of *Reprisal* (*retorsio*) as a satisfaction taken by one people for an offence committed by another, without any attempt being made to obtain reparation in a peaceful way.   Such an act of retaliation would be similar in kind to an outbreak of hostilities without a previous Declaration of War.   For if there is to be any Right at all during the state of war, something analogous to a Contract must be assumed, involving *acceptance* on the one side of the declaration on the other, and amounting to the fact that they both will to seek their Right in this way.

57.

Right during War.

The determination of what constitutes Right *in* War, is the most difficult problem of the Right of Nations and International Law.   It is very difficult even to form a conception of such a Right, or to think of any Law in this lawless state without falling into a contradiction. *Inter arma silent leges.*   It must then be just the right to carry on War according to such principles as render it always still possible to pass out of that natural condition of the states in their external relations to each other, and to enter into a condition of Right.

No war of independent States against each other, can rightly be a war of Punishment (*bellum punitivum*).   For punishment is only in place under the relation of a Superior (*imperantis*) to a Subject (*subditum*); and this is not the relation of the States to one another.   Neither can an international war be ' a war of Extermination ' (*bellum internicinum*), nor even ' a war of Subjugation ' (*bellum subjugatorium*); for this would issue in the moral extinction of a State by its people being either fused into one mass with the conquering State, or being reduced to slavery. Not that this necessary means of attaining to a condition of peace is itself contradictory to the right of a State; but because the idea of the Right of Nations includes merely the conception of an antagonism that is in accordance with principles of external freedom, in order that the State may maintain what is properly its own, but not that it may acquire a condition which, from the aggrandizement of its power, might become threatening to other States.

Defensive measures and means of all kinds are allowable to a State that is forced to war, except such as by their use would make the Subjects using them unfit to be citizens; for the State would thus make itself unfit to be regarded as a person capable of participating in equal rights in the international relations according to the Right of Nations. Among these forbidden means are to be reckoned the appointment of Subjects to act as spies, or engaging Subjects or even strangers to act as assassins, or poisoners (in which class might well be included the so-called sharpshooters who lurk in ambush for individuals), or even employing agents to spread false news. In a word, it is forbidden to use any such malignant and perfidious means as would destroy the confidence which would be requisite to establish a lasting peace thereafter.

It is permissible in war to impose exactions and contributions upon a conquered enemy; but it is not legitimate to plunder the people in the way of forcibly depriving individuals of their property. For this would be robbery, seeing it was not the conquered people but the State under whose government they were placed that

carried on the war by means of them. All exactions
should be raised by regular *Requisition,* and Receipts
ought to be given for them, in order that when peace
is restored the burden imposed on the country or the
province may be proportionately borne.

58.

Right after War.

The Right that follows *after* War, begins at the
moment of the Treaty of Peace and refers to the consequences of the war.   The conqueror lays down the
conditions under which he will agree with the conquered
power to form the conclusion of Peace.   Treaties are
drawn up; not indeed according to any Right that it
pertains to him to protect, on account of an alleged
lesion by his opponent, but as taking this question upon
himself, he bases the right to decide it upon his own
power.   Hence the conqueror may not demand restitu-
tion of the cost of the war; because he would then have
to declare the war of his opponent to be unjust.   And
even although he should adopt such an argument, he is
not entitled to apply it; because he would have to
declare the war to be punitive, and he would thus in
turn inflict an injury.   To this right belongs also the
Exchange of Prisoners, which is to be carried out without
ransom and without regard to equality of numbers.

Neither the conquered State nor its Subjects, lose
their political liberty by conquest of the country, so as
that the former should be degraded to a colony, or the
latter to slaves; for otherwise it would have been a
penal war, which is contradictory in itself.   *A colony* or
a province is constituted by a people which has its own

constitution, legislation, and territory, where persons belonging to another State are merely strangers, but which is nevertheless subject to the supreme *executive* power of another State.   This other State is called the 'mother-country.'   It is ruled as a daughter, but has at the same time its own form of government, as in a separate Parliament under the presidency of a Viceroy (*civitas hybrida*). Such was Athens in relation to different islands; and such is at present [1796] the relation of Great Britain to Ireland.

Still less can *Slavery* be deduced as a rightful institution, from the conquest of a people in war; for this would assume that the war was of a punitive nature. And least of all can a basis be found in war for a *hereditary* Slavery, which is absurd in itself, since guilt cannot be inherited from the criminality of another.

Further, that an *Amnesty* is involved in the conclusion of a Treaty of Peace, is already implied in the very idea of a Peace.

59.

The Rights of Peace.

The Rights of Peace are :—

1. The Right to be in Peace when War is in the neighbourhood, or the Right of *Neutrality*.

2. The Right to have Peace secured so that it may continue when it has been concluded, that is, the Right of *Guarantee*.

3. The Right of the several States to enter into a mutual *Alliance*, so as to *defend* themselves in common against all external or even internal attacks.   This Right of Federation, however, does not extend to the formation

of any League for external aggression or internal aggrandizement.

60.

Right as against an Unjust Enemy.

The Right of a State against an *unjust* Enemy has no
limits, at least in respect of quality as distinguished from
quantity or degree.   In other words, the injured State
may use—not, indeed, *any* means, but yet—all those
means that are permissible and in reasonable measure in
so far as they are in its power, in order to assert its
Right to what is its own.   But what then is an *unjust*
enemy according to the conceptions of the Right of
Nations, when, as holds generally of the state of Nature,
every State is judge in its own cause ?   It is one whose
publicly expressed Will, whether in word or deed, betrays
a maxim which, if it were taken as a universal rule,
would make a state of Peace among the nations impossible, and would necessarily perpetuate the state of
Nature.   Such is the violation of public Treaties, with
regard to which it may be assumed that any such
violation concerns all nations by threatening their freedom, and that they are thus summoned to unite against
such a wrong, and to take away the power of committing
it.   But this does not include the Right *to partition and
appropriate the country,* so as to make a State as it were
disappear from the earth ; for this would be an injustice
to the people of that State, who cannot lose their original
Right to unite into a Commonwealth, and to adopt such
a new Constitution as by its nature would be unfavour-
able to the inclination for war.

Further, it may be said that the expression 'an unjust
enemy in the state of Nature' is *pleonastic ;* for the state

of Nature is itself a state of injustice. A just Enemy would be one to whom I would do wrong in offering resistance; but such a one would really not be my Enemy.

61.

Perpetual Peace and a Permanent Congress of Nations.

The natural state of Nations as well as of individual men is a state which it is a duty to pass out of, in order to enter into a legal state. Hence, before this transition occurs, all the Right of Nations and all the external property of States acquirable or maintainable by war, are merely *provisory ;* and they can only become *peremptory* in a universal Union of States analogous to that by which a Nation becomes a State. It is thus only that a real *state of Peace* could be established. But with the too great extension of such a Union of States over vast regions any government of it, and consequently the protection of its individual members, must at last become impossible; and thus a multitude of such corporations would again bring round a state of war. Hence the *Perpetual Peace*, which is the ultimate end of all the Right of Nations, becomes in fact an impracticable idea. The political principles, however, which aim at such an end, and which enjoin the formation of such unions among the States as may promote a continuous *approximation* to a Perpetual Peace, are not impracticable; they are as practicable as this approximation itself, which is a practical problem involving a duty, and founded upon the Right of individual men and States.

Such a *Union of States,* in order to maintain Peace, may be called a *Permanent Congress of Nations;* and it

is free to every neighbouring State to join in it.   A
union of this kind, so far at least as regards the formalities of the Right of Nations in respect of the
preservation of peace, was presented in the first half
of this century, in the Assembly of the States-General
at the Hague.   In this Assembly most of the European
Courts, and even the smallest Republics, brought forward
their complaints about the hostilities which were carried
on by the one against the other.   Thus the whole of
Europe appeared like a single Federated State, accepted
as Umpire by the several nations in their public differences.   But in place of this agreement, the Right of
Nations afterwards survived only in books; it disappeared from the cabinets, or, after force had been
already used, it was relegated in the form of theoretical
deductions to the obscurity of Archives.

By such a *Congress* is here meant only a voluntary
combination of different States that would be *dissoluble*
at any time, and not such a union as is embodied in the
United States of America, founded upon a political constitution, and therefore indissoluble.   It is only by a
Congress of this kind that the idea of a Public Right
of Nations can be established, and that the settlement
of their differences by the mode of a civil process, and
not by the barbarous means of war, can be realized.

PUBLIC RIGHT.

III.

The Universal Right of Mankind.

(Jus cosmopoliticum.)

62.

Nature and Conditions of Cosmopolitical Right.

The rational idea of a universal, *peaceful,* if not yet friendly, Union of all the Nations upon the earth that may come into active relations with each other, is a *juridical* Principle, as distinguished from philanthropic or ethical principles. Nature has enclosed them altogether within definite boundaries, in virtue of the spherical form of their abode as a *globus terraqueus;* and the possession of the soil upon which an inhabitant of the earth may live, can only be regarded as possession of a part of a limited whole, and consequently as a part to which every one has originally a Right. Hence all nations *originally* hold a community of the soil, but not a *juridical* community of possession (*communio*), nor consequently of the use or proprietorship of the soil, but only of a possible physical *intercourse* (*commercium*) by means of it. In other words, they are placed in such thoroughgoing relations of each to all the rest, that they may claim to enter into *intercourse* with one another, and they have a right to make an attempt in this direction, while a foreign nation would not be entitled to treat them on this account as enemies. This Right, in so far as it relates to a possible Union of all Nations, in respect of certain laws universally regulating their intercourse with each other, may be called 'Cosmopolitical Right' (*jus cosmopoliticum*).

It may appear that seas put nations out of all communion with each other. But this is not so; for by means of commerce, seas form the happiest natural provision for their intercourse. And the more there are of neighbouring coast - lands, as in the case of the Mediterranean Sea, this intercourse becomes the more animated. And hence communications with such lands, especially where there are settlements upon them connected with the mother countries giving occasion for such communications, bring it about that evil and violence committed in one place of our globe are felt in all. Such possible abuse cannot, however, annul the Right of man as a citizen of the world to *attempt* to enter into communion with all others, and for this purpose to *visit* all the regions of the earth, although this does not constitute a right of *settlement* upon the territory of another people (*jus incolatus*), for which a special contract is required.

But the question is raised as to whether, in the case of newly discovered countries, a people may claim the right to settle (*accolatus*), and to occupy possessions in the neighbourhood of another people that has already settled in that region; and to do this without their consent.

Such a Right is indubitable, if the new settlement takes place at such a distance from the seat of the

former, that neither would restrict or injure the other in
the use of their territory.   But in the case of nomadic
peoples, or tribes of shepherds and hunters (such as the
Hottentots, the Tungusi, and most of the American
Indians), whose support is derived from wide desert
tracts, such occupation should never take place by force,
but only by contract; and any such contract ought never
to take advantage of the ignorance of the original
dwellers in regard to the cession of their lands.   Yet
it is commonly alleged that such acts of violent appropriation may be justified as subserving the general good
of the world.   It appears as if sufficiently justifying
grounds were furnished for them, partly by reference to
the civilisation of barbarous peoples (as by a pretext
of this kind even Busching tries to excuse the bloody
introduction of the Christian religion into Germany), and
partly by founding upon the necessity of purging one's
own country from depraved criminals, and the hope of
their improvement or that of their posterity, in another
continent like New Holland.   But all these alleged good
purposes cannot wash out the stain of injustice in the
means employed to attain them.   It may be objected
that had such scrupulousness about making a beginning
in founding a legal State with force been always maintained, the whole earth would still have been in a state
of lawlessness.   But such an objection would as little
annul the conditions of Right in question as the pretext of the political revolutionaries, that when a constitution has become degenerate, it belongs to the people
to transform it by force.   This would amount generally
to being unjust once and for all, in order thereafter to
found justice the more surely, and to make it flourish.

CONCLUSION.

———0———

IF one cannot prove that a thing *is*, he may try to prove that it is *not*. And if he succeeds in doing neither (as often occurs), he may still ask whether it is in his *interest* to *accept* one or other of the alternatives hypothetically, from the theoretical or the practical point of view. In other words, a hypothesis may be accepted either in order to explain a certain Phenomenon (as in Astronomy to account for the retrogression and stationariness of the planets), or in order to attain a certain end, which again may be either *pragmatic* as belonging merely to the sphere of Art, or *moral* as involving a purpose which it is a duty to adopt as a maxim of action. Now it is evident that the assumption (*suppositio*) of the practicability of such an End, though presented merely as a theoretical and problematical judgment, may be regarded as constituting a duty; and hence it is so regarded in this case. For although there may be no positive obligation to believe in such an End, yet even if there were not the least theoretical probability of action being carried out in accordance with it, so long as its impossibility cannot be demonstrated, there still remains a duty incumbent upon us with regard to it.

Now, as a matter of fact, the morally practical Reason

utters within us its irrevocable *Veto : ' There shall be no War.'* So there ought to be no war, neither between me and you in the condition of Nature, nor between us as members of States which, although internally in a condition of law, are still externally in their relation to each other in a condition of lawlessness ; for this is not the way by which any one should prosecute his Right. Hence the question no longer is as to whether Perpetual Peace is a real thing or not a real thing, or as to whether we may not be deceiving ourselves when we adopt the former alternative, but we must *act* on the supposition of its being real. We must work for what may perhaps not be realized, and establish that Constitution which yet seems best adapted to bring it about (mayhap Republicanism in all States, together and separately). And thus we may put an end to the evil of wars, which have been the chief interest of the internal arrangements of all the States without exception. And although the realization of this purpose may always remain but a pious wish, yet we do certainly not deceive ourselves in adopting the maxim of action that will guide us in working incessantly for it ; for it is a duty to do this. To suppose that the moral Law within us is itself deceptive, would be sufficient to excite the horrible wish rather to be deprived of all Reason than to live under such deception, and even to see oneself, according to such principles, degraded like the lower animals to the level of the mechanical play of Nature.

It may be said that the universal and lasting establishment of Peace constitutes not merely a part, but the whole final purpose and End of the Science of Right as viewed within the limits of Reason. The state of Peace is the only condition of the Mine and Thine that is secured and guaranteed by *Laws* in the relationship of men living in numbers contiguous to each other, and who are thus combined in a Constitution whose rule is derived not from the mere experience of those who have found it the best as a normal guide for others, but which must be taken by the Reason *à priori* from the ideal of a juridical Union of men under public laws generally. For all particular examples or instances, being able only to furnish illustration but not proof, are deceptive, and at all events require a Metaphysic to establish them by its necessary principles. And this is conceded indirectly even by those who turn Metaphysics into ridicule, when they say, as they often do, 'The best Constitution is that in which not Men but Laws exercise the power.' For what can be more metaphysically sublime in its own way than this very Idea of theirs, which according to their own assertion has, notwithstanding, the most objective reality? This may be easily shown by reference to actual instances. And it is this very Idea which alone can be carried out practically, if it is not forced on in a revolutionary and sudden way by violent overthrow of the existing defective Constitution; for this would produce for the time the momentary annihilation of the whole juridical state of Society. But if the idea is carried forward by gradual Reform, and in accordance with fixed Principles, it may lead by a continuous approximation to the highest political Good, and to Perpetual Peace.

SUPPLEMENTARY EXPLANATIONS

OF THE

PRINCIPLES OF RIGHT.

[Written by Kant in 1797, and added to the
Second Edition in 1798.]

SUPPLEMENTARY EXPLANATIONS OF THE PRINCIPLES OF RIGHT.

The Occasion for these Explanations was furnished mainly by a Review of this work that appeared in the *Göttingen Journal*, No. 28, of 18th February 1797. The Review displays insight, and with sympathetic appreciation it expresses 'the hope that this Exposition of Principles will prove a permanent gain for juridical Science.' It is here taken as a guide in the arrangement of some critical Remarks, and at the same time as suggesting some expansion of the system in certain points of detail.

Objection as to the Faculty of Desire.

In the very first words of the GENERAL INTRODUCTION the acute Reviewer stumbles on a Definition. He asks what is meant by 'the Faculty of Desire.' In the said Introduction it is defined as 'the Power which Man has, through his mental representations, of becoming the cause of objects corresponding to these representations.' To this Definition the objection is taken, 'that it amounts to nothing as soon as we abstract from the *external* conditions of the effect or consequence of the act of Desire.' 'But the Faculty of Desire,' it is added, 'is something even to the Idealist, although there is no external world according to his view.'—ANSWER: Is there not likewise a violent and yet consciously ineffective form of Desire as a mere mental longing, which is expressed by such words as ' Would to God such a one were still alive ! ' Yet although this Desire is *actless* in the sense of not issuing in overt action, it is not *effectless* in the sense of having no consequence at all ; in short, if it does not produce a change on external things, it at least works powerfully upon the internal condition of the Subject, and even may superinduce a morbid condition of disease. A Desire, viewed as an *active Striving (nisus)* to be a *cause* by means of one's own mental representations, even although the individual may perceive his incapacity to attain the desired effect, is still a mode of causality within his own internal experience.—There is therefore a misunderstanding involved in the objection, that because the consciousness of one's *Power* in a case of Desire may be at the same time accompanied with a consciousness of the *Want of Power* in respect of the external world, the definition is therefore not applicable to the Idealist. But as the question only turns generally upon the relation of a Cause (the Representation) to an Effect (the Feeling), the Causality of the Representation in respect of its object—whether it be external or internal—must inevitably be included by thought in the conception of the Faculty of Desire.

I.

Logical Preparation for the Preceding Conception of Right.

If philosophical Jurists would rise to the Metaphysical Principles of the Science of Right, without which all their juridical Science will be merely statutory, they must not be indifferent to securing completeness in the *Division* of their juridical conceptions. Apart from such internal completeness their science would not be a *rational System*, but only an Aggregate of accidental details. The *topical* arrangement of Principles as determined by the form of the System, must therefore be made complete ; that is to say, there must be a proper *place* assigned to each conception (*locus communis*) as determined by the synthetic form of the Division. And it would have to be afterwards made apparent that when any other conception were put in the place of the one thus assigned, it would be contradictory to itself and out of its own place.

Now Jurists have hitherto received only two formal commonplaces in their Systems, namely, the conceptions of *Real Right* and of *Personal Right*. But since there are other two conceptions possible even *à priori* by a mere formal combination of these two as members of a rational Division, giving the conception of a Personal Right of a Real Kind, and that of a Real Right of a Personal Kind, — it is natural to ask whether these further conceptions, although viewed as only problematical in themselves, should not likewise be incorporated in the scheme of a complete Division of the juridical System ? This in fact does not admit of doubt. The merely logical Division, indeed, as abstracting from the object of Knowledge, is always in the form of *a Dichotomy* ; so that every Right is either a Real or a not-Real Right. But the metaphysical Division, here under consideration, may also be in the fourfold form of a *Tetrachotomy* ; for in addition to the two simple members of the Division, there are also two relations between them, as conditions of mutual limitation arising from the one Right entering into combination with the other ; and the possibility of this requires a special investigation.—But the conception of *a Real Right of a Personal Kind* falls out at once ; for the Right of a *Thing* as against a *Person* is inconceivable. It remains, therefore, only to consider, whether the converse of this relation is likewise inconceivable ; *or* whether the conception of *a Personal Right of a Real Kind* is not only free from internal contradiction, but is even contained *à priori* in Reason and belongs as a necessary constituent to the conception of the external Mine and Thine in its completeness, in order that *Persons* may be viewed so far in the same way as Things ; not indeed to the extent of *treating* them in all respects alike, but by regard to the *possession* of them, and to proceeding with Persons in certain relations as if they were Things.

II.

Justification of the Conception of a Personal Right of a Real Kind.

The Definition of a Personal Right of a Real Kind may be put shortly and appropriately thus : ' it is the Right which a man has to have another *Person* than himself as *his.*' I say intentionally a ' Person ;' for one might have another *man* who had lost his civil personality and become enslaved as *his ;* but such a Real Right is not under consideration here.

Now we have to examine the question whether this conception—described as ' a new phenomenon in the juristic sky '—is a *stella mirabilis* in the sense of growing into a star of the first magnitude, unseen before but gradually vanishing again, yet perhaps destined to return, or whether it is to be regarded as merely a shooting and falling star ! [1]

III.

Examples of Real-Personal Right.

1. To have anything external as one's own, means to possess it rightfully; and Possession is the condition of the possibility of using a thing. If this condition is regarded merely as physical, the possession is called *detention* or holding. But legal detention alone does not suffice to make an object mine, or to entitle me so to regard it. If, however, I am entitled, on any ground whatever, to press for the possession of an object which has escaped from my power or been taken from me, this conception of right is a sign in effect that I hold myself entitled to conduct myself towards it as being mine and in my rational possession, and so to use it as my object.

The 'Mine' in this connection does not mean that it is constituted by ownership of the Person of another; for a man cannot even be the owner of himself, and much less of another person. It means only the right of Usufruct (*jus utendi fruendi*) in immediate reference to this person, as if he were a thing, but without infring-

---

[1] According to the Definition, I do not use the expression 'to have another *Person* as *my Person*,' but as '*mine*' (τὸ *meum*), as if the Person were viewed in this relation as a Thing. For I can say 'this is *my father*' in indicating my natural relationship of connection with him, by which I merely state that I *have* a father. But I may not say 'I have him as *mine*' in this relation. However, if I say '*my Wife*,' this indicates a special juridical relation of a possessor to an object viewed as a thing, although in this case it is a person. But physical possession is the condition of the use of a thing as such (*manipulatio*); although in another relation the object must at the same time be treated as a Person.

ing on the right of his personality, even while using him as a means for my own ends.

These ends, however, as conditioning the rightfulness of such use, must necessarily be moral. A man may neither desire a wife in order to enjoy her as if she were a thing by the immediate pleasure in mere physical intercourse, nor may the wife surrender herself for this purpose; for otherwise the rights of personality would be given up on both sides. In other words, it is only under the condition of a marriage having been previously concluded that there can be such a reciprocal surrender of the two persons into the possession of each other that they will not dehumanize themselves by making a corporeal use of each other.

When this condition is not respected, the carnal enjoyment referred to, is in principle, although not always in effect, on the level of cannibalism. There is merely a difference in the manner of the enjoyment between the exhaustion which may thus be produced and the consumption of bodies by the teeth and maw of the savage; and in such reciprocal use of the sexes the one is really made a *res fungibilis* to the other. Hence a contract that would bind any one for such mere use would be an illegal contract (*pactum turpe*).

2. In like manner, a husband and wife cannot produce a child as their mutual offspring (*res artificialis*) without both coming under the obligation towards it and towards each other to maintain it as their child. This relation accordingly involves the acquisition of a human being as if it were a thing, but it holds only in form according to the idea of a merely Personal Right of a real kind. The parents have a Right against any possessor of the child who may have taken it out of their power (*jus in*

re), and they have likewise a Right to compel the child
to perform and obey all their commands in so far as
they are not opposed to any law of freedom (*jus ad
rem*) ; and hence they have also a Personal Right over
the child.

3. Finally, if, on attaining the age of majority, the
duty of the parents in regard to the maintenance of
their children ceases, they have still the Right to use
them as members of the house subjected to their
authority, in order to maintain the household until
they are released from parental control. This Right of
the parents follows from the natural limitation of the
former Right. Until the children attain maturity, they
belong as members of the household to the *family ;* but
thereafter they may belong to the *domestics (famulatus)*
as servants of the household, and they can enter into
this relation only by a contract whereby they are bound
to the master of the house as his domestics. In like
manner, a relation of master and servant may be formed
outside of the family, in accordance with a personal right
of a real kind on the part of the master ; and the
domestics are acquired to the household by contract
(*famulatus domesticus*). Such a contract is not a mere
letting and hiring of work (*locatio conductio operæ*) ;
but it further includes the giving of the person of the
domestic into the possession of the master, as a letting
and hiring of the person (*locatio conductio personæ*). The
latter relation is distinguished from the former in that
the domestic enters the contract on the understanding
that he will be available for everything that is allowable
in respect of the well-being of the household, and is not
merely engaged for a certain assigned and specified piece
of work. On the other hand, an artisan or a day-

labourer who is hired for a specific piece of work, does not give himself into the possession of another, nor is he therefore a member of his household. As the latter is not in the legal possession of his employer, who has bound him only to perform certain things, the employer, even though he should have him dwelling in his house (*inquilinus*), is not entitled to *seize* him as a thing (*via facti*), but must press for the performance of his engagement on the ground of personal right, by the legal means that are at his command (*via juris*).

So much, then, for the explanation and vindication of this new Title of Right in the Science of Natural Law, which may at first appear strange, but which has nevertheless been always tacitly in use.

IV.

Confusion of Real and Personal Right.

The proposition 'Purchase breaks Hire' (§ 31, p. 131) has further been objected to as a heterodoxy in the doctrine of Natural Private Right.   It certainly appears at first sight to be contrary to all the Rights of contract, that any one should intimate the termination of the lease of a house to the present Lessee before the expiry of the period of occupation agreed upon ; and that the former can thus, as it appears, break his promise to the latter, if he only gives him the usual warning determined by the customary and legal practice.   But let it be supposed that it can be proved that the Lessee when he entered upon his contract of hire knew, or must have known, that the promise given to him by the Lessor or proprietor was naturally (without needing to be expressly stated in the contract, and therefore *tacitly*) connected with the condition '*in so far as he should not sell his house within this time,* or might have to renounce it on the occasion of an action on the part of his creditors.' On this supposition the Lessor does not break his promise, which is already conditioned in itself according to reason, and the Lessee does not suffer any infringement of his Right by such an intimation being made to him before the period of lease has expired. For the Right of the latter arising from the contract of hire, is a *Personal* Right to what a certain person has to perform for another (*jus ad rem*); it is not a *Real* Right (*jus in re*) that holds against every possessor of the thing.

The Lessee might indeed secure himself in his lease and acquire a Real Right in the house; but he could do this only by having it *engrossed* by a reference to the house of the Lessor as attached to the soil. In this way he would provide against being dispossessed before the expiry of the time agreed upon, either by the intimation of the proprietor or by his natural death, or even by his civil death as a bankrupt. If he did not do this, because he would rather be free to conclude another lease on better conditions, or because the proprietor would not have such a burden (*onus*) upon his house, it is to be inferred that, in respect of the period of intimation, both parties were conscious of having made a tacit contract to dissolve their relation at any time, according to their convenience, —subject, however, to the conditions determined by the municipal law. The confirmation of the Right to break hire by purchase, may be further shown by certain juridical consequences that follow from such a naked contract of hire as is here under consideration. Thus the Heirs of the Lessee when he dies should not have the obligation imposed upon them to continue the hire, because it is only an obligation as against a certain person and should cease with his death, although here again the legal period of intimation must be always kept in view.   The right of the Lessee as such can thus only pass to his heirs by a special contract.   Nor, for the same reason, is he entitled even during the life of both parties, to *sublet* to others what he has hired for himself, without express agreement to that effect.

V.

Addition to the Explanation of the Conceptions of Penal Right.

The mere idea of a political Constitution among *men* involves the conception of a *punitive* Justice as belonging to the supreme Power.   The only question, then, is to consider whether the legislator may be indifferent to the *modes* of punishment, if they are only available as means for the removal of crime, regarded as a violation of the Security of property in the State ; or whether he must also have regard to respect for the Humanity in the person of the criminal, as related to the species ; and if this latter alternative holds, whether he is to be guided by pure principles of Right, taking the *jus talionis* as in form the only *à priori* idea and determining principle of Penal Right, rather than any generalization from experience as to the remedial measures most effective for his purpose.   But if this is so, it will then be asked how he would proceed in the case of crimes which do not admit of the application of this Principle of *Retaliation,* as being either impossible in itself, or as in the circumstances involving the perpetration of a penal offence against Humanity generally.   Such, in particular, are the relations of rape, pæderasty, and bestiality. The former two would have to be punished by castration (after the manner of the white or black eunuchs in a seraglio), and the last by expulsion for ever from civil society, because the individual has made himself unworthy of human relations. *Per quod quis peccat per idem punitur et idem.* These crimes are called unnatural, because they are committed against all that is essential to Humanity. To punish them by *arbitrary* penalties, is literally opposed to the conception of a *penal* Justice. But even then the criminal cannot complain that wrong is done to him, since his own evil deed draws the punishment upon himself; and he only experiences what is in accordance with the spirit, if not the letter, of the penal Law which he has broken in his relation to others.

Every punishment implies something that is rightly degrading to the feeling of honour of the party condemned. For it contains a mere one-sided compulsion. Thus his dignity as a citizen is suspended, at least in a particular instance, by his being subjected to an external obligation of duty, to which he may not oppose resistance on his side. Men of rank and wealth, when mulcted in a fine, feel the humiliation of being compelled to bend under the will of an inferior in position, more than the loss of the money. Punitive Justice (*justitia punitiva*), in which the ground of the penalty is *moral* (*quia peccatum est*), must be distinguished from punitive *Expediency*, the foundation of which is merely pragmatic (*ne peccetur*) as being grounded upon the experience of what operates most effectively to prevent crime. It has consequently an entirely distinct place (*locus justi*) in the topical arrangement of the juridical conceptions. It is neither the conception of what is *conducible* to a certain effect (*conducibilis*), nor even that of the pure *Honestum*, which must be properly placed in Ethics.

VI.

On the Right of Usucapion.

Referring to § 33, p. 133, it is said that 'the Right of *Usucapion* ought to be founded on natural right; for if it were not assumed that an *ideal acquisition*, as it is here called, is established by *bona fide* possession, no acquisition would be ever peremptorily secured.'—But I assume a merely provisory acquisition in the state of nature; and, for this reason, insist upon the juridical necessity of the civil constitution.—Further, it is said, ' I assert myself as *bona fide* possessor only against any one who cannot prove that he was *bona fide* possessor of the same thing before me, and who has not ceased by his own will to be such.' But the question here under consideration is not as to whether I can assert myself as owner of a thing although another should put in a claim as an earlier real owner of it, the cognizance of his existence as possessor and of his possessorship as owner having been absolutely impossible; which case occurs when such a one has given no publicly valid indication of his uninterrupted possession,— whether owing to his own fault or not,—as by Registration in public Records, or uncontested voting as owner of the property in civil Assemblies.

The question really under consideration is this : Who is the party that ought to prove his rightful Acquisition ? This obligation as an *onus probandi* cannot be imposed upon the actual Possessor, for he is in possession of the thing so far back as his authenticated history reaches

The former alleged owner of it is, however, entirely separated, according to juridical principles, from the series of
successive possessors by an interval of time within which
he gave no publicly valid indications of his ownership.
This intromission or discontinuance of all public possessory activity reduces him to an untitled claimant. But
here, as in theology, the maxim holds that *conservatio est
continua creatio.* And although a claimant, hitherto
unmanifested but now provided with discovered documentary evidence, should afterwards arise, the doubt
again would come up with regard to him as to whether
a still older claimant might not yet appear and found
a claim upon even earlier possession.—Mere *length of
time* in possession effects nothing here in the way of
finally *acquiring* a thing (*acquirere per usucapionem*).
For it is absurd to suppose that what is wrong, by being
long continued, would at last become right. The use of
the thing, be it ever so long, thus presupposes a Right in
it ; whereas the latter cannot be founded upon the former.
Hence *Usucapion,* viewed as acquisition of a thing merely
by long use of it, is a contradictory conception. The
prescription of claims, as a mode of securing possession
(*conservatio possessionis meæ per præscriptionem*), is not
less contradictory, although it is a different conception as
regards the basis of appropriation. It is in fact a
negative Principle ; and it takes the complete *disuse* of
a Right, even such as is necessary to manifest possessorship, as equivalent to a *renunciation* of the thing (*dere-
lictio*). But such renunciation is a juridical act, and it
implies the use of the Right against another, in order
to exclude him by any claim (*per perscriptionem*) from
acquiring the object ; which involves a contradiction.

I acquire therefore without probation, and without any

juridical act; I do not require to prove, but I acquire by the law (*lege*). What then do I acquire? The *public* release from all further claims; that is, *the legal security of my possession* in virtue of the fact that I do not require to bring forward the proof of it, and may now found upon uninterrupted possession. And the fact that all *Acquisition* in the state of Nature is merely provisory, has no influence upon the question of Security in the *Possession* of what has been acquired, this consideration necessarily taking precedence before the former.

VII.

On Inheritance and Succession.

As regards the ' Right of Inheritance,' the acuteness of the Reviewer has here failed him, and he has not reached the nerve of the proof of my position. I do *not* say (§ 34, p. 136) that 'every man necessarily accepts every *thing that is offered* to him, when by such acceptance he can only gain and can lose nothing;' for there are no things of such a kind. But what I say is, that every one always in fact accepts *the Right of the offer* of the thing, at the moment in which it is offered, inevitably and tacitly, but yet validly; that is, when the circumstances are such that revocation of the offer is impossible, as at the moment of the Testator's death. For the Promiser cannot then recall the offer; and the nominated Beneficiary, without the intervention of any juridical act, becomes at the moment the acceptor, not of the promised inheritance, but of the Right to accept it or decline it. At that moment he sees himself, on the opening of the Testament and before any acceptance of the inheritance, become possessed of more than he was before; for he has acquired exclusively the *Right to accept*, which constitutes an element of property. A Civil state is no doubt here presupposed, in order to make the thing in question the property of *another* person when its former owner is no more; but this transmission of the possession from the hand of the dead (*mort-main*) does not alter the possibility of Acquisition according to the universal Principles of Natural Right, although a Civil Constitution must be assumed in order to apply them to cases of actual experience. A thing which it is in my free choice to accept or to refuse unconditionally, is called a *res jacens*. If the owner of a thing offers me gratuitously a thing of this kind,—as, for instance, the furniture of a house out of which I am about to remove,—or promises it shall be mine, so long as he does not recall his offer or promise, which is impossible if he dies when it is still valid, then I have exclusively a Right to the acceptance of the thing offered (*jus in re jacente*); in other words, I alone can accept or refuse it, as I please. And this Right, exclusively to have the choosing of the thing, I do not obtain by means of a special juridical act, as by a declaration that ' I *will* that this Right shall belong to me;' but I obtain it without any special act on my part, and merely by the law (*lege*). I can therefore declare myself to *this* effect : ' I will *that the thing shall not belong to me*' (for the acceptance of it might bring me into trouble with others). But I cannot will to have exclusively the *choice* as to whether it *shall or shall not belong to me;* for this Right of accepting or of refusing it, I have immediately by virtue of the Offer itself, apart from any declaration of acceptance on my part. If I could refuse even to have the choice, I might choose not to choose; which is a contradiction.   Now this right to choose passes at the moment of the death of the Testator to me ; but although instituted heir by his Will (*institutio hæredis*), I do not yet, in fact, acquire any of the property of the Testator, but merely the *juridical* or rational *possession* of that property or part of it, and I can renounce it for the benefit of others.   Hence this possession is not interrupted for a moment, but the Succession, as in a continuous series, passes by acceptance from the dying Testator to the heir appointed by him ; and thus the proposition *testamenta sunt juris naturæ* is established beyond all dispute.

VIII.

The Right of the State in relation to Perpetual Foundations for the Benefit of the Subjects.

A FOUNDATION (*Sanctio testamentaria beneficii perpetui*) is a voluntary beneficent institution, confirmed by the State and applied for the benefit of certain of its members, so that it is established for all the period of their existence.   It is called *perpetual* when the ordinance establishing it is connected with the Constitution of the State ; for the State must be regarded as instituted for all time.   The beneficence of such a foundation applies either to the people generally, or to a class as a part of the people united by certain particular principles, or to a certain family and their descendants for ever.   Hospitals present an example of the first kind of foundations ; Churches of the second ; the Orders in the State (spiritual and secular) of the third ; Primogeniture and Entail of the fourth.

Of these corporate institutions and their Rights of succession, it is said that they cannot be abolished ; because the Right has been made the property of the appointed heirs in virtue of a *legacy*, and to abrogate such a constitution (*corpus mysticum*) would amount to taking from some one what was his.

A. Hospitals.

Such benevolent institutions as Hospitals and other Foundations for the poor, for invalids, and for the sick, when they have been founded by the property of the State, are certainly to be regarded as indissoluble. But if the spirit, rather than the mere letter, of the will of a private Testator is to form the ground of determination, it may be that circumstances will arise in the course of time such as would make the abolition of such foundations advisable, at least in respect of their form. Thus it has been found that the poor and the sick may be better and more cheaply provided for by giving them the assistance of a certain sum of money proportionate to the wants of the time, and allowing them to board with relatives or friends, than by maintaining them in magnificent and costly institutions like Greenwich Hospital, or other similar institutions which are maintained at great expense and yet impose much restriction on personal liberty. Lunatic asylums, however, must be regarded as exceptions. In abolishing any such institutions in favour of other arrangements, the State cannot be said to be taking from the people the enjoyment of a benefit to which they have a right as their own ; rather does it promote their interest by choosing wiser means for the maintenance of their rights and the advancement of their well-being.

B. Churches.

A spiritual order, like that of the Roman Catholic Church, which does not propagate itself in direct descendants, may, under the favour of the State, possess lands with subjects attached to them, and may constitute a spiritual corporation called the Church. To this corporation the laity may, for the salvation of their souls, bequeath or give lands which are to be the property of the Church. The Roman Clergy have thus in fact acquired possessions which have been legally transmitted from one age to another, and which have been formally confirmed by Papal Bulls. Now, can it be admitted that this relation of the clergy to the laity may be annulled by the supreme power of the secular State; and would not this amount to taking violently from them what was their own, as has been attempted, for example, by the unbelievers of the French Republic?

The question really to be determined here is whether the Church can belong to the State or the State to the Church, in the relation of property; for *two* supreme powers cannot be subordinated to one another without contradiction. It is clear that only the *former consti-tution (politico - hierarchica)*, according to which the property of the Church belongs to the State, can have proper existence; for every Civil Constitution is *of this world*, because it is an earthly human power that can be incorporated with all its consequences and effects in experience. On the other hand, the believers whose *Kingdom* is in Heaven as *the other world*, in so far as a hierarchico-political constitution relating to this world is conceded to them, must submit themselves to the sufferings of the time, under the supreme power of the

men who act in the world.   Hence the former Constitution is only in place.

Religion, as manifested in the form of belief in the
dogmas of the Church and the power of the Priests who
form the aristocracy of such a constitution, even when
it is monarchical and papal, ought not to be forced upon
the people, nor taken from them by any political power.
Neither should the citizen—as is at present the case in
Great Britain with the Irish Nation—be excluded from
the political services of the State, and the advantages
thence arising, on account of a religion that may be
different from that of the Court.

Now, it may be that certain devout and believing
souls, in order to become participators of the grace
which the Church promises to procure for believers even
after their death, establish an institution for all time,
in accordance with which, after their death, certain lands
of theirs shall become the property of the Church.
Further, the State may make itself to a certain extent,
or entirely, the vassal of the Church, in order to obtain
by the prayers, indulgences, and expiations administered
by the clergy as the servants of the Church, participa-
tion in the boon promised in the other world.   But
such a Foundation, although presumably made for all
time, is not really established as a perpetuity; for the
State may throw off any burden thus imposed upon it
by the Church at will.   For the Church itself is an
institution established on faith, and if this faith be an
illusion engendered by mere opinion, and if it disappear
with the enlightenment of the people, the terrible
power of the Clergy founded upon it also falls.   The
State will then, with full right, seize upon the presumed
property of the Church, consisting of the land bestowed

upon it by legacies. However, the feudatories of the hitherto existing institution, may of their own right demand to be indemnified for their life interests.

In like manner, Foundations established for all time, in behoof of the poor as well as educational Institutions even supposing them to have a certain definite character impressed by the idea of their founder, cannot be held as founded for all time, so as to be a burden upon the land. The State must have the liberty to reconstitute them, in accordance with the wants of the time. No one may be surprised that it proves always more and more difficult to carry out such ideas, as for instance a provision that poor foundationers must make up for the inadequacy of the funds of their benevolent institution by singing as mendicants; for it is only natural that one who has founded a beneficent institution should feel a certain desire of glory in connection with it, and that he should be unwilling to have another altering his ideas, when he may have intended to immortalize himself by it. But this does not change the conditions of the thing itself, nor the right, and even the duty of the State, to modify any foundation when it becomes inconsistent with its own preservation and progress; and hence no such institution can be regarded as unalterably founded for all time.

C. The Orders in the State.

The nobility of a country which is not under an aristocratic but a monarchical Constitution, may well form an institution that is not only allowable for a certain time, but even necessary from circumstances. But it cannot be maintained that such a class may be established for all time, and that the Head of the State should not have the right entirely to abolish the privileges of such a class; nor, if this be done, can it be held that thereby what belonged to the Nobility as Subjects, by way of a hereditary possession, has been taken from them. The Nobility, in fact, constitute a temporary corporation or guild, authorized by the State; and it must adapt itself to the circumstances of the time, nor may it do violence to the universal right of man, however long that may have been suspended. For the rank of the nobleman in the State is not only dependent upon the Constitution itself, but is only an accident, with a merely contingent inherence in the Constitution. A nobleman can be regarded as having a place only in the Civil Constitution, but not as having his position grounded on the state of Nature. Hence, if the State alters its constitution, no one who thereby loses his title and rank would be justified in saying that what was his own had been taken from him; because he could only call it his own under the condition of the continued duration of the previous form of the State. But the State has the right to alter its form, and even to change it into a pure Republic. The Orders in the State, and the privilege of wearing certain insignia distinctive of them, do not therefore establish any right of *perpetual* possession.

D. Primogeniture and Entail.

By the Foundation of *Primogeniture and Entail* is meant that arrangement by which a proprietor institutes a succession of inheritance, so that the next proprietor in the series shall always be the eldest born heir of the family, after the analogy of a hereditary monarchy in the State. But such a Foundation must be regarded as always capable of being annulled with the consent of all the Agnates; and it may not be held to be instituted as for all time, like a hereditary Right attaching to the Soil. Nor, consequently, can it be said that the abrogation of it is a violation of the Foundation and Will of the first ancestral Founder. On the contrary, the State has here a Right and even a duty, in connection with gradually emerging necessity for its own Reform, if it has been once extinguished, not to allow the resuscitation of such a federative system of its subjects, as if they were viceroys or sub-kings, after the analogy of the ancient Satraps and Heads of Dynasties.

IX.

Concluding Remarks on Public Right and Absolute Submission to the Sovereign Authority.

With regard to the ideas presented under the Heading of PUBLIC RIGHT, the Reviewer says that ' the want of room does not permit him to express himself in detail.' But he makes the following remarks on one point: ' So far as we know, no other philosopher has recognised this most paradoxical of all paradoxes, that the mere *idea* of a Sovereign Power should compel me to obey as my master any one who gives himself out to be my master, without asking who has given him the Right to command me? That a Sovereign Power and a Sovereign are to be recognised, and that the one or the other whose existence is not given in any way *à priori* is also to be regarded *à priori* as a master, are represented so as to be one and the same thing.' Now, while this view is admitted to be *paradoxical*, I hope when it is more closely considered, it will not at least be convicted of *heterodoxy*. Rather, indeed, may it be hoped that this penetrating, thoughtful, and modestly censuring Critic may not grudge to make a second examination of this point, nor regret to have taken the whole discussion under his protection against the pretentious and shallow utterances of others. And this all the more, in view of his statement that he 'regards these Metaphysical Principles of the Science of Right as a real gain for the Science.'

Now, it is asserted that obedience must be given to whoever is in possession of the supreme authoritative and legislative power over a people; and this must be done so unconditionally by right, that it would even be penal to inquire publicly into the title of a power thus held, with the view of calling it in doubt, or opposing it in consequence of its being found defective. Accordingly it is maintained, that ' *Obey the authority which has power over you* ' (in everything which is not opposed to morality), is a Categorical Imperative. This is the objectionable proposition which is called in question; and it is not merely this principle which founds a right upon the fact of occupation as its condition, but it is even the very idea of a sovereignty over a people obliging me as belonging to it, to obey the presumptive right of its power, without previous inquiry (§ 44), that appears to arouse the reason of the Reviewer.

Now every fact is an object which presents itself to the senses, whereas what can only be realized by pure Reason must be regarded as an *idea* for which no adequately corresponding object can be found in experience. Thus a perfect *juridical Constitution* among men is an ideal Thing in itself.

If then a people be united by laws under a sovereign

power, it is conformable to the idea of its unity *as such* under a supreme authoritative will, when it is in fact so presented as an object of experience.   But this holds only of its phenomenal manifestation.   In other words, a juridical constitution so far exists in the general sense of the term ; and although it may be vitiated by great defects and coarse errors, and may be in need of important improvements, it is nevertheless absolutely unallowable and punishable to resist it.   For if the people regarded themselves as entitled to oppose force to the Constitution, howeyer defective it may be, and to resist the supreme authority, they would also suppose they had a right to substitute force for the supreme Legislation that establishes all rights.   But this would result in a supreme will that would destroy itself.

The *idea* of a political Constitution in general, involves at the same time an absolute command of a practical Reason that judges according to conceptions of right, and is valid for every people ; and as such it is holy and irresistible.   And although the organization of a State were defective in itself, yet no subordinate power in the State is entitled to oppose active resistance to its legislative Head.   Any defects attaching to it ought to be gradually removed by reforms carried out on itself ; for otherwise, according to the opposite maxim, that the subject may proceed according to his own private will, a good Constitution can only be realized by blind accident.   The precept, ' *Obey the authority that has power over you*,' forbids investigating into how this power has been attained, at least with any view to undermining it.   For the Power which already exists, and under which any one may be living, is already in possession of the power of Legislation ; and one may, indeed, rationalize about it, but not set himself up as an opposing lawgiver.

The will of the people is naturally un-unified, and consequently it is lawless; and its unconditional subjection under a *sovereign* Will, uniting all particular wills by one law, is a *fact* which can only originate in the institution of a supreme power, and thus is public Right founded.   Hence to allow a Right of resistance to this sovereignty, and to limit its supreme power, is a contradiction; for in that case it would not be the supreme legal power, if it might be resisted, nor could it primarily determine what shall be publicly right or not.   This principle is involved *à priori* in the idea of a political Constitution generally as a conception of the practical Reason.   And although no example adequately corresponding to this principle can be found in experience, yet neither can any Constitution be in complete contradiction to it when it is taken as a standard or rule.

APOLOGIA.

KANT'S VINDICATION OF HIS PHILOSOPHICAL STYLE.

[IN THE PREFACE TO THE FIRST EDITION, 1796-97.]

KANT'S VINDICATION OF HIS PHILOSOPHICAL STYLE.

THE reproach of obscurity, and even of a studied indefiniteness affecting the appearance of profound insight, has been frequently raised against my philosophical style of exposition. I do not know how I could better meet or remove this objection than by readily accepting the condition which Garve, a philosopher in the genuine sense of the term, has laid down as a duty incumbent upon every writer, and especially on philosophical authors. And for my part, I would only restrict his injunction by the condition, that it is to be followed only so far as the nature of the science which is to be improved or enlarged will allow.

Garve wisely and rightly demands, that every philosophical doctrine must be capable of being presented in a *popular* form, if the expounder of it is to escape the suspicion of obscurity in his ideas; that is, it must be capable of being conveyed in expressions that are universally intelligible. I readily admit this, with the exception only of the systematic Critique of the Faculty of Reason, and all that can only be determined and unfolded by it; for all this relates to the distinction of the sensible in our knowledge from the supersensible, which is attainable by Reason. This can never be made popular, nor can any formal Metaphysic as such be popular; although their results may be made quite intelligible to the common reason, which is metaphysical without its being known to be so. In this sphere, popularity in expression is not to be thought of. We are here forced to use scholastic *accuracy*, even if it should have to bear the reproach of troublesomeness; because it is only by such technical language that the precipitancy of reason can be arrested, and brought to understand itself in face of its dogmatic assertions.

But if pedants presume to address the public in technical phraseology from pulpits or in popular books, and in expressions that are only fitted for the Schools, the fault of this must not be laid as a burden upon the critical philosophers, any more than the folly of the mere wordmonger (*logodœdalus*) is to be imputed to the grammarian. The laugh should here only turn against the man and not against the science.

It may sound arrogant, egotistical, and, to those who have not yet renounced their old system, even derogatory, to assert 'that before the rise of the Critical Philosophy, there was not yet a philosophy at all.' Now, in order to be able to pronounce upon this seeming presumption, it is necessary to resolve the question as to *whether there can really be more than one philosophy*. There have, in fact, not only been various modes of philosophizing and of going back to the first principles of Reason in order to found a system upon them, with more or less success; but there must be many attempts of this kind of which every one has its own merit at least for the present. However, as objectively considered there can only be one human Reason, so there cannot be many Philosophies; in other words, there is only one true System of Philosophy founded upon principles, however variously and however contradictorily men may have philosophized over one and the same proposition.   Thus the Moralist rightly says, there is only one virtue, and only one doctrine regarding it; that is, one single system connects all the duties of virtue by one principle.   The Chemist, in like manner, says there is only one chemistry, that which is expounded by Lavoisier.   The Physician, in like manner, says there is only one principle, according to Brown, in the system of classifying Diseases.   But because it is held that the *new systems* exclude all the others, it is not thereby meant to detract from the merit of the older Moralists, Chemists, and Physicians; for without their discoveries, and even their failures, we would not have attained to the unity of the true principle of a complete philosophy in a system.   Accordingly, when any one announces a system of philosophy as a production of his own, this is equivalent to saying that 'before this Philosophy there was properly no philosophy.'   For should he admit that there had been another and a true philosophy, it would follow that there may be two true systems of philosophy regarding its proper objects; which is a contradiction.   If, therefore, the Critical Philosophy gives itself forth as that System before which there had been properly no true philosophy at all, it does no more than has been done, will be done, and even must be done, by all who construct a Philosophy on a plan of their own.

Another objection has been made to my System which is of *less* general significance, and yet is not entirely without importance.   It has been alleged that one of the essentially distinguishing elements of this Critical Philosophy is not a growth of its own, but has been borrowed from some other philosophy, or even from an exposition of Mathematics. Such is the supposed discovery, which a Tübingen Reviewer thinks he has made, in regard to the Definition of Philosophy which the author of the *Critique of the Pure Reason* gives out as his own, and as a not insignificant product of his system, but which it is alleged had been given many years before by another writer, and almost in the same words.[1] I leave it to any one to judge whether the words: '*intellectualis quædam constructio*,' could have originated the thought of the presentation of a given conception in an *intuitive perception a priori*, by which Philosophy is at once entirely and definitely distinguished from Mathematics. I am certain that Hausen himself would have refused to recognise this as an explanation of his expression ; for the possibility of an intuitive perception *à priori*, and the recognition of Space as such an intuition and not the mere outward coexistence of the manifold objects of empirical perception (as *Wolf* defines it), would have at once repelled him, on the ground that he would have felt himself thus entangled in wide philosophical investigations. The presentation, *constructed, as it were, by the Understanding*, referred to by the acute Mathematician, meant nothing more than the (empirical) *representation* of a Line corresponding to a conception, in making which representation attention is to be given merely to the Rule, and abstraction is to be made from the deviations from it that inevitably occur in actual execution, as may be easily perceived in the geometrical construction of Equalities.

And *least of all* is there any importance to be laid

[1] Porro de actuali constructione hic non quæritur, cum ne possint quidem sensibiles figuræ ad rigorem definitionum effingi ; sed requiritur cognitio eorum, quibus absolvitur formatio quæ *intellectualis quædam constructio est*. C. A. Hausen, *Elem. Mathes.* Pars I. p. 86 (1734).

upon the objection made regarding the spirit of this Philosophy, on the ground of the improper use of some of its terms by those who merely ape the system in words. The technical expressions employed in the *Critique of the Pure Reason* cannot well be replaced by others in current use, but it is another thing to employ them outside of the sphere of Philosophy in the public interchange of ideas. Such a usage of them deserves to be well castigated, as Niçolai has shown; but he even shrinks from adopting the view that such technical terms are entirely dispensable in their own sphere, as if they were adopted merely to disguise a poverty of thought. However, the laugh may be much more easily turned upon the *unpopular pedant* than upon the *uncritical ignoramus;* for in truth the Metaphysician who sticks rigidly to his system without any concern about Criticism, may be reckoned as belonging to the latter class, although his ignorance is voluntary, because he will only not accept what does not belong to his own older school. But if, according to Shaftesbury's saying, it is no contemptible test of the truth of a predominantly practical doctrine, that it can endure *Ridicule,* then the Critical Philosophy must, in the course of time, also have its turn; and it may yet laugh *best* when it will be able to laugh *last.* This will be when the mere paper systems of those who for a long time have had the lead in words, crumble to pieces one after the other; and it sees all their adherents scattering away,—a fate which inevitably awaits them.